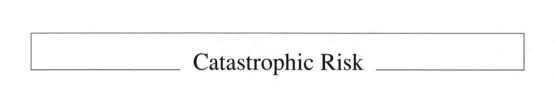

Catastrophic Risk

For other titles in the Wiley Finance Series
please see www.wiley.com/finance

Catastrophic Risk

Analysis and Management

Erik Banks

John Wiley & Sons, Ltd

Other Wiley Editorial Offices

John Wiley & Sons Inc., 111 River Street, Hoboken, NJ 07030, USA

Jossey-Bass, 989 Market Street, San Francisco, CA 94103–1741, USA

Wiley-VCH Verlag GmbH, Boschstr. 12, D-69469 Weinheim, Germany

John Wiley & Sons Australia Ltd, 33 Park Road, Milton, Queensland 4064, Australia

John Wiley & Sons (Asia) Pte Ltd, 2 Clementi Loop #02–01, Jin Xing Distripark, Singapore 129809

John Wiley & Sons Canada Ltd, 22 Worcester Road, Etobicoke, Ontario, Canada M9W 1L1

Wiley also publishes its books in a variety of electronic formats. Some content that appears
in print may not be available in electronic books.

British Library Cataloguing in Publication Data

A catalogue record for this book is available from the British Library

ISBN-13 978-0-470-01236-9 (HB)
ISBN-10 0-470-01236-6 (HB)

Typeset in 10/12pt Times by TechBooks, New Delhi, India
Printed and bound in Great Britain by Antony Rowe Ltd, Chippenham, Wiltshire
This book is printed on acid-free paper responsibly manufactured from sustainable forestry
in which at least two trees are planted for each one used for paper production.

Contents

Acknowledgments

I would like to express my sincere thanks to Samantha Whittaker, publishing editor at John Wiley, for her support on this project; her enthusiasm and comments throughout were of tremendous help. Thanks are also due to Carole Millett, Peter Baker, and the production and marketing teams at Wiley.

Various professionals at the Insurance Service Office, Insurance Information Institute, Risk and Insurance Management Society, Aon, Merrill Lynch, and Swiss Re deserve thanks for their help in providing information and constructive comments on various aspects of the text.

And, as always, my greatest thanks go to Milena.

About the author

Erik Banks, an independent risk consultant, writer, and lecturer, has held senior risk management positions at several global financial institutions over the past 20 years, including Merrill Lynch, Citibank, and XL Capital. He is the author of 18 books on risk, derivatives, governance, and merchant banking, including the John Wiley titles *Alternative Risk Transfer*, *Exchange-Traded Derivatives*, *The Simple Rules of Risk*, and *E-Finance*.

Part I
Identification and Analysis
of Catastrophic Risk

1

Catastrophe and Risk

1.1 INTRODUCTION

Risk, which we define as the uncertainty surrounding the outcome of an event, is an integral and inevitable part of business. Companies and governments operating in the complex economic environment of the 21st century must contend with a broad range of risks. Some do so in an ad hoc or reactive fashion, responding to risks as they appear, while others are proactive, planning in advance the risks that they wish to assume and how they can best manage them. Since it has become clear over the past few years that risk can be financially damaging when neglected, anecdotal and empirical evidence suggests that institutions increasingly opt for formalized processes to manage uncertainties that can lead to losses.

Risk can be classified in a number of ways and, though we do not intend to present a detailed taxonomy of risk, a brief overview is useful in order to frame our discussion. To begin, risk can be divided broadly into financial risk and operating risk. Financial risk is the risk of loss arising from the movement of a market or performance of a counterparty, and can be segregated into market risk (the risk of loss due to movement in market references, such as interest rates, stock prices, or currency rates), liquidity risk (the risk of loss due to an inability to obtain unsecured funding or sell assets in order to make payments), and credit risk (the risk of loss due to non-performance by a counterparty on its contractual obligations). A rise in funding costs, an inability to sell financial assets at carrying value, or the default by a counterparty on a loan are examples of financial risks. Operating risk, in contrast, is the risk of loss arising from events that impact non-financial business inputs, outputs, and processes. Lack of electricity needed to power assembly lines, collapse of a computer network, disruptions in the sourcing of raw materials, or misdirection of payments or orders are examples of operating risks.

Risk can also be classified in pure or speculative form. Pure risk is any exposure that results either in a loss or in no loss, but can never generate a gain; speculative risk is an exposure that can result in a gain, a loss, or no loss. In general, operating risks are often pure risks (e.g., if an assembly line fails to function as expected a loss results, and if it functions as it should no loss occurs), while financial risks are often speculative risks (e.g., if interest rates rise the cost of funding rises and a loss occurs, if interest rates decline the cost of funding declines and a saving, or 'gain,' results).

Risk can also be classified by frequency and severity. Though the specter of risk is present in virtually all business activities, the frequency of occurrence can vary widely. Some exposures can create losses (or gains) every day, week, or month. For instance, currency rates move every day, and a firm with unhedged foreign exchange risk that revalues its operations to daily closing rates will experience a loss (or gain) each business day. In general, however, these frequent losses (or gains) are likely to be relatively modest in size, as the foreign exchange market can only move by a certain amount on a given business day.[1] The same is true for many other

---

[1] In extremely rare circumstances a financial event such as a devaluation might cause a currency rate to move by a large amount; this is quite exceptional, however, and not part of the normal pattern of markets.

financial risks, which are collectively considered to be high frequency/low severity risks – that is, a loss or gain may occur every day, but the absolute size is almost certain to be quite small.

Other exposures create losses (or gains) much less frequently, perhaps every few years or decades. For example, an energy company operating a natural gas-fired generator is exposed to the risk of mechanical failure, which might cause the generator to cease producing power. Given the design of the equipment such a shut down is not expected to occur, but if it does happen the financial consequences from interrupted business revenues may be significant. Similarly, a violent tornado may strike an agricultural area and destroy an agricultural cooperative's crops; the tornado is not expected to occur very often, but if it does, the crop damage may be substantial. Or, a very large systemic liquidity crisis may occur in the banking sector as a result of a unique confluence of micro- and macro-economic events; again, although the event is not expected to happen very frequently, it may cause substantial economic damage. These types of natural or man-made events, often termed catastrophic, or disaster, risks, are considered to be low frequency/high severity risks – they do not occur very often, but they have the potential of creating very large losses. The focus of our discussion in this book is on such catastrophic risks.

The basic classification of risk by type, result, and frequency/severity is summarized in Figure 1.1.

Catastrophe risk is a broad topic that must be viewed holistically, as it can impact many facets of society – human, social, political, cultural, scientific, and economic. The very breadth of its impact means a specialist focus on the individual components is generally necessary. In fact, this book is centered specifically on the financial/economic impact of catastrophic risks, and how exposures can be analyzed and managed in order to minimize losses. While the management of all financial and operating risks is critical to continued prosperity in the private and public sectors, we shall not address the high frequency/low severity exposures that affect daily business activities; these are beyond our purview and are treated in many other works. Neither shall we attempt to address the social, cultural, or scientific issues of catastrophes, or those surrounding crisis management and disaster recovery. Again, these are vital issues, but well beyond our scope. In the balance of this chapter we consider the nature of catastrophe and its potential scope of impact; we also introduce the concept of catastrophe risk in the conventional risk management framework, and provide an overview of the structure of the text.

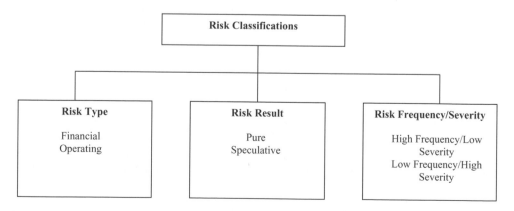

Figure 1.1   Basic risk classifications

1.2   THE NATURE OF CATASTROPHE

1.2.1   A definition

Catastrophe does not lend itself to a simple, universal definition. While we have mentioned that a catastrophic event is a low frequency/high severity risk, it may be sudden or prolonged, and natural or man-made; it may affect valuable financial/physical assets in a densely populated city, or it may impact a desolate and unpopulated region; and, it may be measured by arbitrary guidelines or very precise metrics. Despite room for interpretation we shall develop certain definitions and concepts that provide us with the necessary tools to evaluate catastrophe and catastrophe risk (with some caution to the reader that other alternatives and extensions may be perfectly acceptable).

For our purposes we define a catastrophe as a low probability natural or man-made event that creates shocks to existing social, economic, and/or environmental frameworks, and has the potential of producing very significant human and/or financial losses. Though a catastrophe is traditionally viewed as a single large event that causes sudden change – such as an earthquake or terrorist attack – we can expand the definition to include instances where a gradual accumulation of many small incidents, perhaps precipitated by the same catalyst, leads to the same scale of damage/losses; such events may not actually be recognized as catastrophes until a long period of time has passed and many losses have accumulated.[2]

Although the potential for large losses exists, a catastrophic event does not always lead to losses. While we are primarily concerned with events that might produce losses and considering what can be done to mitigate or minimize them, we would be remiss in excluding events that occur without creating losses. Accordingly, a large earthquake striking in an unpopulated region of the Aleutian Islands and a similar earthquake striking in the densely populated city-center of Kobe are both catastrophic events.

The catastrophe is the event itself, and not the specific human or financial outcome of the event; this is important because each new event, whether or not it creates social/economic damage, becomes part of the historical data record that is so vital in developing an analytic framework. Naturally, from a pure risk management perspective we are primarily interested in situations that have the potential of creating real event losses.[3]

1.2.2   Frequency

Many types of financial and operating risks appear on a regular basis – so regularly, in fact, that their impact can be estimated with a high degree of accuracy through standardized tools. Automobile accidents, household fires, stock price declines, standard medical procedures, and other non-catastrophic risk events occur every day, and the severity of each individual event is generally quite small. They can be quantified through statistical frameworks and actuarial processes, allowing exposed parties to make cost/benefit decisions with a high degree of confidence.

The same does not necessarily apply to catastrophes. Most catastrophes occur very infrequently, and they may be quite severe. For instance, although some 700 significant natural

---

[2] Some exposures with very long 'tails' or duration may be subject to changes in regulations or legal terms that create large-scale liabilities and losses that only become evident over time (e.g., asbestos, environmental disposal).

[3] We can define an event loss as the sum of all individual losses for a single catastrophic occurrence; for example, an earthquake is considered to be a single catastrophic occurrence, while the sum of the individual losses the earthquake creates for 1000 (or 10 000, or 50 000) homeowners becomes the event loss.

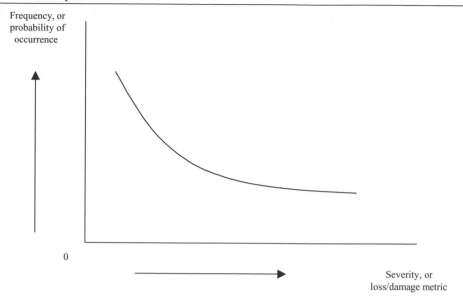

Figure 1.2   Frequency and severity

disasters occur in an average year, this figure is quite small given the number of vulnerable areas around the world; one of these 700 events may only appear in a given location once every ten, hundred, or five hundred years – and sometimes even longer. The tools and rich history of past events that are used to evaluate frequently occurring risks are not available to help in the quantification process. These differences, as we shall note later, make financial modeling, decision-making, and ongoing management more challenging. Despite this relative lack of frequency, some types of catastrophes recur, meaning that they can be anticipated – though not predicted. In the short term catastrophes are non-routine, often appearing as random events; in the very long term, however, certain classes are routine.

The probability that a particular type of catastrophe will occur is generally expressed as an annual occurrence frequency, e.g., there may be a 0.01% probability of an 8.0 magnitude earthquake occurring in City XYZ in a given year. This can be depicted in graph form, as in Figure 1.2, where frequency is conveyed as a probability of occurrence and severity as a metric of loss or damage (e.g., dollar losses, magnitude, intensity). Events that occur very frequently and have low severity outcomes dominate the left-hand portion of the curve; those that appear infrequently and have higher severity outcomes comprise the right-hand portion of the curve; the two relationships are depicted in Figure 1.3.[4]

An associated frequency measure is the recurrence interval (or return period), or the average time within which an event equal to, or greater than, a designated severity occurs; this is simply the time-independent inverse of the occurrence frequency, i.e., the recurrence interval of the 8.0 earthquake in City XYZ is 100 years (1/100 years = 0.01%). Occurrence frequency and return period are typically held constant from year to year in analytic frameworks, apart from any condition changes owing to man-made influences. A related concept is the non-encounter

---

[4] Note that there is no single *ex ante* 'dividing point' between non-catastrophic and catastrophic events; the classification on the curve is for illustrative purposes, and depends on individual circumstances.

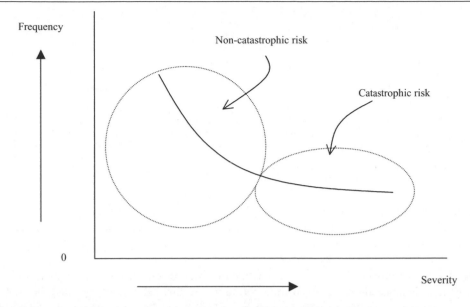

Figure 1.3   Catastrophic and non-catastrophic frequency and severity

probability, or the probability that no event greater than, or equal to, a given magnitude will occur over a particular period, i.e., there is a 99.9% annual non-encounter probability of an 8.0+ earthquake striking in City XYZ. All three measures of frequency are widely used in catastrophe risk management, and we shall revisit them throughout the book.

Knowing that catastrophes occur infrequently is an important consideration when evaluating the potential for losses, as a large magnitude event that occurs only rarely must be managed differently from a small magnitude event appearing regularly. It is not sufficient, of course, to say that catastrophes occur infrequently; within this broad classification we can divide frequency even further, into non-repetitive, irregular, regular, and seasonal events (further granularity is possible, but this categorization is detailed enough for our purposes).

- *Non-repetitive catastrophe*: a disaster that occurs only once in a particular area and can never be repeated in the same location to yield the same results. Examples include the collapse of a dam (which forever changes the channel, floodplain, and discharge dynamics above and below the dam), a massive landslide from a mountain slope (which permanently alters the landscape and potential for a repeat event), or a terrorist bombing (which obliterates a landmark structure in a particular location permanently). It is important to note that non-repetitive catastrophes can recur, but always in different locations and/or under different circumstances (e.g., another dam can collapse, another building can be bombed); the time and location of future events remain unknown.
- *Irregular catastrophe*: a disaster that does not appear with any degree of statistical regularity, but which can occur repeatedly in a general location or marketplace, though time and specific location are generally unknown. Examples of irregular catastrophe include a tsunami generated by an earthquake, or a very large stock market collapse.
- *Regular catastrophe*: a disaster that is characterized by the regular, if sometimes very long and gradual, accumulation of forces that lead to the triggering of an event. Though the

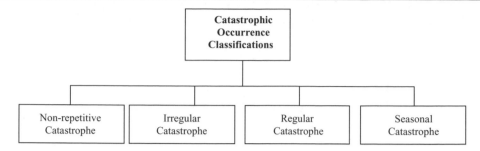

Figure 1.4 Catastrophic occurrence classifications

pattern of buildup occurs on a regular basis and can be accommodated within a statistical framework, the precise timing of event occurrence remains unknown. Examples of regular catastrophe include an earthquake on a known fault line or a volcanic eruption from an active volcano.

- *Seasonal catastrophe*: a disaster that has the potential of occurring on a regular basis in a general location during a given time period; while this helps limit the time and space of occurrence, the precise location, severity, and moment of occurrence remain unknown. Examples include hurricanes, extra-tropical cyclones, floods, and droughts, all of which can occur in particular areas during specific seasons.

Catastrophes that feature a dimension of repetition, such as regular or seasonal events, can be described by statistical distributions, which allows for better estimates of severity and frequency. Those that are non-repetitive or irregular are more challenging to quantify. We shall consider this point at greater length in Chapter 4. Figure 1.4 summarizes the classifications noted above.

Some observers have noted that the frequency of disasters appears to have increased over the past few decades. In fact, there is little scientific evidence to support such a claim: the frequency of disasters such as earthquakes, flooding, tornadoes, extra-tropical cyclones, industrial contamination, or terrorism does not appear to be accelerating, nor is it necessarily expected to. While global warming and changes in the hydrological cycle have alternately increased and decreased certain hazards that have the potential of creating disasters (e.g., spring flooding and winter storms, respectively), and though certain man-made events appear to be on the rise as a result of geopolitical tensions (e.g., large-scale terrorist-related activities), the incidence of disasters has not actually increased. In fact, growing media coverage and larger damages may be contributing to the perception of increased frequency.

1.2.3   Vulnerability

As we explore dimensions of low frequency/high severity risks, we want to consider the element of the topic that is most important to our theme – the management of losses. In particular, we consider the concept of economic vulnerabilities. From a risk management perspective, we are interested in understanding the interaction between catastrophe and vulnerabilities in order to determine the potential for losses of a given size, and ways of minimizing such losses.

A vulnerability exists when humans and/or infrastructure are present and 'at risk' when a catastrophe strikes, or has the potential of striking. Vulnerabilities represent the potential for losses from casualty, damage, destruction, and/or business interruption. When vulnerabilities are present and a catastrophe occurs, some amount of losses will result; when no vulnerabilities exist, no losses can occur. Thus, the unpopulated region of the Aleutians has no vulnerabilities – when the earthquake strikes, no losses will ensue, as human life and infrastructure are not exposed to the risk. But the densely populated center of Kobe is highly vulnerable to loss; when the earthquake hits, as it did in January 1995, the combination of the actual catastrophe and the vulnerability generates losses. The existence of vulnerability can be estimated without precise knowledge of risk levels, but the size of a loss cannot be quantified without also estimating the strength of a particular catastrophic event.

Vulnerability is a dynamic variable. As society grows and changes, new technologies are developed, new construction techniques are introduced, and demographic and migration patterns fluctuate, associated vulnerabilities change – sometimes dramatically. In general, vulnerability increases as the world's population grows and the value of assets and infrastructure multiply (even if technical/engineering advances can help reduce the amount of damage that occurs); though the frequency of catastrophe may not increase, losses continue to expand as greater wealth is built.

In fact, population growth, which tends to generate asset and wealth expansion, is a key driver of vulnerability growth. Exponential population growth over the past 2000 years means that vulnerabilities have increased rapidly and continue to expand (e.g., global population of 3b in 1960 is predicted to reach 7b by 2012); an estimated current annual growth rate of approximately 1.4% leads to population doubling time of 50 years, meaning ever-larger human and financial exposure to catastrophic risk.[5] Many areas that are exposed to a range of perils – such as the coastal USA, Japan, Taiwan, France, China, and Mexico – have grown rapidly over the past century and are expected to grow at a similar pace for the foreseeable future.

In some instances vulnerabilities can be controlled and managed by limiting participation or development in at-risk areas or introducing mitigation or loss financing techniques. In other cases they cannot be controlled as there is simply no alternative but to permit development; this is particularly true in nations that face limited regional development alternatives. Interestingly, in some instances individuals and societies willingly increase their vulnerabilities by developing at-risk areas. This tends to occur primarily in wealthier nations, where development opportunities in safe or low-risk areas exist, but where it may be regarded as desirable to live and work in a peril-prone region (e.g., a coastal area exposed to hurricanes or flooding, or a mountain area prone to earthquakes and land mass movement). Thus, despite knowledge of risk and vulnerability reduction techniques, political, social, and economic forces foster expansion and development in risky areas. Under this scenario economic progress and free selection dominate scientific knowledge and environmental conditions. Only when a major disaster strikes might such behavior change – though even this is not guaranteed, as legislative efforts may not succeed in banning development, or those impacted may simply choose to return to the status quo (believing, perhaps, that the 'big one' has passed and that they will be safe for the next 10, 50, or 100 years). In some instances exposed parties prefer to deny the threat of the peril, believing that nothing will occur, or that loss control schemes and construction standards will provide necessary protections. These beliefs may increase vulnerability over time, and make any incident that much more devastating. Catastrophe, vulnerability, and loss can therefore be viewed as a combination of cause and effect. One extreme view suggests that humans who

---

[5] This may be partly offset by the fact that industrialized nations, with greater concentrations of asset wealth, exhibit stable population patterns (though continued expansion in asset accumulation); it is also partly offset by technical/engineering advances.

choose, or are forced, to develop in areas that are exposed to catastrophe, cause losses; the 'fault' lies with human development, rather than the event itself. A more moderate view indicates that losses occur because of joint interaction between human motivations and catastrophes. Regardless of perspective or semantics, it is clear that catastrophe exists independent of losses, but the interesting issues of financial management arise when vulnerabilities are introduced. A related point is that vulnerabilities may occasionally be underestimated as a result of the dynamism that characterizes progress and development. This can lead to greater than expected losses in the event of disaster, rendering post-loss financing programs inadequate. Consider, for instance, that prior to the arrival of devastating Hurricane Andrew in Florida in 1992, the single largest loss estimate for a hurricane was $7b; this was based, in part, on previous worst case losses from other disasters,[6] along with some extrapolation on population and asset value growth in sensitive regions. To the surprise of many, Andrew generated $26b in total losses (including $15.5b of insurable losses), multiples of the previous 'conservative' loss estimate, because of the force of the event and a general underestimate of the vulnerabilities in the affected region. Not surprisingly, many homeowners, business owners, insurers, and reinsurers were financially unprepared for the losses and experienced financial distress.

Just two years later the California Northridge earthquake struck, causing $40b in total losses ($14b of insurable losses) – again, well in excess of any expectations (had Andrew and Northridge occurred in the same year, the insurance/reinsurance sectors would have faced devastating losses and a very high incidence of insolvency). Similarly, though insurers and reinsurers had actively estimated the potential for economic loss from terrorist activities since the 1970s, few expected an event equal to the magnitude of the 9/11 events: the $90b in direct and indirect losses that resulted from the four airplane strikes was underestimated by any measure.

Gauging vulnerabilities is thus a crucial and complex process – and one that is essential to effective risk management. Fortunately, improvements in modeling techniques, accumulation of historical data points, refinements in the construction of loss distributions, and compilation of more granular information regarding assets and structures has permitted development of better loss estimates. While just a decade ago the world was surprised that a single hurricane could generate $26b of damage, there is now widespread agreement among academics and practitioners involved in disaster management that if Andrew had turned northwards by a mere 30 miles it would have caused damage of $60b to $100b. Similarly, research suggests the possibility that future hurricanes impacting the Northeast USA and Florida could create losses of $20b and $75b, respectively, a California earthquake or continental European windstorm could lead to losses of $50b to $100b, an 8.5 magnitude earthquake in the New Madrid Seismic Zone of the central USA could create $100b of losses, and a repeat of the devastating 1923 Tokyo earthquake in today's market could lead to losses of $500b to $1t. The US General Accounting Office has compiled insurance industry estimates that suggest a hurricane striking a densely populated area could cost $110b, while a large earthquake could cost over $225b. Modeling firm Risk Management Solutions (RMS) has estimated the 100-year and 250-year return period losses of Florida hurricanes at $30b and $41b, respectively, Southern California earthquakes at $15b and $27b, and US multi-peril events at $59b and $115b. Applied Insurance Research (AIR), another leading modeling firm, has estimated that a repeat in the millennium of the relatively rare New England hurricane of 1938 would cause nearly $30b of damage. The

---

[6] Reference points included $4.4b from windstorm 87J in the UK in 1987, $5.6b from Hurricane Hugo in the Caribbean in 1989, and $6.9b from Typhoon Mireille in Japan in 1991.

growth of human and economic vulnerability has made these figures seem less unrealistic than they would have seemed only a few years ago.

1.2.4 Measuring severity

Catastrophes are generally measured by physical, social, and economic severity in order to provide an estimate of potential and actual damage. This provides useful information for both analytic assessment and exposure management. Ranking the physical severity of a catastrophe can be a complex undertaking. In some instances the metrics are clear, well established and widely accepted (if based, in some cases, on rather arbitrary thresholds).[7] This is particularly true of natural disasters, which use recognized metrics such as the Richter scale, Shindo scale, and moment magnitude scale (earthquake), Saffir–Simpson scale (hurricane), Fujita scale (tornado), volcanic explosivity intensity (volcano), and so on; we shall consider these measures in the next chapter. In other cases metrics are far less clear, or of limited application to other events; indeed, there may be no established gauge of physical severity. This may apply in the case of both natural and man-made disasters (e.g., a land mass movement, crude oil spill, or bomb explosion may be unique to time and location, it may not be measurable with any degree of precision, or it may provide no meaningful comparative data). Nevertheless, some effort at measuring physical severity is necessary in order to supplement data used in the quantitative process.

Measuring the social/economic severity of a catastrophe is also a complicated task that depends largely on the perspective of the analyst, researcher, or risk manager. Public sector organizations often measure severity based on the number of injuries, casualties, or displaced persons so that they can provide appropriate medical care, aid, or shelter. Companies, insurers, reinsurers, financial institutions, and government authorities responsible for assessing financial losses, settling claims, or providing reimbursements or loans to affected parties gauge severity by tabulating total economic losses. In some instances measuring economic losses can take months or years. Again, the determination of financial severity is an essential element of risk quantification. Without de-emphasizing or reducing the critical importance of the human consequences of physical catastrophes, our discussion will focus primarily on the direct economic implications of such events.

1.3 THE SCOPE OF IMPACT

Expanding on our brief introduction of vulnerability, we know that catastrophic events can generate significant damage. From a social perspective thousands, or tens of thousands, of casualties can devastate a community and a nation, and a state of emergency may be declared as the social framework is temporarily or permanently disrupted. From a financial perspective a disaster can place a tremendous burden on citizens, the private corporate sector, and the public sector, creating financial distress and slowing economic progress for weeks, months, or years.[8]

---

[7] For instance, in order for a tropical storm to be elevated to tropical cyclone status it must achieve a minimum (arbitrary) wind speed of 74 mph.

[8] Even a relatively moderate catastrophe can have a major impact on a small national economy. Consider, for instance, that Hurricane Gilbert (1988) caused $1b of damage in Jamaica; though modest compared with other instances of regional hurricane damage, it was large relative to the size of the local economy. In fact, the losses were equivalent to 25% of Jamaica's gross domestic product (based primarily on agriculture and tourism); export earnings declined by 15%, the public sector deficit increased by 5 times, and inflation accelerated dramatically.

The long-term economic impact of any catastrophe depends on the size of the direct losses, whether direct losses influence indirect losses and secondary costs, and how well an affected company/country can cope with the losses. For purposes of our discussion we can define direct loss as financial damage to capital assets, indirect loss as business interruption resulting from loss of capital assets (and measured by lost output and earnings), and secondary costs as costs associated with disruption of development plans and increased debt/public sector deficits. While direct and indirect losses can generally be estimated *ex ante* and reconciled *ex post*, secondary losses are much more difficult to ascertain (*ex ante* and *ex post*), since a national economy is a complex system of linkages, some of which may or may not be affected by the onset of a disaster.

The scope of impact is directly related to the severity of the event and the level of vulnerability. As we have noted above, a severe event in an area with little or no vulnerability will not produce social or financial losses of consequence. Similarly, a moderate event in a vulnerable area will have a modest impact, while a severe event in the same area will have a significant impact. This relationship becomes important when we consider various risk management solutions in Part II.

The depth and breadth of economic and social impact is dynamic, and driven largely by human progress (development and vulnerability) and action (mitigation and management). Let us assume that a region is exposed to catastrophic events that range in severity from an arbitrary 1 (weak) to 3 (strong), and that we can apply to this the scope of vulnerability to determine financial losses. Our result is a matrix of economic losses where the impact is driven primarily by the level of vulnerability – a direct function of human progress and action. Assuming complete economic loss of vulnerable assets if an event occurs and a linear relationship between severity and loss, we can consider several scenarios to illustrate our point. If vulnerability is equal to 100 and an event of force 1 occurs, the resulting economic loss is 100; if a severe event 3 occurs, the loss rises to 300. Thus, the catastrophe can cause a loss ranging from 100 to 300; nothing worse can happen. Assume next that the state continues to develop its community and infrastructure so that the value of local assets increases from 100 to 300; in developing such assets it does not alter its actions (i.e., it does not change its mitigation or management policies). If a catastrophe strikes, the economic loss will now range from 300 to 900 – significantly greater than in the previous state of development, despite the fact that the actual severity of the disaster remains bounded. It is simple to extend the example by reflecting increases in development that expand the vulnerable asset base from 300 to 500 to 1000, and so on. Assuming that the severity of the catastrophic event remains constant within the range of 1 to 3, and presuming no change in mitigation or management, economic losses will continue to grow – that is, the scope of impact will continue to grow. In fact, this is precisely what has occurred in recent decades. Empirical evidence indicates that, apart from certain weather-related events associated with global warming and geopolitical issues related to terrorism, the frequency of catastrophes has not increased – yet the scope of social and financial impact has increased dramatically. This is attributable almost exclusively to growing vulnerabilities, which often expand without any meaningful change in mitigation or management behavior. Urbanization, social progress, and technological advancement have led to increased development over the past decades, and the pace of progress shows no sign of slowing.[9] However, if development continues without a

---

[9] Insurer Swiss Re's review of national disasters of the past 30 years suggests that insurance losses caused by disasters have risen dramatically as a result of higher property values and greater population densities in high-risk areas, rather than increased frequencies. Indeed, apart from spikes in terrorist activities and a growing incidence of certain types of storms owing to intensification of the hydrological cycle through global warming, there is no evidence to suggest the frequency of catastrophic events is rising. Loss growth

corresponding increase in risk management activities, a point must eventually be reached where the actual or potential losses become so large that mitigation/management must be employed – this state might be characterized as one of sustainable mitigation. Whether this will eventually occur is unknown. Ultimately, progress can be viewed as a form of risk amplification that can only be checked by proper risk mitigation/management.

Catastrophe risk must therefore be managed – failure to do so can have a tangible impact on the health and safety of society, and the supporting financial and economic structures that allow society to function. Since vulnerabilities have increased steadily during the latter part of the 20th century and into the millennium, the micro and macro implications of disasters are becoming more apparent. Consider, for example, that during the 1950s, total global losses attributable to natural disasters amounted to less than $50b. By the 1960s that figure had increased to over $70b, by the 1980s to more than $200b, and by the 1990s to more than $700b.[10] Losses in the early part of the millennium have continued to grow larger – including $90b in direct and indirect losses associated with the terrorist incidents of 9/11, and tens of billions of dollars attributable to hurricanes/typhoons in Florida and Japan and tsunamis in Asia. The trend towards increasing losses is on the rise, making active management more essential than ever.

Though the largest dollar amount of losses occur in industrialized nations (given their urbanization, development, and asset value/concentrations), the greatest financial impact is typically felt in developing nations, where the economic base is generally small and the ability to absorb losses is limited. Indeed, the resilience of an economy is a key factor in determining precisely how a nation will cope with an event. A moderate catastrophe has the potential of consuming up to 1% of a developing nation's gross domestic product, which has significant implications on long-term economic expansion; years of potential progress might be threatened by a single event.

1.4   CATASTROPHE AND THE RISK MANAGEMENT FRAMEWORK

The management of risk is a difficult endeavor, partly because risk is an abstract and dynamic issue. Risk cannot be seen or touched, though its ultimate impact can certainly be detected after physical or financial damage has been wrought. Catastrophic risk is even harder to manage, because its relative infrequency makes it difficult to measure. In addition, its low frequency/high severity characteristics can create a mindset that allows exposed parties to believe that the 'worst case scenario' will not occur. In fact, hazard perception is an important element of the risk management process; if individuals or firms do not believe that an event is likely to happen, risk management decisions will be very different than if they believe otherwise. Though media coverage has expanded awareness, much more education remains to be done.

Disasters cannot be eliminated. A tornado, cyclone, chemical spill, or terrorist bomb explosion will occur at some time. The event cannot be stopped, as it is a force of natural energy or human motivations; though there is some possibility of reducing certain types of disasters, rarely can they be eliminated completely. Accordingly, the only way for a risk-averse institution

---

is largely, if not exclusively, a function of vulnerability growth. Separately, insurance broker Guy Carpenter estimates that growth in hazard areas over the past few decades has led to a doubling of real dollar damages every 14 years. Munich Re's estimates are even more striking, suggesting that economic damage from catastrophe has been doubling every 7 years since the 1960s.

[10] The Red Cross and Red Crescent estimate that during the 1990s alone, 2800 significant natural disasters created $700b of direct and indirect losses at the personal and institutional level; the human toll during this period was significant as well, with more than 500 000 lives claimed and over 1b indirectly affected.

to cope with this inevitability is to create a risk management program that is based on economically rational mitigation, loss financing, or reduction measures; in fact, it is incumbent upon those responsible for managing risk to consider the potential impact of an event, however remote, on financial resources, and construct a plan for dealing with the consequences.

The risk management discipline has become well established in the business world over the past few decades. Many companies and sovereigns are now accustomed to dealing with the high frequency/low severity financial and operating risks that impact their operations, and often do so through a multi-stage process centered on identification, quantification, management, and monitoring. This process allows exposures and financial resources to be managed in a diligent and efficient manner, and minimizes the likelihood of 'surprise losses.' The same type of risk management framework is applicable to catastrophic risks. Catastrophe risks can be identified, quantified, managed, and monitored, and adjustments to the program can be made as vulnerabilities increase or new exposures expand. We will develop a catastrophic risk management framework in the balance of the book by focusing on the nature of the perils and the specific locations where they can occur (identification), the deterministic and probabilistic models that can be used to evaluate catastrophe risks and their relative economic consequences (quantification), and the range of private and public sector techniques, mechanisms, and products that help exposed parties reduce potential losses (management and monitoring).[11] Though risk management tools and techniques exist, it will come as no surprise that they differ from those applied to high frequency/low severity risks, and depend heavily on assumptions and estimates. Throughout the text we shall highlight some of the challenges that exist when trying to evaluate and manage catastrophic risks through a formal framework.

While risk management is generally conducted by individual entities at a micro level, certain catastrophic events have the potential of generating such large direct and indirect losses that government authorities must participate in pre-loss crisis planning and post-loss emergency management and financing. This is especially critical when a regional or national disaster creates significant casualties and property destruction, or when the financial burden of reconstruction is so great that it overwhelms the capabilities of the private sector. It is therefore critical for government entities to create a risk management process that can be enacted quickly. Certain aspects of disaster recovery can only be conducted effectively at a regional or national level, as local efforts may prove inadequate, duplicative, or disorganized. Evidence suggests that governmental authorities in some hazard-prone countries have developed emergency risk management programs that can be implemented at short notice; they also have the necessary resources on hand to provide rapid access to post-loss financing. However, many others do not, and are susceptible to considerable difficulties should a disaster occur. This is particularly true of developing nations, which tend to lack the financial resources and risk management capabilities of the industrial world.

The state of the local economy dictates how quickly a crisis can be absorbed. Ultimately, a resilient economy that is capable of handling the financial shock of a catastrophe will fare better than one that is already in the midst of a contraction or structural dislocation, or which lacks the resources necessary to assist those that have been affected. Since major catastrophes may require a reallocation of financial resources from existing economic programs and planned

---

[11] Concerns can arise when risk decisions are made largely on the basis of subjective beliefs or reactions to recent occurrences, rather than objective measures and analysis; this increases the potential of taking overly conservative or liberal actions. Furthermore, in some societies the risk management process is regarded as irrelevant or a novelty, particularly when viewed in the context of larger social issues such as poverty, disease, or famine; a catastrophe is simply another element of the social condition – one that is more likely to be managed through external sovereign aid rather than coordinated micro-level risk management actions.

investments, economic goals can be jeopardized. Exports may also be disrupted, causing deterioration in the country's trade balance and a worsening of the balance of payments account.[12] Public borrowing may also be required if insufficient government funds exist, increasing the local/national interest burden (and possibly lowering the credit rating/increasing the general cost of funding at the sovereign level).

We shall discover in Part II of the book that the actual management of catastrophic risk is a multi-faceted approach that requires the expertise and resources of various private and public sector mechanisms. The natural reaction for those attempting to actively manage exposure to earthquake, hurricane, terrorism, or a sovereign financial event is to utilize insurance. In fact, insurance is one of the most efficient and resilient mechanisms available for dealing with low frequency/high severity risks. But insurance alone is not a sufficient solution. The growing scope of impact means that there is simply not enough insurance-based capital to provide coverage for all those seeking protection. Accordingly, alternative solutions must be factored into the process, including *ex ante* measures such as loss control/mitigation, and *ex post* loss financing via reinsurance, capital markets instruments, and public funding. Only when combined is an economy likely to be able to withstand the onset of one or more large disasters.

1.5 OVERVIEW OF THE BOOK

With this brief overview of catastrophe risk in hand, we are now prepared to examine the topic in greater detail. In the balance of Part I we continue with our focus on identification and quantification:

- In Chapter 2 we commence our discussion of specific catastrophic perils, focusing on both natural and man-made disasters and how they occur. We do not intend to provide a technical, scientific, or socio-political discussion on why disasters happen, or an exhaustive catalog of all the events that have occurred in the past few decades. Rather, we illustrate some of the basic concepts of disasters and support the topic by providing select examples.
- In Chapter 3 we extend the discussion on identification by considering vulnerable areas by geographic region. Since disasters may or may not be constrained by natural or geopolitical boundaries, a regional perspective provides an understanding of areas that are at risk, which is an important consideration when attempting to determine the scope of potential losses.
- In Chapter 4 we consider the second essential element of the risk management process, quantification. Once risk exposures have been identified it is necessary to consider the financial impact they can have on operations, and our discussion on catastrophe risk modeling provides direction in this area.

In Part II we will utilize the analysis tools developed in Part I to understand how catastrophic risks can be managed:

- In Chapter 5 we consider catastrophic exposures in light of the holistic risk management framework, examining the concepts of enterprise value maximization, solvency, and liquidity in relation to loss control, loss financing, and risk reduction. This approach helps us understand the relative advantages, disadvantages, opportunities, and limitations of the private and public risk management efforts that form our discussion in the balance of Part II.

---

[12] As an example, one research study has found that in the 5-year period following the devastating Mexico City earthquake of 1985, the country's balance of payments deficit increased by $8.6b.

- In Chapter 6 we analyze the insurance and reinsurance mechanisms that are available to ceding companies and ceding insurers attempting to manage their catastrophic exposures. We examine issues related to mechanics, structure, pricing, and market cycles, as well as challenges and limitations.
- In Chapter 7 we continue the discussion of management solutions by examining alternatives from the capital markets. Gradual convergence of the insurance and financial sectors has led to the creation of new mechanisms for transferring and hedging risk exposures, and we analyze several of the most significant, including catastrophe bonds and contingent capital. In order to understand how such solutions interact with, or substitute for, insurance/reinsurance, we also consider structure, pricing, and capital supply characteristics, as well as challenges and shortcomings.
- In Chapter 8 we extend our discussion of capital markets risk management by analyzing the role of derivatives, with a specific review of the features and limitations of exchange-traded and over-the-counter catastrophe contracts.
- In Chapter 9 we shift our focus from the private sector to the public sector by examining programs that are funded and directed by federal, regional, or local governments. As noted, some disasters are so large (and/or are located in countries lacking private sector transfer mechanisms) that the role of sovereign authorities in providing financial and technical assistance is imperative.
- In Chapter 10 we conclude our work by examining challenges facing the catastrophic risk management sector in the dynamic social and economic world of the millennium.

2

Risk Identification I: Perils

Identifying the nature of risk is a prerequisite for the subsequent stages of quantification, management, and monitoring that comprise a standard risk management framework. Expanding on the theme introduced in the last chapter, we are interested in identifying risk events that occur infrequently and have the potential of generating large losses; this process represents a combination of hazard/peril assessment and vulnerability assessment.[1]

In this chapter we consider hazard/peril assessment by focusing on various classes of natural and man-made catastrophes. Within the class of natural catastrophes we consider geophysical, meteorological/atmospheric, and other events, while in the class of man-made catastrophes we consider terrorism, industrial contamination, technological failure, and financial dislocation. We will also briefly discuss mega-catastrophes, rare events that create exceptionally large losses and affect various classes of risk coverage simultaneously. Our aim is to acquaint the reader with basic issues surrounding catastrophes. We do not intend to provide a detailed scientific or technical discussion of natural or man-made disasters, or a comprehensive catalog of disasters that have occurred over the years; while such information is important, it is beyond the scope of our discussion and is well treated by several of the works listed in the Bibliography. These categories are summarized in Figure 2.1. Note that in the next chapter we expand the discussion by considering vulnerability assessment – analyzing specific geographic regions that are susceptible to disaster and losses by virtue of their location and population/asset concentrations. Both elements are vital inputs into the modeling framework we discuss in Chapter 4.

Before commencing our discussion we note that any analysis regarding the nature of risk must focus on both hazards and perils; the two are related, but distinct. A hazard is an event that can lead to, or intensify, a peril. A peril, in turn, is the actual event that causes damage to an area. Thus, gasoline spilled on the floor of a warehouse is a hazard that can lead to an increased probability of damage by fire, which is the peril. Similarly, a fault line in the Earth's crust is a hazard that can lead to earthquakes, the peril. Perils are determined and defined by location, time, magnitude, and frequency. Some are limited by location and time (e.g., North Atlantic hurricanes are bounded by the area between 5–25 degrees north of the Equator and the months of August to October), while others are not (e.g., a terrorist strike can theoretically occur at any time, and in any location). Some perils adhere to the magnitude–frequency rule, which indicates that over a sufficiently long period of time small catastrophes will recur frequently and large ones only periodically; this rule is consistent with the frequency/severity curve presented in the last chapter. However, contrary to established notions, not all perils follow the magnitude–severity rule, which indicates that the larger the event, the more severe the damage/losses: in some cases the severity of the disaster (in human or financial terms) is independent of the

---

[1] Hazard/peril assessments, based on scientific and geopolitical knowledge and historical experience, define the natural and social boundaries of a vulnerable area and possible event intensity and frequency; once defined, at-risk assets can be identified in the vulnerability phase to determine potential losses. It is important to stress that catastrophic hazard/peril identification is not about predicting the time and occurrence of an event, which is essentially impossible, but signaling areas of danger and vulnerability.

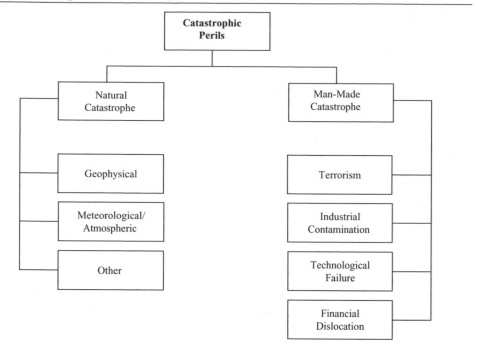

Figure 2.1   Natural and man-made catastrophes

magnitude of the disaster, meaning that a large magnitude event can cause little damage, while a small magnitude event can cause significant damage. This, of course, relates directly to the concept of vulnerability.

2.1   NATURAL CATASTROPHE

Natural catastrophes are disasters originating from nature or natural forces. The Earth is home to complex forces that are driven by energy from internal heat (e.g., impact energy, radioactive decay), external heat (e.g., the Sun), and gravity/rotation/extra-terrestrial motion. Major flows of energy are in a constant state of activity. In some instances they become very concentrated and must be released; this creates events of moderate or significant force that can disrupt physical conditions, geography, and weather. Although there are various ways of classifying and considering natural catastrophes, we divide them into three broad categories for the purposes of our discussion: geophysical catastrophes, meteorological/atmospheric catastrophes, and other natural catastrophes. Within each of these broad classes we consider certain subclasses, including earthquake and volcanic eruption (geophysical), tropical cyclone/hurricane, extra-tropical cyclone, thunderstorm and tornado (meteorological/atmospheric), and fire, mass movement, and flood (other, which can occur independently, or arise from events in other classes). Naturally, other natural catastrophes exist, such as frost, drought, and so forth; we shall not consider these in detail. From a pure economic perspective (and ignoring any direct social/human toll), earthquakes, tropical cyclones, and flooding account for approximately 90% of all catastrophic economic losses; windstorm, extra-tropical cyclones, tornadoes, fire, and other events account for the balance.

2.1.1   Geophysical

2.1.1.1   *Earthquake*

An earthquake is defined as a rapid dislocation or displacement of land/rock mass, which typically occurs along a fault line. A fault line, in turn, is a fracture in the Earth's surface where rock slides. The dislocation or rupture leads to the release of energy from the hypocenter via the fault plane, creating seismic waves from the origin outward; seismic waves may be categorized as body waves (planetary) or surface waves.

Much of the study of earthquakes is based on the science of plate tectonics. Tectonic plates are massive slabs of moveable, yet rigid, continental or oceanic rock sitting atop the Earth's crust (lithosphere). As these plates pull apart (diverge), collide (converge), or slide (shear), they create the dislocations that lead to energy release. Different motions create different types and sizes of earthquakes: divergent motions cause rocks to rupture and lead to small, frequent earthquakes; sliding motions cause plate fractures to move around the surface and create large, though infrequent, earthquakes; and convergent motions cause plate overrides (at subduction zones) or crashes (at collision zones), creating the largest, and least frequent, events.[2] Though plate movement earthquakes are most common, events can also be caused by intraplate faults and crustal fractures; intraplate seismicity is not as well understood as tectonic activity, but the destructive force of such earthquakes can be significant.

The actual area of an earthquake's wave dispersal depends on the amount of energy released and the nature of the surrounding landscape and geology. Depending on the strength of the release, the earthquake may or may not be perceptible to humans, though it will almost certainly be 'felt' by highly sensitive seismic instrumentation capable of gauging even the smallest motions. Harder, or denser, terrain delivers seismic waves over longer distances, thus affecting a larger area; for instance, an earthquake of a given magnitude affecting the hard base New Madrid Seismic Zone (NMSZ) in the Midwestern USA would create damage over a larger area than an equivalent event over the softer base California coast. While most earthquake damage comes from ground motion, further destruction can come through liquefaction, a process that occurs when contact pressure between individual particles of sand/earth is removed via shaking, turning seemingly hard ground into a dense, fluid-like substance. Tsunamis, or seismic tidal waves, are an associated feature of certain earthquakes; a tsunami is generated by ocean fractures and can strike a shoreline quite unexpectedly, creating additional destruction.

Every earthquake can be described by certain key parameters, including location, depth, magnitude, and intensity. An earthquake begins at the hypocenter and spreads through the fault rupture plane. The epicenter is the vertical point above the hypocenter and defines the location; the distance between the epicenter and hypocenter is a measure of depth. Magnitude measures the amount of energy that is released at the hypocenter and radiated outward from the rupture plane; intensity, in contrast, measures the observed effects of energy release on the surface.

In general, the greater the amount of energy release, the greater the magnitude, and the greater the intensity and potential damage (though this depends ultimately on both the nature of the surrounding geology and the degree of regional vulnerability). As an earthquake becomes larger the actual physical sensation may not increase noticeably, though diffusion to a broader area will result. The magnitude of an earthquake, which is measured through seismographs,

---

[2] As in Tokyo (1923), New Zealand (1931), and Alaska (1964), for example.

Table 2.1   Descriptive terms of the modified
Mercalli intensity scale

Category	Description
I	Imperceptible
II	Very Slight
III	Slight
IV	Moderate
V	Fairly Strong
VI	Strong
VII	Very Strong
VIII	Destructive
IX	Devastating
X	Annihilating
XI	Catastrophic
XII	Cataclysmic

Guide: X events destroy smaller wooden frame structures,
XI events destroy masonry/concrete buildings, and XII
events create widespread leveling across all structures.

can be expressed via the moment magnitude scale,[3] Richter scale,[4] Shindo scale,[5] body wave magnitude, and surface wave magnitude. Intensity is generally measured through the modified Mercalli intensity (MMI) scale, a 12-point scale of observable damage that is influenced primarily by magnitude, distance from hypocenter/epicenter, duration, ground surface type, and construction type (see Table 2.1).

Though many earthquakes occur on a random, or time-independent, basis, some faults are characterized by time-dependent probabilities; that is, the faults build up stress levels at a given rate and release energy once a certain threshold is attained. This means that the probability of event occurrence at a particular location increases as the time since the last event at the same location lengthens. This does not mean that the precise time of the next event can be predicted, simply that the probability of occurrence increases with the passage of time. Not surprisingly, recurrence intervals increase with the magnitude of an earthquake; for large events the interval may span decades or centuries (e.g., the recurrence interval of the 1906 San Andreas 7.9 Richter earthquake is 210 years, the interval of the 1992 Landers 7.3 earthquake is 5000 years; historical event data on these and other earthquakes is generally limited and must be supplemented by geological and geodetic information). The level of devastation that can be caused when an earthquake of a given magnitude strikes in a particular location can be determined with some precision through tectonic models and local geology. Similarly, the overall degree of seismic hazard (low to high) and the probability that an earthquake will occur in a location can be determined with reasonable accuracy. What remains unknown in advance is the precise timing, location, and intensity of a strike; short-term prediction is simply not feasible.

---

[3] A scale used to measure large or distant earthquakes that is related directly to the physical characteristics of the event and energy release.

[4] A logarithmic scale that is used primarily for local earthquakes of moderate magnitude.

[5] A scale measuring intensity of shaking on a scale of 0–7, where an event of 6 leads to the collapse of less than 30% of structures and an event of 7 to the collapse of more than 30%.

2.1.1.2   Volcanic eruption

Volcanic activity is influenced by many of the same forces that create earthquakes, namely divergence, convergence, or shear of tectonic plates, which creates energy release from the Earth. In fact, more than 90% of volcanism is related to plate tectonics, and 80% of magma expelled during eruptions is done through divergences in fault lines (e.g., so-called spreading centers), a rather tranquil form of volcanic energy release. Volcanic activity can also be created via hot spots, which are masses of slowly rising mantle rock that lead to volcanic formation and eruption. Hot spots occur in the center of tectonic plates, and can last for up to 100 million years each; researchers estimate that there are approximately 120 hot spots globally (more than 50 under the ocean).

Like earthquakes, volcanic eruption tends to occur infrequently; indeed, it is sometimes difficult to determine whether a volcano is active, dormant, or extinct, and extended periods of inactivity lasting several centuries can give rise to the sometimes mistaken belief that a volcano has become extinct. A volcano can remain technically active for hundreds of thousands, to millions, of years, and fall into a state of dormancy lasting several centuries before reactivating. Unfortunately, significant population centers tend to develop around certain dormant volcanoes (e.g., as in Japan, Colombia, the Philippines, Montserrat, Mexico, Washington state); this can increase the level of vulnerability, and widespread damage (and fatalities) can occur when volcanic activity resumes.[6] The probability of any single person being impacted by a volcanic eruption in his or her lifetime is remote; however, the development of towns and cities, which are designed to remain *in situ* for many decades or centuries, means that the probability of impact over time is much greater.[7]

Most volcanic activity occurs along ocean ridge spreading of sea floors; in fact, many eruptions occur below sea level, making monitoring difficult or impossible. Those occurring on land can be quite dramatic and damaging. Eruption begins when superheated rock at depth rises towards the Earth's surface; as it travels upward pressure declines, causing expansion. In some instances the rock changes to magma, a molten, liquefied form of rock. Fractures in a volcano allow more rock/magma to rise to lower pressure levels, causing solid material to liquefy further. As more of the rock/magma rises, gases form bubbles within the mass, helping push material through fractures and into the pipe of the volcano, until eruption draws nearer. When the gas bubble volume exceeds 75%, magma is fragmented into smaller pieces, which are carried out by a strong gas jet in an eruption; once the magma has been expelled, the gas jet draws in more air, increasing the buoyancy. The actual speed and flow of the magma post-eruption depends on both viscosity and mineral composition. Magma that reaches the surface moves in the form of lava if the gas can easily escape. If the gas is not released it remains trapped within the magma until it is blasted into the air in the form of pyroclastic debris; when it reaches the surface and cools it forms volcanic glass (e.g., pumice or obsidian).

There are many different types of volcanic land formations and eruption styles, some of which are more dangerous than others. For instance, Icelandic eruption is relatively benign as gas escapes freely and lava has low viscosity. Other forms of eruption, including Hawaiian, Vulcanian, Vesuvian, Plinian, Pelean, and Strombolian, can be much more violent

---

[6] For instance, Montserrat, a once-popular Caribbean tourist center, was heavily damaged in 1997 when a dormant, though not extinct, volcano completed a multi-year cycle of eruptions.

[7] For instance, Mount Rainier in Washington state is deemed to be a high-risk volcano as a result of its height, weak internal structure, and proximity to fault lines; though the volcano is surrounded by national parks the risk of extensive ash and land mass damage in the rapidly expanding Seattle–Tacoma region is all too real.

and explosive; indeed, the largest eruptions expel so much magma that they can create enormous craters. Lava, ash, debris, and explosive material can create considerable damage; the aftermath of such eruptions can also give rise to lahars, damaging earth and debris landslides caused by post-event rainfalls.[8]

Volcanic intensity is generally measured through the volcanic explosivity index (VEI), which calibrates eruptions on a scale of 0 (inactive) to 8 (extreme). The VEI measures the volume of material erupted, the height of the column, and the length of the major burst. Globally, a large volcanic explosion (e.g., VEI of at least 3) occurs approximately every 3 years; more than 125 significant eruptions have been recorded in the modern era (i.e., 1800 on). However, over the past three centuries there has only been one VEI 7 event and four VEI 6 events.

2.1.2   Meteorological/atmospheric

2.1.2.1   Tropical cyclone/hurricane

Tropical cyclones, which are also known as hurricanes (in the Atlantic), cyclones (in the Indian Ocean), and typhoons (in the Pacific), are intense, seasonal cyclonic storm systems that convert the heat energy of a tropical ocean into waves, wind, and storms. They have the potential of creating heavy precipitation, damaging winds, and tornadoes; if a system reaches land it can also create coastal flooding through storm surge.

Tropical cyclones develop when air movements and water temperatures are in a particular state of readiness. Specifically, the ocean surface must be warm (e.g., 80° Fahrenheit to a depth of approximately 200 feet) and the upper atmosphere cannot feature shear winds that might suppress cyclonic outflow. Tropical cyclones begin as disorganized thunderstorms. As low pressure draws them together, they form a tropical disturbance, and as surface winds strengthen and flow around the storm an organized center is created; at this stage the disturbance becomes a tropical depression. As water vapor from humid air rises through the moist center of the depression (to an altitude of more than 18 000 feet), air pressure continues to drop and wind speed increases. Condensation continues, generating more latent heat and forcing the air to rise up through the center column at an increasingly rapid rate. Air is ventilated at the top, allowing new humid, moist air to enter from the surface and replace the exiting air; this process continues until the depression strengthens to a tropical storm (i.e., sustained winds above 39 mph) and, ultimately, a tropical cyclone (i.e., winds above 74 mph).

The strength of the storm is ultimately determined by the speed of surface winds flowing into, and up, the center; the greater the efficiency and strength of this action, the greater the power of the storm. A fully developed tropical cyclone is essentially a band of extremely intense thunderstorms arrayed in a spiral fashion around the eye (e.g., meso-vortex); the eye itself is extremely calm as no wind can enter, while the surrounding eye wall is the location of the most intense wind activity. The entire lifecycle of a tropical cyclone, from disturbance to maximum strength, can last from 5 to 15 days.[9]

---

[8] In fact, volcanism can impact short-term weather patterns via blasts of ash and gas that block sunlight for extended periods of time, e.g., tons of SO_2 gas injected into the atmosphere can reflect shortwave solar radiation, causing a lowering of temperatures for several months (or longer). For instance, the massive Mount Pinatubo eruption in the Philippines led to a decline of 2° Fahrenheit in the Northern Hemisphere; similar findings were recorded in the eruptions of Tambora (Indonesia) and El Chichon (Mexico).

[9] Oscillations (oceanic/atmospheric patterns) play a role in determining temperature, precipitation, and winds. Though various oscillations exist, one of the most significant is the El Nino Southern Oscillation (ENSO), which appears in the tropical Pacific every few years; ENSO is comprised of El Nino, the warm extreme of the cycle, and La Nina, the colder extreme – both of which contribute to interannual climate variability. The ENSO cycle appears to repeat every 2 to 7 years, with each segment lasting 1 to 2 years. According to researchers, the frequency, intensity, and persistence of the cycles has become more apparent since the 1970s, affecting patterns of

Table 2.2   Saffir–Simpson scale

Category	Barometric pressure (mbar)	Wind speed (mph)	Surge (ft)	Description
1	>980	74–95	4–5	Minimal
2	965–979	96–110	6–8	Moderate
3	945–964	111–130	9–12	Expansive
4	920–944	131–155	13–18	Extreme
5	<920	155+	18+	Catastrophic

Table 2.3   Tropical cyclone activity, by region

Region	Average tropical cyclones per year	Hurricane/typhoon strength per year
Atlantic	9.7	5.4
NE Pacific	16.5	8.9
NW Pacific	25.7	16.0
Indian Ocean	10.4	4.4

The intensity of a tropical cyclone is based on the difference between low pressure in the eye of the storm and ambient pressure outside the storm. In general, storms are classed by central barometric pressure and/or wind speed according to the Saffir–Simpson scale, summarized in Table 2.2.

The most intense tropical cyclones (i.e., Category 5 hurricanes or equivalent super-typhoons) can cause extreme damage. In addition to the destructive force of wind and rain,[10] vulnerable areas must also contend with damage from storm surge, large quantities of seawater that accumulate beneath the eye of the storm and pour on to the shore when landfall occurs; the surge can temporarily elevate coastal water levels by 4 to 20 feet, causing significant damage to proximate structures. Storms may also spawn tornadoes, as discussed below. Note that tropical cyclones are characteristically different from storms forming at higher latitudes (e.g., the extra-tropical cyclones described in the section below), as they draw their energy primarily from the release of heat within the storm, weaken quickly over land, and feature less power as they increase in height.

Tropical cyclones are seasonal events that only form during a set period of time. For instance, Northern Hemisphere events form between July and October, with peak activity occurring in August and September; if storms have not occurred by September the risk of landfall declines dramatically until the following season. Similarly, the peak season for Southern Hemisphere events is in February and March. Tropical cyclones occur with relative frequency compared to other catastrophic events such as earthquakes – though the actual number achieving hurricane/cyclone strength is relatively small, and the actual number of those making landfall and impacting a vulnerable area is smaller still. Table 2.3 summarizes the average number of

---

precipitation, flooding, drought, fire, tropical cyclones, and extra-tropical cyclones. For instance, when the warm cycle is in observance, storm conditions in the Atlantic are suppressed (e.g., less hurricane and extra-tropical cyclone activity), while those in the South Pacific are enhanced (e.g., more typhoons and cyclones). The reverse occurs when the cool cycle is in motion.

[10] Most physical damage from tropical cyclones arises from poorly constructed buildings; roofs are generally susceptible to damage (particularly when windows are open/blown out).

tropical cyclones, including those of hurricane/typhoon strength, which occur in an average year (based on data drawn from the past five decades).

2.1.2.2   Extra-tropical cyclone/winter storm

Extra-tropical cyclones form in the mid-latitudes, just outside the tropical zone, when differences between cold and warm air masses create atmospheric instability. Specifically, high and low pressure systems create changes in horizontal pressure gradients, primarily in the late fall and into the winter (hence the common association with winter storms), leading to sometimes significant disturbances. These storms are often characterized by very strong winds and drenching rain.

Like tropical cyclones, extra-tropical cyclones typically pass through several distinct phases of strength, including storm creation, tracking, strengthening, and subsidence. Using European storms as an example, in the first phase a disturbance on the polar front (the Icelandic low) develops in the mid-latitudes of the Atlantic as a result of temperature differentials between the North Pole and the Equator, and begins moving quickly in an easterly direction.[11] To balance the temperature differences low-pressure vortexes, which are essentially secondary cyclones, mix the humid subtropical air masses with colder Arctic air masses; a storm is created within these vortexes once a certain momentum is reached. In the second phase intensity grows as low-pressure vortexes expand over water into a low-pressure system with counter-clockwise air mass movement. The storm in this phase is characterized by very distinct cold and warm fronts, which add force to the entire system and create strong winds. In the third phase the storm passes overland; peak force is reached as the cold front overtakes the warm front in the center of the low-pressure area, with strong winds and precipitation covering large areas – this is the point of maximum force and destruction, and once the peak is reached the storm begins to lose energy. In the final stage the remaining energy within the storm dissipates and the system dies out.

Though extra-tropical cyclones are not as intense as tropical cyclones, they can affect much larger geographical areas, and can last overland for a period of up to several days – meaning damages are sometimes much greater. Indeed, extra-tropical cyclones reaching land can range from 700 to 1400 miles in width and carry sustained wind speeds of 50 to 110 mph. A typical overland storm can travel at speeds in excess of 60 mph and last for 2 to 5 days before dying out.[12]

2.1.2.3   Thunderstorms and tornadoes

Like other meteorological/atmospheric events, thunderstorms and tornadoes can threaten life and property. Thunderstorms occur frequently in many parts of the world and are not typically considered catastrophic; however, extremely severe thunderstorms, super-cells, and microbursts, which are rather more rare, can create a large amount of destruction. In fact,

---

[11] Solar radiation at the mid-latitudes follows a seasonal cycle, meaning temperature differentials follow the same cycle; in fact, the largest temperature differences occur in the winter months.

[12] There is much research underway to determine whether the frequency of extra-tropical cyclones impacting Europe is affected by global warming. In general, a positive North Atlantic Oscillation (NAO) is associated with mild, but wind-intensive, winters, while a negative NAO is linked to cold, but calm, winters. Until the 1960s the negative NAO was in observance quite frequently; since then the positive NAO scenario has dominated, leading to a greater incidence of storms. Researchers are still attempting to determine the linkages between global warming, the NAO, and storm frequency.

the most devastating events feature hail, lightning, winds, ice, and snow, any of which can lead to catastrophic damage.[13] Most storm events are based on cyclones that rotate around a low-pressure center. Cyclonic action depends on the presence of wind shear, which arises when a layer of compressed air develops between slow surface winds and fast high-altitude winds. As warm air masses move toward the stratosphere, the air layer is tilted; updrafts then start spinning the column of air into a meso-cyclone, leading to thunderstorms and tornadoes.

Thunderstorms generally form when a warm air mass absorbs heat and moisture and remains less dense than the surrounding air. As warm air rises through the atmosphere, large clouds are created through a convection process (e.g., the vertical transfer of heat in a rising air mass). Latent heat is released as water vapor in the air mass condenses, adding warmth to the air and forcing it higher. When the mass of water ultimately becomes too heavy for the updrafts of air, upper level precipitation begins, causing downdrafts and rain and drawing in cool air. The process can bring drenching rains and strong winds, which only dissipate when sufficient cool air is brought into the system. Super-cells are extremely powerful thunderstorms that form when strong winds from different directions and altitudes create an intense meso-cyclone; air rising and falling within the cyclone intensifies the storm's energy and keeps rain and hail from falling for a period of time. When sufficient force is built, rain, hail, and even tornadoes can be unleashed in a storm event that can travel rapidly and remain at full strength for several hours. Microbursts, which appear in the final stages of certain thunderstorms, are sudden, violent downdrafts of cold air, rain, and hail, which can reach up to 2 miles in diameter; though generally short-lived (e.g., sub 5 minutes), they are still capable of creating significant damage.

A tornado, which is a rapidly rotating column of air that forms along a narrow line of thunderstorms (often known as a squall line), occurs through a unique confluence of regionally unstable weather events. For instance, in the central USA (site of much of the world's tornado activity), tornadoes can develop when tropical air from the Gulf of Mexico moves northward, cold, dry air from Canada or the Rocky Mountains moves southeast, and strong jet streams move from west to east. The three air masses, moving in different directions, create large thunderclouds, some of which can spawn tornadoes. In fact, scientists remain uncertain about why some storms lead to tornadoes and others do not, but at least one theory suggests that wind shear tilts thunderclouds sufficiently to allow warm air to rise on the advancing side, creating downdrafts on the trailing side, and generating tornadic activity through rotating motions. As the rotating core tightens, it accelerates and creates the familiar funnel column that characterizes the tornado. The core of a tornado's vortex is typically less than 1/2 mile wide; funnel clouds driving the system form thousands of feet up in the atmosphere and often do not even reach the ground. Those reaching the ground can do so very suddenly, and tend to follow very erratic tracks that last from several minutes to several hours.

In fact, tornadoes feature stronger winds than any other weather phenomenon, with minimum speeds of 72 mph and bursts of over 300 mph; they can be more intense than tropical cyclones, though they impact a much smaller area.[14] Small tornadoes account for the majority of observed activity (e.g., in the USA 90% of tornadoes have paths of less than 3 miles and moderate wind speeds of 70 to 90 mph); any damage they cause is likely to be isolated and rather modest, and

---

[13] Ice storms are periodically responsible for widespread damage as falling snow, ice particles, and/or freezing rain create thick frozen precipitation coatings on structures and power lines. For instance, the costliest natural disaster in Canadian history was an 80-hour ice storm in 1998 that killed 25 people and downed 130 power transmission towers.

[14] It is worth noting that tornadoes are not strictly a rural phenomenon; urban tornadoes, such as those appearing in Nashville, Fort Worth, Salt Lake City, Oklahoma City, and Miami, can create significant destruction.

Table 2.4   Fujita scale

Category	Wind speed (mph)	Path length (mi)	Description
F0	<72	—	Light
F1	73–112	<1	Moderate
F2	113–157	1–3.1	Considerable
F3	158–206	3.2–9.9	Severe
F4	207–260	10–31	Devastating
F5	261–318	32–99	Incredible
F6	319+	100–315	Unexpected

generally not of catastrophic proportions (though the sum total of many discrete events can lead to the same economic consequences as a single large event). Only the strongest tornadoes, typically spawned by super-cells, are classed as catastrophic events. Though rare, they account for the majority of death and destruction; for instance, in the USA only 1% of tornadoes have wind speeds of over 200 mph, but these events account for approximately 70% of damage and fatalities. Tornado strength is most commonly measured by the Fujita scale, which incorporates wind speed and path length (see Table 2.4).

2.1.3   Other natural disasters

Fire, mass movements, and flood are additional perils that can reach catastrophic proportions. In fact, the three classes are often (though not always) associated with earthquakes, tropical cyclones, extra-tropical cyclones, and thunderstorms.

2.1.3.1   Fire

Fire, like certain other perils, need not necessarily be catastrophic in nature. Small fires are a regular, non-catastrophic risk that can be analyzed and managed in the same manner as other high frequency/low severity exposures. But some fires can assume catastrophic qualities: intense and widespread forest fires can burn hundreds of thousands of acres, and urban firestorms can destroy entire city blocks or residential enclaves.

Fire, which produces flame, heat, and light, is the result of the rapid combination of oxygen with carbon, hydrogen, and other organic agents. Fuel, oxygen, and heat are the necessary ingredients in any fire; if one of the three is missing, a fire cannot start (e.g., a lightning strike can supply the required heat for a fire, but if there is no dry wood, scrub, or kindling, the essential fuel element will prevent a fire from starting). The process begins with a preheating phase where water is expelled from the fuel source and the surface temperature increases. Thermal degradation through preheating then leads to flaming combustion and energy release; this can occur through convection (transfer through air via electrons or particle waves), conduction (transfer through physical contact), or diffusion (transfer from hot to cool regions). Fire can spread along the ground, as a wall along a flaming combustion front, or via treetops as a crown fire. The actual area and speed of the spreading depends on the presence of fuel, the nature of weather conditions (including wind and rain), the topography, and the construction of the fire itself. Fire often spreads through cold front winds, local winds, or foehn winds (warm, dry, high-speed winds descending from the mountains). For instance, in the USA foehn winds such as the Chinook, Diablo, and Santa Ana regularly create strong, warm airflows that can

Table 2.5   Common mass movements

Speed	Dry conditions	Wet conditions
Slow	Creep	Earth flow
Intermediate	—	Mudflow, subside, landslide
Fast	Rock fall	Avalanche

expand fire zones by raising ground temperatures, lowering humidity, and pushing fire fronts forward at speeds of up to 60 mph. Fire tornadoes, mini-cyclones of fire and burning debris, are particularly hazardous as they can move at speeds of up to 150 mph and deposit flammable material in distant locations. Firestorms are also a threat; these can occur when a fire is large enough to inject excess heat into the atmosphere, creating hot winds that propel the system forward. Major fires often occur in groups; though infrequent, they can be especially damaging (e.g., 2–3% of major fires cause up to 95% of fire damage in a given year). A responsible policy is generally required to help manage the risk of major fires; this typically includes allowing naturally starting fires to burn (thus reducing the accumulated fuel supply), starting fires under controlled conditions to help destroy fuel, or actually removing elements of the fuel supply through clearing.[15]

2.1.3.2   Mass movement

Mass movement, or the movement of large sections of land under the force of gravity, creates billions of dollars worth of damage every year and results in hundreds of casualties; those that occur rapidly can be extremely dangerous as there is often little, or no, time to prepare or evacuate.[16] Mass movements are generally triggered by another peril, such as an earthquake, hurricane, flood, or tornado. As such, they are often grouped with other perils, meaning some of their unique details can be overlooked.

Mass movements can arise from slope failure created by a sudden movement (e.g., earthquake, lahar) or through a gradual 'creep process' that impacts the soil and bedrock. They can be influenced by the presence and speed of water, or they may occur in completely dry conditions; if water is present, the speed and movement help determine the potential path and degree of damage (e.g., water movement ranges from very slow [1 ft/yr] to very rapid [10 ft/sec]). Common mass movements are summarized in Table 2.5.

Landslides, a relatively common form of wet mass movement, are caused by the slope angle and instability of a hill or mountain. Contributing factors may include removal of slope supports, addition of mass on top of a slope, internal foundation weakness (e.g., clay, silt), or presence of water. In practice, most landslides are the result of a complex set of interactions; when a trigger event occurs, a chain reaction leads to a landslide.

A subside, or collapse of portions of earth into a void, occurs when slow or instant compression of sediments underneath weight or pressure leads to failure of the surrounding area. Slow subsidence from groundwater pumping often appears in river delta/coastal areas that have

---

[15] There is still a risk in following this approach, of course. Consider the case of Yellowstone National Park in the USA, which in the 1970s shifted to a 'natural burn' policy. The new approach was successful through 1988, with an average of 100 acres lost to natural fires each year. In 1988, however, difficult weather conditions led to massive spreading that ultimately consumed 1.4m acres (versus 146 000 acres in the previous 116 years).

[16] For instance, sudden landslides in Peru in 1970 killed 70 000; those in Venezuela, Honduras, and Nicaragua in 1998–1999 killed over 10 000.

become heavily populated and developed (e.g., Bangkok, Houston, Nagoya, Tokyo, Shanghai). Sudden subsidence events, such as sinkholes, occur when buoyant support is drained from underneath the supporting material. Avalanches, mudflows, and rock falls are mass movements of boulders, rocks, sand, clay, and/or snow that convert into a fluid motion, allowing debris to travel over reasonably long distances. Loess flows, large silt deposit shifts, can be quite damaging as they can move quickly;[17] sturzstorms, large rock flows that can move rapidly over great distances (e.g., 175 mph over distances of up to 25 miles), can also create widespread destruction.[18]

2.1.3.3   Flood

Floods occur when an area is unable to discharge a stock or flow of water to accommodate a new inflow of water. They are random events characterized by uncertain timing and intensity – though certain at-risk areas, such as floodplains, can be identified in advance, and forecasting tools can indicate when threatening weather might strike.[19]

In general, a river (or other body of water) seeks equilibrium of input and output, where the equilibrium depends on the amount of input, channel pattern, channel gradient, and level of sediment. When there is too much water, excess energy builds, extra sediment is collected, erosion and meandering commence, and the water flow slows. If a river has too much sediment and insufficient water, the stream bottom and gradient increase, causing water flow to accelerate. When an excess of water is introduced into such a system the equilibrium is disrupted; the amount of flooding that results is a function of the state of the river at that time. Flooding is also influenced by the nature of the floodplain, which is a series of streambeds that appear during wet conditions and 'disappear' in dry conditions; the beds, which are created by streams through erosion and deposits, can be reoccupied when needed (e.g., when excess water builds).

Floods occur in rivers, streams and other bodies of water (e.g., lakes, sea coasts), and they can be triggered by various events: thunderstorms with drenching rains can create a flash flood that generally dissipates very quickly; several days of steady rainfall can lead to ground saturation that leads to days or weeks of regional flooding; natural or man-made dams can create a water backup that causes a rise in water levels and flooding into proximate areas; dams and levees designed to hold water back can fail, causing flooding downriver; storm surges from tropical cyclones can create coastal floods; urbanization can prevent water from soaking into the ground, leading to faster excess discharge through urban waterways and the onset of urban flash floods; and decomposition of winter ice on rivers can lead to ice jam floods.

Though many floods are minor and thus non-catastrophic, others are significantly larger and capable of creating widespread death and destruction. From a human perspective, flash floods are especially dangerous, accounting for 50% of all flood-related deaths. Slow-moving regional floods, though less costly in human terms, can cause very extensive structural damage over a period of days or weeks. Such events tend to occur in large river valleys with low topography. Indeed, populated floodplains with significant development are at high

---

[17] For instance, in the 1920 Gansu Province earthquake, loess flows from surrounding dry hills and mountains contributed to the deaths of more than 200 000.

[18] In a sturzstorm at Turtle Mountain in Alberta several tons of limestone dropped approximately 1/2 mile downward and then flowed an additional 2 miles into the valley, killing 70.

[19] The availability of historical data allows a flood frequency curve to be developed for a particular region; a plot of peak water discharge versus recurrence allows engineers and developers to plan their development activities accordingly, e.g., avoiding areas with a frequent return period.

risk.[20] Development in the floodplain is hardly surprising: proximity to rivers and other bodies of water is important as a local population needs to be near agriculture, transportation, and power; this means vulnerabilities rise, making risk mitigation essential (e.g., dams, levees, channels, zoning). But attempts at mitigation can also contribute to problems. Dams and levees, for instance, are routinely overtopped or suffer from structural weakness that can lead to collapse – creating even more flooding. Indeed, hundreds of major dams have failed over the decades, and dam integrity is a pervasive concern.[21] Levees can occasionally do more harm than good, increasing the risk of flooding; a barrier that attempts to constrain or control the force of water in a floodplain can easily be challenged. An area that has expanded on the basis of a belief that a levee will provide adequate security can suffer significant losses.

It is important to note that while the natural catastrophes we have described in this section are the result of geophysical or meteorological forces, some can also be influenced by human activities. For instance, there is now significant evidence that greenhouse gas emissions generated by human activities lead to global warming; global warming, in turn, has been linked to an increased incidence of tropical storm activity, flooding, and drought, some of which have produced (and will continue to produce) extreme social and economic losses.[22] Similarly, mass development of urban areas and growing population density, coupled with insufficient rainfall and/or supply of water, can lead to severe urban drought conditions and associated losses. Man-made activities can thus induce, promote, accelerate, or intensify the onset of certain naturally occurring events.

2.2   MAN-MADE CATASTROPHE

Man-made catastrophes are disaster events originating from human activities or forces. Such events are important to analyze and manage in a society that has become heavily dependent on capital, technology, and industry to accomplish its daily activities, and which suffers from geopolitical conflicts that increase the threat of violent action. In this section we consider four broad categories of man-made catastrophes, including terrorism, industrial contamination, technological failure, and financial dislocation.

2.2.1   Terrorism

Terrorism can be defined as a premeditated, illegal, and covertly planned act of violence on life, property, and/or social/political/economic structures, with the intent of influencing authority or instilling shock, fear, or panic in the public. Indeed, the impact on public psyche is a central goal of terrorism – fear and insecurity can be damaging for open societies accustomed to trust and freedom.[23] A terrorist act may be perpetrated by an individual or group, with or without political, religious, or social affiliations, and may impact a city or region, or cross borders to

---

[20] In the USA, 2.5% of floodplain land is developed (and supports 6.5% of the country's population) and is therefore considered to be at risk.

[21] In the USA, the Army Corps of Engineers has estimated through surveys that approximately 25% of 8500 US dams have structural defects that may make them unsafe under stressed conditions.

[22] The class of general circulation models created in the 1990s to examine hydrological and atmospheric cycles has predicted a rise in storms and extreme events as a result of climate change, i.e., global warming. Some models and practitioners, however, have not seen a direct linkage between global warming and the incidence of Atlantic hurricanes, for example. In practice, natural variability, rather than climate change, may be a more relevant driver of hurricanes over the coming decades.

[23] Consider, for instance, that while the release of a few grams of radioactive cobalt-60 in a city center would kill only a few people, the act would lead to mass evacuation and create widespread, and enduring, social panic and instability – key goals of certain terrorist organizations.

affect a broader area. The process is necessarily covert as the relatively small number of those involved cannot generally challenge authority in a direct manner. Unlike many of the other disasters we have noted above, terrorism has no spatial or temporal boundaries; attacks can theoretically occur anywhere, and at any time (though in practice target locations are likely to be ranked by security vulnerability, economic/social significance, human/financial damage potential, and attack method requirements). Note that not all terrorist acts are catastrophic; indeed, most are not, when measured by loss of life, economic damage, or social instability. Only a small number of events assume catastrophic proportions.

Terrorists can operate across borders, their motives and methods may not always be fully understood, and they can act in a highly unpredictable and elusive manner. Groups that are centralized may be more susceptible to counter-terrorism measures but may also be able to accumulate greater resources for a larger attack; decentralized cells stand a better chance of avoiding capture but may have less destructive capability.[24]

In general, terrorism risk increases as actions become more coordinated and access to increasingly destructive materiel improves (e.g., nuclear, biological, chemical, radiological (NBCR) devices); use of communication and transportation mechanisms of the modern era can help facilitate coordination, planning, and execution. Safety matters are complicated by the large number of potential targets, the density of people and asset values associated with the targets, and the willingness by some terrorists to engage in suicide/martyrdom actions (which are especially difficult to defend against). Though terrorism has existed for many centuries, its potential social and financial impact started to become more significant during the 1990s and into the millennium, when numerous groups began carrying out larger and bolder actions; in fact, some studies suggest that larger attacks are consistent with a growing number of groups that advocate mass human, social, and economic destruction.[25] Naturally, not all terrorist activity is based on physical destruction for religious, socio-political, or geopolitical reasons; some is associated with economic gain, e.g., via cyber crime (including computer-based fraud, embezzlement, and theft) and industrial espionage.

While certain parallels exist between terrorism and the natural disasters we have described above – namely, relative infrequency and potentially large severity – there is a key distinguishing feature between the two: specifically, while natural disasters occur randomly and without intent, terrorism is driven by human intent. This means human behaviors must be considered. Indeed, terrorism cannot be viewed in the same way as a natural force that must adhere to the laws of science and nature, or as a complex mechanical system that has particular failure points – it must be considered in light of both subjective and objective factors, which we shall consider in greater detail in Chapter 4.

Though terrorists act unexpectedly (just as an earthquake or flash flood might appear unexpectedly) they do not do so randomly – events are planned and have some end goal. While terrorists seek to destabilize, their reasons for wanting to do so, and the specific aims they hope to achieve, are often quite unique (e.g., claiming victims, destroying symbolic targets, inflicting economic damage). Ultimately, the success of a terrorist act is generally influenced by two factors, detection and execution, each of which can be assessed separately. A plot that

---

[24] Some decentralized organizations operate with independent hubs that control individual cells; others have no such hubs, meaning they can be assembled and dismantled rapidly.

[25] For instance, the first World Trade Center bombing of 1993 caused $725m of insured property damages, the City of London car bombings of 1992 and 1993 registered at just under $1.4b, and the 1996 Manchester car bombing at $745m. Events such as the simultaneous attacks of 9/11 demonstrate that a single terrorist campaign, which claimed over 3000 lives and caused over $90b in direct and indirect insured/uninsured losses, can have the same destructive power as a single massive earthquake or hurricane.

is not detected can proceed until the execution phase; one that is detected fails before damage can be done. An undetected plot can result in damage if the execution phase is perfect, or it can lead to no damage if some execution failure occurs.

Unlike various natural disasters we have discussed, where frequency of occurrence remains relatively constant over time, terrorism has the potential of growing in frequency. While this depends ultimately on available resources, motivations, and counter-terrorism responses, there appear to be no apparent natural constraints that prevent frequencies from increasing.[26]

Human intervention via loss control measures (e.g., increased security, checkpoints, and so on) can reduce the probability of an occurrence; this is not a certainty, of course, and increased security measures in one area may simply cause terrorists to shift their focus to a secondary target with less protection. However, in a world of infinite resources, it is possible for human intervention to actually succeed in reducing the probability of a terrorist event. National governments can influence terrorist activity by their actions and defensive assets; depending on the nature of the assets and the threat, terrorist activities can be reduced, delayed, and perhaps eliminated (in a narrow sense).

2.2.2   Industrial contamination

Industrial contamination is a man-made peril that is driven largely by society's use of chemical and biological agents with toxic or harmful by-products, which must be used, handled, stored, treated, and disposed of with care. Industrial contamination can take various forms, including direct spillage or discharge of pollutants into the environment, accidental explosion leading to release or dispersal of toxic materials,[27] use of materials thought to be safe that ultimately prove harmful (e.g., asbestos and lead paint), and flawed disposal/storage which results in degradation of the containment facility and release of harmful agents into the environment. Minor instances of contamination are not considered catastrophic. For instance, localized contamination of a building or parts of a town or port through the release of medical waste, low-level radioactive material, industrial by-products, or marine toxins would not be classified as a disaster.

In some cases contamination can reach catastrophic proportions, particularly when toxicity of the contaminant is high and the affected region is large and/or densely populated; the latter dimension reverts, once again, to the level of vulnerability. For example, if a manufacturing company accidentally spills a large amount of highly poisonous chemicals into the local water supply, it may create significant physical and economic damage in the surrounding commun-ities; if the chemicals lack odor and color, the spillage may remain undetected for an extended period of time, compounding the effects of the disaster.[28]

---

[26] There may, of course, be certain constraints related to repeated activity in a single location, as security and counter-terrorism measures are likely to expand in a location that has been the target of some action.

[27] Intentional explosion would more appropriately be considered an act of crime or terrorism, even though the physical damage might be equivalent.

[28] Various examples reinforce the point. For instance, in late 1984 chemical company Union Carbide accidentally released 40 tons of methyl isocyanate used in fertilizer production from its chemical manufacturing facility in Bhopal, India. The catastrophic contamination caused more than 2000 immediate deaths (along with an estimated 6000 deaths several weeks/months later, and more than 150 000 injuries); the company ultimately paid $500m in restitution. In 1989, the oil tanker Exxon Valdez spilled 11m gallons of crude oil into Prince William Sound off the coast of Alaska, creating an environmental disaster of significant proportions; more than 1200 miles of coastline suffered damage and hundreds of thousands of birds and fish were destroyed. Exxon, prior to its merger with Mobil, eventually paid $300m in damages and $2.2b for clean-up, and contributed $1b to state and federal government programs; it was also served with a punitive damage penalty of $4b. More generally, the use of asbestos in building construction materials prior to the discovery of its harmful (and often fatal) effects resulted in catastrophic losses for companies (and insurers) that were required to compensate victims.

Nuclear accidents can also lead to catastrophic damage and contamination. Though the probability of a nuclear accident is extremely small given the safeguards and loss control mechanisms that are incorporated into the design and operation of reactor facilities, the resulting damage may be significant and include immediate deaths from radiation poisoning, and indirect deaths over time from cancer and contaminated food and water.[29]

2.2.3 Technological failure

Technological failure, which we define to include failure of mechanical or structural processes, including computers, communication networks, infrastructure, buildings, and mechanical or engineering devices, is another peril that can lead to catastrophic losses. This has become especially true in the latter part of the 20th, and early 21st, centuries, where many economic sectors have become extremely dependent on mechanical/technological infrastructure and advanced engineering to conduct business. Automation, aviation, transportation, information processing, satellite tracking/imaging, networking/communications, power generation/distribution, product design/assembly, and so forth, are often based solely or primarily on technological processes. With increasingly sophisticated computing and communication technologies, dependence (i.e., vulnerability) grows ever larger, meaning that any failure can lead to disastrous consequences that may be on a financial (if not human) par with an earthquake or hurricane. Indeed, the depth and breadth of personal and commercial losses due to business interruption can be substantial, and increases as society becomes more reliant on technology to conduct its affairs; in fact, vulnerability to technological failure may be increasing more rapidly than vulnerability to other perils.

Technological failure may be accidental or deliberate, and attributable to human error, lack of control, or criminal intent (when failure is designed to intentionally destabilize social mechanisms, the peril is more appropriately considered an act of terrorism, as above). For instance, in developed nations electric power grids are finely tuned technological mechanisms that must be managed and balanced properly in order to deliver power when, and where, needed. Any failure of the process for engineering or technological reasons can leave communities and businesses without power for a period lasting from hours to days, leading to hundreds of millions, if not billions, of dollars in losses from interrupted business.[30] As dependence on both energy and automation grow in the future, the potential for increasingly severe events rises and financial costs may become extremely large.

Similarly, technological failure from engineering faults can lead to structural collapse of buildings and bridges (with or without a catalyst such as an earthquake); those related to mechanical faults or maintenance failures can create malfunctions leading to disaster.[31] Computer network malfunctions serve as another important example. Though technical collapse can occur

---

[29] While the USA and Japan have experienced low level nuclear accidents in the past (e.g., at Three Mile Island in 1979 and Tokaimura in 1999, respectively), the example of the nuclear meltdown at Chernobyl in the Ukraine serves as a potent reminder of the catastrophic proportions of the peril. Specifically, in 1986 human error led to a power surge in one of Chernobyl's four reactors, causing the 1000-ton reactor roof to blow off and a partial core meltdown to release a significant amount of uranium dioxide and fissionable by-products into the atmosphere. Contamination levels of 185m curies (a measure of radioactive strength) were of fatal proportions, and well in excess of the mere 17 curies released during the Three Mile Island incident; dozens of deaths occurred in the immediate vicinity. Tragically, the atmospheric dispersal of the contaminants led to an estimated 165 000 deaths in the Ukraine and surrounding areas of Europe over the ensuing decade, as well as widespread loss of crops and livestock.

[30] We can again point to various examples of such large-scale technological grid failure, including those in the US West Coast (1996), Auckland (1998), and New England/Mid-Atlantic (2003); in each case engineering, computing, and/or communications technologies failed, causing massive (and sometimes prolonged) power outages.

[31] Examples include the space shuttle disasters, explosion of the Piper Alpha oil rig in the North Sea, and so forth.

for a number of reasons, there has already been evidence in the 21st century of flawed computer code causing significant data problems and computer viruses spreading rapidly through computer networks, disabling communications and destroying data. While past incidents have been large, they have not yet been catastrophic; many experts believe, however, that a significant technological collapse is inevitable, particularly as network connectivity and penetration continue to expand. Unlike other catastrophes, this sector represents 'uncharted territory;' there is no meaningful historical data reflecting the financial losses of such a technical collapse.

2.2.4   Financial dislocation

Traditional financial asset markets, including those related to equities, fixed income securities, currencies, and certain types of commodities, are an essential element of economic and financial progress. Indeed, the financial system of the 21st century is a complex system of cross-border capital flows that requires stability in order to function effectively. This is particularly true of deregulated industrialized financial markets, which account for much of the world's capital raising and investment. Since these markets are freely accessible by a large number of investors and intermediaries, it is not surprising that they are susceptible to periodic volatility and pressure. The ability for buyers and sellers to quickly enter a particular market, execute strategies/orders, and reallocate funds to other sectors is at once a benefit and a liability; the efficiency injects liquidity and makes possible activity, but also increases the specter of instability. During periods of intense leveraged speculation or economic weakness, crisis conditions can build; risky assets may no longer be considered favorably, causing bouts of selling and a large migration into relatively risk-free assets. Such one-way activity may create illiquid conditions and heighten the overall sense of panic in the marketplace. The financial dislocation that ensues may be fuelled by counterparty or sovereign defaults, bank runs, and/or stopped payments. The 'worst-case' scenario manifests itself in systemic dislocation affecting participants in a large number of countries. In the most extreme cases direct or indirect government intervention may be required to stave off a deeper crisis.

Financial dislocations of the most severe type are catastrophic events that are created by human activity. That said, the catalyst for the dislocation could come from any number of sources, including natural and man-made events. For instance, it is possible that an exceptionally large earthquake striking Tokyo or Los Angeles could create significant financial instability in the global markets;[32] a large terrorist event in a major capital might produce similar reactions.[33] In fact, any significant event that causes investors to lose capital and take protective actions (including reducing leverage and shifting to low-risk assets) can increase volatility, create illiquid conditions, and generate financial losses.[34] Although financial crises lack the human tragedy of natural catastrophes and terrorist acts, they can be financially devastating to a large number of individuals and institutions.

There are, of course, other types of man-made and natural catastrophes, some of which manifest themselves in widespread mortality and/or financial loss. Internal political conflict leading to genocide, spreading of communicable diseases (e.g., SARS, HIV, respiratory pandemics), starvation, and so forth, are all tragic events that can assume catastrophic

---

[32] In fact, the 1995 Kobe earthquake caused a very significant sell-off in the Japanese stock market.

[33] For instance, the events of 9/11 halted trading on the New York Stock Exchange for several days and led to a period of uncertainty, illiquidity, and price volatility in the financial markets at large.

[34] Such catastrophic financial dislocations are not, of course, theoretical; they occur every few years or decades, as in 1929 (the Great Crash), 1987 (global stock market crash), and 1998 (the Russian crisis and hedge fund crisis).

proportions – human, social, and economic. While these are obviously of vital importance, particularly in a social context, we shall not consider them in further detail.[35]

2.3   MEGA-CATASTROPHE AND CLASH LOSS

There are instances when disasters are so large that they cause extremely devastating losses; these are known as mega-catastrophes and, while they are fortunately very rare, they do occur. Though definitions vary, a mega-catastrophe typically generates more than $50b of direct and indirect losses, and very often occurs when a single peril triggers associated damage-inducing events. For instance, a hurricane may strike a coastal area, causing damage from wind and storm surge; once overland the storm may spawn tornadoes and additional rainfall, causing even greater amounts of damage. Or, a large earthquake in a metropolitan area can initially create widespread physical damage and fatalities from ground motion, and may then trigger land mass movements and urban fires, which compound the damage and losses. A terrorist bomb that destroys a building may also create destruction and fire in proximate areas and lead to suspension of transportation and communication services, mass evacuation, and business interruption.

Clash losses, or losses impacting several areas of insurable risk simultaneously, often accompany a mega-catastrophe. Indeed, the sheer scope and scale of mega-catastrophes often leads to direct losses related to property and life, and indirect losses related to liability, business interruption, workers' compensation, and health. Mega-catastrophes and associated clash losses represent the pinnacle of disaster.[36] As noted in Chapter 1, there now appears to be greater sensitivity among many parties that further mega-catastrophes costing $50b–100b are quite likely to occur in the coming years and decades.

While the source and nature of perils is a vital dimension of the identification process, it must be supplemented by vulnerability assessment to be truly accurate and useful; we consider this topic in the next chapter.

---

[35] In fact, some insurers/reinsurers (e.g., Swiss Re through Vita Capital) have securitized excess mortality arising from large-scale biological terrorism and diseases, essentially transferring the risk of excess payouts on life insurance policies from the insurance market to the capital markets.

[36] Perhaps the most vivid example of clash loss relates to the events of 9/11, when the four airplane hijackings and crashes created significant losses on several fronts: property, aircraft hull, liability, workers' compensation, health, and life. The $90b in direct and indirect losses were approximately 50% covered by insurance, making it the single largest insurance-related settlement in history.

3
Risk Identification II:
Regional Vulnerability

In order to properly manage the catastrophic perils we have described in the last chapter it is necessary to expand the identification process by highlighting regions that can be impacted by natural or man-made disasters. This provides essential information regarding the human and economic damage that can be wrought by a particular event; indeed, knowledge of regional vulnerabilities is an important input in the quantitative process we discuss in the next chapter, and is useful when considering the private and public sector risk management solutions covered in Part II.

A proper understanding of the regional impact of disaster allows institutions to map the value of 'at-risk' areas and identify which human/economic centers are likely to face the most significant losses. Not surprisingly, the more granular the regional analysis the better the identification and assessment process. Thus, it is not sufficient (or particularly helpful) to indicate that the USA is exposed to hurricane risk; the USA is a large country featuring areas that are very developed and densely populated, as well as those that are quite rural and unpopulated, so the information tells us little. Instead, it is essential to know that the Southeastern and Gulf states of the USA (Texas, Louisiana, Mississippi, Florida) are exposed to Gulf and lower Atlantic hurricanes, while the Mid-Atlantic and Northeastern states (Carolinas, Virginia, Maryland, New Jersey, New York, the balance of New England) are exposed to North Atlantic hurricanes; much of the coastal region is well developed and therefore potentially at risk. From there, further regional clarification is necessary (e.g., within the state of Florida, Dade, Broward, Palm Beach, and various other counties are at risk). More granular information (e.g., ZIP codes/postal codes, individual commercial buildings) makes the vulnerability identification process even more accurate, allowing development of meaningful loss assessments based on property, buildings, infrastructure, and contents.[1]

Our aim in this chapter is to highlight general regions that are exposed to natural and man-made disasters; in the interest of space we shall not explore in detail the specific metropolitan or suburban centers that are at greatest risk. In fact, most of the regions we cite in this chapter contain densely populated centers with concentrated wealth and asset values – meaning many of these locations are vulnerable to significant loss. While our discussion is necessarily an overview, it should be clear detailed analysis, to the level of ZIP codes/postal codes or individual structures, is an essential requirement of the quantification process that any company, sovereign, or insurer might undertake.

---

[1] The vulnerability assessment process improves with information regarding the resistive capacity/strength of buildings and other structures, which may be classified by structure type and construction material. Structural engineers generally examine these characteristics in light of natural and man-made forces in order to determine how they will perform in the face of an event of a given magnitude.

3.1 SPATIAL IMPACT OF NATURAL CATASTROPHES

3.1.1 Bermuda and the North American Atlantic Coast

Bermuda and the Atlantic coast of the USA and Canada are susceptible to very strong hurricanes. A North Atlantic hurricane can have a storm diameter ranging from 100 to 800 miles (with an eye of 10 to 40 miles), and can last from 1 to 15 days (longer duration events can occur, but are far less common). Though storm track depends on the specific atmospheric conditions present as a storm evolves, most Atlantic hurricanes follow a westerly path and then veer northwards. Hurricanes that commence as tropical storms off Cape Verde on the Western coast of Africa are most likely to impact the Atlantic coast. These storms move quickly across the Atlantic via the trade winds, accumulating heat and energy from warm water along the way. Once in the Atlantic their precise track depends on varying pockets of pressure (e.g., the size of the Bermuda high pressure zone, which is influenced by the North Atlantic Oscillation). For instance, if the Bermuda High is weak and centered far to the north the hurricane moves to the northwest, avoiding the coastline; if the Bermuda High is strong and located in a more southerly position, the storm continues to move in a westerly direction until it makes landfall, either in the Mid-Atlantic or the Northeast. Areas at risk include the island of Bermuda and the US Atlantic/Northeast seaboard, running from Georgia up through Maine and into Nova Scotia. In fact, much of the Atlantic coast is very developed, with commercial, residential, and tourist centers prevalent all along the shoreline; vulnerabilities are very significant.

Over the past century the region has averaged a minimum of 2, and a maximum of 12, hurricanes per year; those making landfall have created significant destruction, ranging from hundreds of millions to billions of dollars in property damage and business interruption. This is particularly true of storms reaching the New England coast,[2] as the relative infrequency of a hurricane landfall means emergency preparedness and risk mitigation are not as prominent as in other hurricane-prone regions.

3.1.2 Florida

The state of Florida is exposed to significant hurricane risk, and has experienced several very damaging events over the years, including Hugo (1989), Andrew (1992), and Ivan, Frances, Charley, and Jeanne (2004). The eastern and western coasts of the state, which are at risk to direct landfall, feature significant vulnerabilities as a result of dense population centers and heavily developed commercial, residential, and tourist infrastructure. Hurricanes first striking Florida often continue to track into other regions, affecting neighboring states such as Georgia and the Carolinas to the north, and Mississippi, Louisiana, Alabama, and Texas to the west.

Hurricane Andrew was a watershed event for the insurance and crisis management sectors as the level of devastation it created was unprecedented (and largely unexpected). The storm developed off the west coast of Africa in mid-August 1992, becoming an Atlantic tropical storm three days later. The storm gathered strength over the next five days, achieving hurricane status, and by the time it passed through the Bahamas (causing $250m of damage) it was a Category 4 storm with sustained winds of more than 140 mph. Andrew reached Florida 10 days after it developed, making landfall in the area of Biscayne Bay and Homestead Air Force Base. Though it was originally classed as a Category 4 hurricane, it was later upgraded to Category 5,

---

[2] The 1938 New England hurricane remains one of the most devastating in US history, with major damage discovered as far inland as upstate New York, interior Connecticut, Massachusetts, and Vermont.

making it only the third Category 5 storm to make landfall in the USA in the 20th century. After sweeping through Florida for three days, creating widespread destruction, it reached the Gulf of Mexico, reintensified, and tracked towards Louisiana, where it caused further damage before finally dying out. The extent of the destruction became clear in the aftermath of the storm: 90 direct and indirect deaths, 25 000+ destroyed homes, and 100 000 damaged structures; the total insurance claim estimate amounted to $15.5b (total losses reached $26b), well in excess of any amount estimated by the insurance industry or analytic firms. Unfortunately, during the claims settlement process it became clear that 25–40% of the damage could have been avoided by following the voluntary standards set forth by the State of Florida Building Code.

3.1.3 North American West Coast

The west coast of North America, extending from Alaska, through Canada, and southwards to Washington, Oregon, and California, is one of the most seismically active regions of the world. The region, which features major conurbations such as Vancouver, Seattle/Tacoma, Portland, San Francisco, Los Angeles, and San Diego, has experienced very large earthquakes over the years, including notable events such as San Fernando (1971), Loma Pietro (1989), and Northridge (1994).[3] Northridge was particularly devastating and surprised many seismologists: the earthquake, a blind thrust fault event, occurred on a previously unrecognized fault line, causing widespread physical damage in an area previously believed to be quite safe.[4] The earthquake, a 6.7 magnitude event, impacted a 30-mile area in north Los Angeles/south Ventura counties. More than 4000 buildings were destroyed (a further 8500 were moderately damaged), and seven freeway bridges collapsed; steel beams and welding joints cracked at a much higher rate than expected, and structural engineering and construction designs proved in some cases to be wholly inadequate.[5] Fortunately, the earthquake struck at 4.30 a.m., meaning loss of life was limited to 60 people; had it occurred three hours later, during the morning commute on the freeways, estimates suggest that as many as 3000 may have been killed. Total direct and indirect losses were ultimately estimated at $40b, with insurable losses of $14b.

In the aftermath of the event more stringent building codes and construction standards were created, retrofits were completed, and new structural designs were introduced. Further significant earthquakes are expected along the west coast of North America (e.g., analytics firm RMS estimates that there is a 65% probability of at least one very significant earthquake occurring in a metropolitan center of California by 2013).

Given the strong linkage between plate tectonics and volcanic activity, it is no surprise that the region features active volcanoes. Indeed, the Cascade Range in the Pacific Northwest and proximate sites such as Mount Saint Helens, Mount Shasta, Glacier Peak, and Mount Rainier, have erupted on multiple occasions over the past few centuries. For example, in May 1980 Mount Saint Helens erupted, blowing off the top 1300 feet of its cone, killing more than 60

---

[3] In fact, the strongest earthquake ever recorded on the North American continent, a 9.2 event, occurred 120 miles east of Anchorage, Alaska; fortunately, the area was relatively sparsely populated, meaning the death and damage toll were relatively minor for an event of that size.

[4] In fact, the combination of the surprise event and the resulting economic losses was a catalyst in the development of new modeling techniques. The unique characteristics of the blind thrust fault led researchers to discover similar faults in the Los Angeles Basin, San Fernando Valley, and other areas. The US Geological Service eventually concluded that up to 15% of seismic activity in the region could be based on similar blind thrust faults. Commercial modelers updated their models to reflect blind thrust faults, as well as additional data obtained from soil response and liquefaction.

[5] However, the 1971 San Fernando earthquake, which led to the creation of new building codes, undoubtedly helped reduce some amount of damage.

and causing widespread damage. The event was triggered by a 5.1 earthquake, which created a landslide and caused a drop in pressure in the gaseous magma in the volcano; the pressure led to a large blast of pyroclastic debris, an opening of the volcano's throat, and a violent Plinian eruption that lasted more than 9 hours.

The region is also at risk to fire and hurricane. With regard to fire, the region features ample supplies of fuel (e.g., dry forest, scrub, dead wood), foehn winds (e.g., Santa Anas), and generally arid conditions – all ideal for fires. In fact, large fires have impacted the residential and commercial areas around San Diego, Los Angeles, San Francisco, and Oakland over the past few decades. For instance, on a single day in October 1991 the Oakland/Berkley fire, fuelled by a five-year drought and large amounts of dead vegetation, left 25 people dead, 2500 homes destroyed, and $1.5b of property destruction. With regard to hurricanes, events affecting the west coast are relatively infrequent compared with those in the Western Pacific or Atlantic, as trade winds push most storms westward into the central Pacific. In addition, most storms lack the intensity of Atlantic or mid-Pacific storms as they are fueled by cold water from Alaska rather than warm Gulf, Caribbean, or mid-Pacific waters. Nevertheless, the potential for strike and damage exists.

3.1.4   US Great Plains/Midwest

The Plains and Midwestern states of the USA, including Nebraska, Oklahoma, Texas, Kansas, Missouri, Iowa, Illinois, Indiana, Kentucky, and adjacent regions are the site of various perils, including tornadoes, flooding, and earthquakes. Each state has major centers of population, commercial development, and agriculture, suggesting that human and economic vulnerabilities are high.

The broad region accounts for roughly 70% of all tornado strikes recorded globally, pointing to an undue concentration of risk. Approximately 1000 tornadoes are recorded in an average year, though most are classified as non-catastrophic F0–F2 events.[6] Oklahoma and Texas have historically featured the largest absolute number of tornadoes, while Kansas has been the site of the largest number of F5 and F6 tornadoes. Interestingly, a series of F2–F3 tornadoes occurring in the Plains or Midwest can, in any given year, account for $1–4b of damages; several years of such activity (which is not uncommon) can generate economic losses that are on a par with a single earthquake or hurricane event in a populated zone. Certain episodes of tornadic activity have been very devastating. For instance, in 1925 the 'Tri-State Tornadoes' of Illinois, Indiana, and Mississippi traveled 219 miles, destroyed portions of 23 towns and cities, and killed more than 700 people. In April 1974, 148 tornadoes struck in 13 Midwestern states over 16 hours, causing 330 deaths and the destruction of 2500 structures. In May 1999, 76 tornadoes were spawned by storms in 18 Plains/Midwestern states (at least two tornadoes attained F5 and F6 classification); the event, which lasted several hours, damaged 10 000 homes, killed 46 people, and caused $1.5b of destruction.

The Midwest is also the site of significant flooding as a result of its river systems and developed floodplains. For instance, the Great Midwestern Flood of 1993, the largest upper Mississippi River basin flood in 140 years, occurred when very wet seasonal conditions led to ground saturation, rising water levels, and overtopping of levees and dams. Iowa and eight

---

[6] Some studies have suggested that tornadic activity in the central USA has tripled since the early 1950s, but this is almost certainly attributable to improvements in monitoring and reporting; apart from a slight relationship with ENSO cycles, many climatologists continue to believe that tornadic activity is relatively stable over time.

other states suffered extensive damage, including 48 deaths, 75 submerged towns, 50 000 damaged/destroyed homes, and a total of $12b in reconstruction costs.

The New Madrid Seismic Zone (NMSZ) in the central USA covers a region comprising Illinois, Indiana, Missouri, Kentucky, and bordering areas. Unlike California, Japan, and other plate-based regions, the NSMZ is an intraplate region, susceptible to large, though infrequent, events. In fact, the NMSZ has been at the center of several devastating earthquake events in the past two centuries. For instance, in a two-month period in 1811–1812, three powerful earthquakes (8.1, 7.8, 8.0) struck, leaving considerable devastation. Although the return period of the 1811–1812 earthquakes is estimated at approximately 1000 years, a repeat in the millennium would create extensive financial and social damage as a result of the economic development that has appeared over the years (e.g., as noted in Chapter 1, estimated costs of a severe NMSZ event run as high as $100b). Though events of the magnitude experienced in the early 19th century have not yet reappeared, NMSZ remains very active seismically, with over 4000 earthquakes recorded between 1974 and the early part of the millennium (most of them very small, and not noticeable to human senses).

3.1.5   Caribbean

The islands of the Caribbean are exposed to a range of perils, including hurricane, windstorm, earthquake, volcanic eruption, and flooding. Though not all islands are impacted by all perils, the region as a whole is at high risk to natural disaster; since many of the islands rely on tourism and agriculture to drive economic growth, significant vulnerabilities exist. Islands such as St. Lucia, Jamaica, Belize, Barbados, Antigua, Anguilla, Trinidad, Haiti, Grenada, Dominican Republic, Tobago, St. Kitts, and the Bahamas have been impacted repeatedly in recent decades by hurricane and flooding, while the tourist island of Montserrat was devastated by volcanic eruption in mid-1997 and has become largely uninhabitable.[7]

Caribbean/Gulf hurricanes are a major threat to the region. Most storms form in the Intertropical Convergence Zone when westerly trade winds converge with air flowing from the Equator to the north. Tropical depressions can develop where convergence occurs; the strongest of these can ultimately develop into hurricanes and sweep through the Outward and Leeward islands of the Caribbean, creating damage along the way. Once a hurricane moves through the Caribbean it can regenerate in the Gulf of Mexico and strike the Mexican coast, or it can veer northwards to the Southeastern coast of the USA. Islands such as Grenada, Haiti, Dominican Republic, Cuba, Jamaica, and the Caymans, among others, have all been affected over the years by hurricanes (e.g., Haiti was heavily impacted by Hurricane Jeanne in 2004, suffering at least 2000 deaths and hundreds of millions of dollars in damages from winds and flooding).

3.1.6   Mexico

Mexico is heavily exposed to a number of catastrophic perils and has experienced significant disasters over the years, including more than 80 of consequence between 1980 and the early part of the millennium (which together caused more than 30 000 deaths and at least $12b

---

[7] Specifically, between 1992 and 1997 the Soufrierre Hills volcano erupted on a regular basis; as events became more intense, more than 80% of the island's population was evacuated. Even after the major eruptions of 1997 the volcano has remained active.

of direct economic losses). These disasters have destroyed aspects of the country's social and physical infrastructure, and affected human and financial conditions; given accelerating population growth and urban migration, vulnerabilities remain high.

Mexico's disaster exposure and experience includes earthquakes, hurricanes, and floods (the dominant perils), along with drought, volcanic activity, and land mass movement. The country is seismically active, sitting atop four tectonic plates that create significant geophysical instabilities; the most active sites include the Guererro coast, Jalisco, Chiapas, and Tehuantepec, all of which are heavily populated. Over the past century Mexico has featured more than 85 7.0+ magnitude earthquakes; the 1985 earthquake that struck Mexico City was particularly devastating, resulting in the death of more than 10 000 people and the collapse of more than 6000 structures. The epicenter was relatively far from the capital (i.e., 200+ miles), but since the city is built atop a dry lakebed, seismic waves were amplified (some amount of liquefaction also occurred). Given its seismic construct, the country also features significant volcanic activity. In recent decades 14 major volcanoes have erupted, creating damage through lava, ash discharge, and lahars. For instance, the Chichon volcano erupted in 1982, killing 2000 and creating more than $100m in crop damage and deforestation.

Mexico is also vulnerable to tropical cyclones on both of its coasts, with the coastal regions of Tehuantepec, Campeche, Eastern Caribbean and tropical Atlantic most susceptible. In fact, 40% of the population of the five Mexican states most prone to hurricane lives on the coast, suggesting considerable vulnerabilities and potential for loss. The country's tropical cyclone season, which extends from June to October, typically brings heavy rainfall and the threat of additional damage from flooding and land mass movement. Between 1970 and 1980 the country experienced more than 150 tropical storms and cyclones, including 50 strong enough to create significant damage; an additional 40 events followed between 1980 and the millennium. The country also features urban flash floods, which arise from construction on the floodplain, deforestation, and erosion; between 1970 and the millennium flash floods claimed more than 2000 lives and caused economic losses of $8b.

3.1.7 Japan

Japan, like portions of the USA and Mexico, is at risk to several major classes of natural disasters, including earthquakes, volcanic eruption, and typhoons. All of these perils have impacted the island nation repeatedly over the years, and the heavy concentration of population and asset values makes it especially vulnerable.

Japan's earthquake and volcanic risks are due to the fact that the country is formed atop three tectonic plates (the Pacific, Eurasian, and Philippine); it is susceptible to regular, and sometimes very significant, plate movement. The Tokyo earthquake of 1923 was exceptionally damaging: the 8.2 event, centered in Sagami Bay southwest of the Tokyo/Yokohama region, created massive ground-shaking that leveled large portions of the city. Unfortunately, many of the buildings that were unaffected by the initial earthquake were later destroyed by fire: in the aftermath of the earthquake the city burned for nearly three days as shifting winds hampered relief efforts. Coastal regions around Yokohama and outer Tokyo were further impacted by a 36-foot tsunami. The extent of the damage became clear after the disaster: 71% of the houses in Tokyo, and 100% of those in Yokohama, were destroyed by the combined effects of earthquake, fire, and tsunami, and rebuilding took years to complete.

In January 1995 the Kobe earthquake, a 14-second event measuring 7.2, killed approximately 5500 people and damaged over 150 000 buildings (primarily wooden housing structures and buildings made of reinforced concrete). More than $100b of direct and indirect losses occurred (only $3b covered by insurance), raising questions about the efficacy of engineering and construction methods. In fact, extensive post-event analysis suggests that human and economic damage would have been much worse but for enforcement of acceptable building standards. The actual earthquake occurred less than 10 miles from the Earth's surface in a rupture approximately 35 miles long in the Akashi Strait; the relatively shallow event concentrated damage in the immediate vicinity of Kobe. The earthquake also spawned urban fires (particularly among the many small wooden structures in the residential zone), which added to the overall damage; though only 1% of Kobe was destroyed by fire, it represented Japan's largest urban fire in decades.

The features that give rise to Japan's seismicity also create volcanic activity. Though far less common than earthquakes, the country has experienced various eruptions in areas proximate to population centers. For instance, Mount Unzen, one of the most active pyroclastic flow volcanoes in the world, has featured regular eruptions of debris (e.g., a 1991 event led to 42 deaths and significant financial damage in nearby towns).

Typhoons also strike the Japanese coast with some frequency, though the actual number making landfall in populated centers is relatively small. For instance, an average of 28 typhoons form in the vicinity of the Japanese archipelago during a given year; three of those actually cross land (though in 2004 a record eight typhoons made landfall). Several large events have crossed the islands over the past few decades. For instance, a large typhoon striking the Ise Bay in 1959 caused more than 5000 deaths. Typhoon Mireille (#19, 1991) and Typhoon Yancy (#13, 1993) were also devastating, and caused government agencies, insurers, and modeling firms to re-evaluate their view of typhoon threats and refine their modeling approaches.

3.1.8 South Asia/Southeast Asia

The broad region of South and Southeast Asia is exposed to a number of natural perils; indeed, over the past 30 years the region has been impacted by 15 of the world's 40 largest disasters. Virtually every major peril we have described in Chapter 2 has the potential of affecting the region: earthquake is prevalent in China, India, Pakistan, Nepal, and Indonesia, severe typhoons regularly hit the Philippines, Indonesia, Bangladesh, Taiwan, the South China coast, and India, volcanic eruptions occur in the Philippines and Indonesia, and flooding from heavy rains, typhoons, and general subsidence occurs in China, Bangladesh, the Philippines, Thailand, and Indonesia. The entire region is very densely populated, and commercial/residential development is extensive throughout; human and economic vulnerabilities are thus very significant. Indeed, the toll from these events has been enormous, and has added to the considerable financial strain many of these countries already operate under: low per capita output and wages, and instances of widespread poverty add to the financial pressures of post-disaster reconstruction. Given locational attributes and population growth rates, vulnerabilities are expected to expand further over the coming years.

China has been the location of many devastating earthquakes, including those produced by continental collisions between the enormous South Asian and Tibetan plates (which move each year by approximately 2 inches along a 1250-mile front in the region of India, Nepal, Bhutan, and China/Tibet). Indeed, the country is so seismically active and has such a large population that it accounts for approximately half of all global earthquake fatalities. For instance, the largest number of earthquake-related deaths ever recorded occurred in Shanxi Province in 1556, when an estimated 830 000 were killed. Unfortunately, similar devastation has occurred in modern times: China experienced more than 150 earthquakes during the 20th century that collectively killed 600 000 and caused billions of dollars of damage (e.g., the 1920 and 1932 earthquakes at Gansu killed a total of 270 000, the 1927 event at Xining more than 200 000, and the 1976 Tangshan earthquake 240 000 (though unofficial estimates suggest multiples of that amount)). China is also very susceptible to floods as a result of erosion, deforestation, and soil degradation. It is common to find river beds that have risen well above their natural levels as a result of these factors, creating a high incidence of flooding – some of it catastrophic. For instance, the Huang River is believed to be the source of more deadly floods than any other location in the world (e.g., the 1887 flood caused more than 1m deaths); other parts of the country feature significant flood risk as well.

Bangladesh is extremely vulnerable to cyclones and flooding. The country, which is very densely populated and has been developed on a very large and complex system of floodplains that cover 80% of the country, is in the direct path of many powerful tropical storms; every year approximately 20% of the country is submerged from tropical storms, heavy monsoon rains, and cyclones. Bangladesh experiences an average of 10 tropical storms and cyclones per year; half enter the Bay of Bengal before the monsoon season, the other half immediately after. Tragically, many of these events are cataclysmic, leaving behind widespread death and destruction. For instance, a November 1970 cyclone with 155 mph winds and 23-foot storm surge killed approximately 400 000 people. In April 1990 a cyclone featuring 145 mph winds and 20-foot storm surge drowned 140 000 people and left approximately 10m more homeless. The combination of powerful natural disasters and extremely high vulnerabilities (e.g., over-crowding, construction in the floodplain, lack of building standards/codes) means the country remains extremely susceptible to loss of life and assets.

Indonesia is impacted by various perils, including earthquakes, typhoons, and volcanic eruptions. The entire archipelago of islands has experienced repeated disasters over the past few decades, some resulting in widespread death and property damage. For instance, the country is at the center of considerable volcanic activity, and has experienced several significant eruptions (e.g., Krakatoa, Tambora). One of the most dramatic and historically famous events occurred in 1883 on Krakatoa, a group of small islands between Sumatra and Java: a series of eruptions over several days caused the volcano to collapse, creating a massive subterranean hole and killing more than 36 000. The Aceh region was the site of a devastating earthquake and tsunami in December 2004, which killed more than 150 000 throughout Indonesia and Southeast Asia.

Like Indonesia, the Philippines is at risk to volcanic eruption, earthquakes, and typhoons. The country has experienced many volcanic events over the past centuries. For instance, Mount Mayon has produced 40 major eruptions over the past four centuries (e.g., one every 10 years), each one resulting in casualties and losses. Mount Pinatubo has also been the site of considerable damage. Following 500 years of dormancy, Pinatubo began to reactivate in early 1991; after several months of increasingly strong expulsions, the volcano underwent a final cataclysmic eruption in the middle of the year. The eruption propelled 3.5 mi^3 of magma, rock, and ash 22 miles into the atmosphere. By unfortunate coincidence, the eruption was followed by a strong typhoon, which created a massive lahar that swept away entire towns and villages (though only 300 of a population of 20 000 were killed as a result of evacuation efforts). The country is also impacted by earthquakes (including 25 major events occurring during the 20th century alone) and experiences approximately 20 typhoons per year, including 10 that cross over the islands, causing damage through wind, coastal flooding, mass movement, and storm surge; two-thirds of the country's population live in seven regions that are particularly exposed to typhoons, suggesting high vulnerabilities.

3.1.9   Middle East/Near East

Turkey is exposed to earthquakes, particularly along the North Anatolian Fault, which is on the borderline of a large plate; the fault line is approximately 700 miles long and features right lateral strike slips. Seismic activity is relatively frequent and occasionally quite severe (e.g., eight 7.0+ earthquakes have occurred since 1900), and losses are compounded by lack of robust building standards; even moderate earthquakes have the potential of creating significant human and financial destruction. The Turkish topography, geology, and development is such that damage can come from ground-shaking, liquefaction, and land mass movement, along with fire and flooding; relatively new earth deposits amplify seismic waves, causing them to radiate a considerable distance. The 1939 earthquake in Erzinsan killed more than 100 000, while the 1999 Izmit earthquake resulted in the deaths of 19 000 and the collapse of more than 77 000 homes and structures; the actual ground-shaking was felt in Istanbul, more than 70 miles away (tragically, there is evidence suggesting that many of the deaths, and much of the structural damage, could have been avoided through application of building codes). Other countries in the region, including Iran, Iraq, and Afghanistan, are also at risk to earthquakes (e.g., earthquakes in Iran in 1990 and 2003 killed a combined 80 000 and leveled many villages and towns).

3.1.10   Europe

The UK and continental Europe are exposed primarily to extra-tropical cyclones and associated winter storms, windstorms (particularly in France, Spain, and Italy), mass movement, and flooding (especially in parts of Central Europe, along the Danube, Rhine, and Rhone); certain locations, such as Russia, Monaco, and the south coast of France and Italy/Sicily are also vulnerable to earthquake. Most of the areas at risk feature rather significant concentrations of population and commercial/residential development, meaning vulnerabilities are high.

Extra-tropical cyclones can be particularly damaging as they have the potential of blanketing a large area with strong winds and heavy precipitation. The path of a European extra-tropical cyclone depends heavily on the position of the Icelandic Low and the Azores High; if the Icelandic Low is well developed, low-pressure systems head directly towards continental Europe. An average of two to three storms can impact the continent in a given year; each storm, lasting from two to five days, is characterized by storm fronts ranging from 700 to 1500 miles in width, with sustained wind speeds ranging from 50 to over 110 mph. The storms affect France, Germany, Switzerland, Spain, and Italy, and can also create additional damage in Denmark, the Benelux region, and the UK. For instance, in late 1999, just weeks after a smaller, but still damaging, storm (Anatol) struck Denmark, the continent was impacted by two major events: Lothar, which hit Northern France, Germany, and Switzerland, and Martin, which struck Southern France, Northern Spain, and Italy. Lothar reached its maximum intensity off the French Atlantic coast, but remained very strong even as it reached Paris and the outlying suburbs (with sustained winds of approximately 100 mph). Martin, following a southerly route, featured wind speeds of just under 100 mph. The two storms damaged structures (small buildings, rooftops), power supply (200+ toppled pylons), and agricultural properties. Lothar created losses of more than $12b (approximately $5.8b insured), while Martin's damage reached $6b ($2.4b insured), surpassing the storms of 1990 to become the costliest in Europe's history. Although the UK often avoids the full effect of extra-tropical cyclones, it is by no means immune. The country suffered considerably during the storms of 2000, and has a long history of similar events.[8]

Parts of Europe are quite susceptible to flooding as a result of significant development in floodplains and alongside coastal/port areas. Indeed, continental Europe has an extensive history of flood damage that includes coastal areas such as the Netherlands, Northern Germany, and Denmark, and landlocked floodplain areas such as Austria, Czech Republic, southern Germany, and Slovakia. For instance, in August 2002 heavy rainstorms throughout central Europe triggered sequential flood waves on the Danube River in Austria and the Vltava, Elbe, and Labe rivers in the Czech Republic and Germany. The resulting floods soon reached 500-year return period levels, leading to 100 deaths and more than $15b in damages. Much of the flooding impacted major urban areas, including Dresden and Prague, adding significantly to the total costs. The event was triggered by 10 inches of regional rainfall in early August, which led to local flooding; this would have been manageable, but an extra-tropical cyclone struck several days later, creating additional heavy rains in the Czech/Southern Germany border area and in South Bohemia/Austria. The additional 5 to 10 inches of rainfall created flood waves on major rivers, causing significant reservoir overtopping and levee damage. Flash floods and landslides contributed to the overall problems and major rivers such as the Elbe peaked 20 to 30 feet above normal levels. Hundreds of thousands of people were evacuated throughout the region, tens of thousands of homes and buildings were partly or totally destroyed, major telecommunication and transportation arteries were crippled, and portions of the region became uninhabitable for weeks to months after waters finally receded. Germany bore the bulk of the financial damage (e.g., $9b).[9]

This list of regional at-risk areas is obviously not all-inclusive. Certain other countries and regions of the world periodically experience disasters of their own, e.g., earthquakes appear in Chile, Guatemala, Colombia, Peru, Morocco, Israel, New Zealand, and Australia, typhoons and forest fires impact Australia, hurricanes periodically hit the New England coast,[10] strong winter storms affect New England and the central USA, ice storms and flooding can appear throughout parts of Canada,[11] concentrated drought can affect large portions of the Saharan and sub-Saharan regions of Africa, and so forth. It should be clear that many parts of the world are exposed to natural disasters, and when relevant vulnerabilities are factored into the equation the potential loss of life and economic value can mount rapidly. In fact, most of the regions outlined above feature significant centers of population, asset concentration, and economic development – hence the extensive losses that often result. Table 3.1 summarizes regions/states and their exposure to natural perils.

3.2   SPATIAL IMPACT OF MAN-MADE CATASTROPHES

Man-made catastrophes, including terrorism, industrial contamination, technological failure, and financial dislocation, can impact relatively small geographic areas (e.g., towns, cities, counties), large areas (c.g., states or provinces), and cross-border areas (e.g., multiple nations).

---

[8] Contemporary reconstruction by RMS of a devastating storm that hit the UK in 1703 suggests that a repeat in the millennium would create $16b of direct damage in the UK, and an additional $3b on the continent.

[9] Unfortunately, German flood insurance penetration at the homeowner level is very low (less than 10%), and many commercial businesses operate without coverage. Accordingly, the government was called on to provide financial assistance.

[10] For instance, analysis suggests that a Category 3 hurricane striking New England (as in 1938) has an annual occurrence frequency of 0.9%, or a return period of approximately 100 years.

[11] For instance, in 1997 the Red River bordering Canada and the USA was the site of extensive flooding: heavy rainfalls in late 1996, coupled with an early freeze, heavy winter snow, and early thaw created record flooding in parts of North Dakota; the 225-year return event caused over $1b in damages.

Table 3.1   Regions/states and exposure to natural perils

Region	Natural peril
Bermuda/North Atlantic	Hurricane, flood
Florida	Hurricane, flood
North America West Coast	Earthquake, volcano, mass movement, fire, hurricane
US Plains/Midwest	Tornado, flood, earthquake
Caribbean	Hurricane, windstorm, earthquake, volcano, flood
Mexico	Earthquake, hurricane, flood, volcano
Japan	Earthquake, volcano, typhoon
South/Southeast Asia (China, Taiwan, Indonesia, Philippines, Bangladesh, India)	Earthquake, flood, typhoon/cyclone, volcano, mass movement
Middle East/Near East (Turkey, Iran, Iraq, Afghanistan)	Earthquake, mass movement, fire
Europe (UK, France, Germany, Austria, Czech, Monaco, Benelux, Scandinavia, Russia)	Extra-tropical cyclone, flood, earthquake

The scope of spatial impact depends largely on the nature of the catastrophe and its severity. Unlike natural disasters, virtually every nation with an industrial, technological, and financial base is exposed to the risk of a catastrophe. To be sure, countries that have a larger base of chemical, fuel, or nuclear production stand a greater chance of being impacted by a catastrophic event than those with a smaller base, all else equal. Similarly, those with poor safety standards, environmental controls/monitoring, and disposal facilities are at greater risk than those with higher standards. Some generalization is possible: industrialized nations feature much larger stocks and use of chemicals and hazardous materials than developing nations and are thus at greater risk, but they typically spend more effort and resources on building proper frameworks of safety and control than developing nations, and are therefore better able to mitigate the risks.

The risk of technological failure can be viewed in a similar light. The most industrialized and advanced nations of the world are much more reliant on leading edge mechanical and technological processes to conduct daily activities than developing nations that have not yet attained (or even required) the same level of sophistication; industrialized nations are therefore at greater risk. That said, they are more likely to use technology wisely by incorporating proper loss controls and mitigants, and improve the ability of their infrastructure to withstand the forces of the natural disasters mentioned above.

The risk of financial dislocation can be divided into two broad segments. Advanced financial markets, primarily those of North America, Western Europe, Japan, and Australia, are complex, efficient, and generally resilient, mechanisms that function very well under most circumstances. They are, however, vulnerable. The sheer size of the markets and the systemic interdependencies they create mean that the possibility of a 'chain reaction' or 'domino effect' surfaces under certain worst-case scenarios. Forms of this have occurred in the past, such as the 1987 global stock market crash, where sudden and deep selling created massive portfolio losses and a general feeling of instability, and the 1998 Russian/hedge fund crisis which created billions of dollars of losses for financial intermediaries and very nearly resulted in the collapse of several major institutions (which would have had profound systemic effects). Vulnerabilities also exist in certain emerging nations. Although the markets are not as large and sophisticated, the specter of instability is greater owing to more pronounced economic/financial weakness. Many large emerging markets, such as Brazil, Mexico, Argentina, Russia, and Venezuela, have defaulted on their debt, injecting uncertainty and volatility into their financial systems; recouping the loss of financial resources and credibility can take years to achieve – meaning the local population can suffer from lower standards of living, while external creditors suffer from lost capital.

Terrorism has become a global phenomenon. Prior to the millennium terrorist activities tended to be concentrated within national borders and were relatively minor and unsophisticated in scope. Countries such as the UK, Spain, Israel, Russia, and Peru, among others, dealt with terrorist incidents arising from nationalist, separatist, or religious forces as relatively manageable domestic problems. However, the events of 9/11 appear to demonstrate that the terrorist problem is a much larger global phenomenon. Cross-border activities appear to be on the rise, with countries such as Indonesia, Philippines, Spain, Kenya, Tanzania, Yemen, Saudi Arabia, and others caught in the same maelstrom as the USA. As coordination increases and access to more damaging materiel expands, the terrorist threat appears likely to continue on two fronts: national causes confined to localities and regions within a country, and larger international causes operating on a global scale. No country appears to be immune from the effects of terrorism. The actual selection of locations and targets is, of course, dependent on the goals and means of each terrorist organization, but items of importance appear to include the nature of the target (e.g., scale, symbolic impact), security around the target (e.g., the relative ease or difficulty of accessing the target), and required materiel (e.g., the actual device or method needed to destroy a target).

While we have mentioned in broad terms the potential impact of broad classes of man-made catastrophe, we provide some additional background on certain regions/countries to reinforce the points above.

3.2.1   North America

The USA and Canada are vulnerable to a range of man-made perils, including industrial contamination, technological failure, financial dislocation and, more recently, terrorism. The sophisticated nature of the countries, their underlying industrial and economic processes, their heavy reliance on energy to propel growth, and their development and use of complex financial transactions via a web of intermediaries, leaves them at risk to failure. Both countries have, over the years, experienced industrial accidents and technological failures of significant proportions (e.g., asbestos, chemical spills, space shuttle disasters, bridge and building collapses, and so on), and the USA has been very vulnerable to financial dislocations such as bank runs, liquidity crises, and financial institution/corporate failures (e.g., the S&L crisis alone cost US taxpayers hundreds of billions of dollars – a financial catastrophe by any measure).

While internal terrorism has appeared sporadically in the USA[12] it was not historically considered to be a significant problem. Larger fears have arisen as a result of the 9/11 Al Qaeda attacks, which created widespread social and economic damage;[13] there is now widespread belief that such events will recur in the future, which intensifies the economic burden of *ex ante* protection, and *ex post* loss funding.

---

[12] For instance, the Oklahoma City bombings caused the deaths of 169 civilians and nearly $150m in damages, the anthrax exposures in Florida and the mid-Atlantic contaminated 21 postal facilities and killed 5, and so on.

[13] Estimates by Tillinghast Towers Perrin indicate insurable losses of up to $12b for property, $7b for business interruption, $5b for workers' compensation, $6b for aviation hull, $20b for liability, $6b for life/health, and $2b for other claims, for a total insurable maximum of $58b; total economic losses (insured and uninsured) are estimated to have reached $90b.

3.2.2   Europe

Like North America, the European continent is exposed to a broad range of man-made catastrophes. Indeed, since European growth and advancement in industrial, financial, and technological matters parallels that of the USA and Canada, it is no surprise that the very same risk factors are at work. As events have shown, Europe is susceptible to industrial accidents/contamination (e.g., Piper Alpha, Chernobyl), financial dislocation (e.g., collapse of the European Exchange Rate Mechanism, default by Russia and others on debt). It is also vulnerable to terrorism. Indeed, many countries have been impacted by repeated terrorist acts over the years, including the UK (IRA, responsible for many incidents over the years, including the City of London, Docklands, and Manchester bombings), Spain (Basque separatists), Russia (Chechen rebels), Italy (Red Guard activists), and so forth; some of these countries are also at risk to global terrorism (e.g., the 2004 Madrid train bombings and Beslan school massacre associated with Al Qaeda/radical Islamic fundamentalists).

3.2.3   Asia/Pacific

Since countries in Asia/Pacific feature varying levels of economic and technological advancement, vulnerability to man-made disaster varies accordingly. Economically advanced nations, such as Japan and Australia, are highly dependent on industrial and technological processes and are therefore exposed to any associated failures. Japan, for instance, has suffered from several minor nuclear accidents in recent years. Developing nations are not quite as reliant on the same processes, but are not necessarily in an advanced state of safety control and readiness. Financial dislocation is a significant risk throughout Asia. For example, Japan has suffered tremendous economic damage over the course of a decade as a result of its speculative asset policies and resulting bad loan crisis. Countries such as Korea, Thailand, Indonesia, and the Philippines promoted speculative capital inflows that led to collapsing asset prices and severe economic recession (e.g., the Asian financial crises of 1997–1998). Terrorism is a reality throughout the region. Japan, for example, suffered a significant attack in 1995 at the hands of the Aum Shin Rikyo sect, which released sarin gas in the subway system;[14] the event was unique in being the first time a non-state group used a chemical weapon against civilians. Other countries, including the Philippines, Thailand, Malaysia, Sri Lanka, Pakistan, India, and Indonesia, have been the center of regional or cross-border terrorist attacks associated with separatist or religious causes (e.g., the 2003 Bali nightclub bombings associated with Al Qaeda).

3.3   URBAN VULNERABILITIES

We have already noted the importance of vulnerabilities in assessing the potential economic and social impact of a catastrophe. Regions with significant centers of population, development, infrastructure, and agricultural production are more exposed to losses than those without them. In fact, many exposed regions of the world are highly urbanized; a steady pattern of migration from rural to urban centers over the past two centuries has intensified the level of vulnerability. Approximately 75% of the population of industrialized nations is concentrated in urban and suburban areas, versus only 33% in undeveloped and developing nations. This statistic is consistent with our point from Chapter 1: though the incidence of catastrophe is

---

[14] Liquefied sarin disseminated on five trains killed 12 and hospitalized over 1000; the attack could have been much worse, as authorities eventually discovered the sect had 'battlefield quantities' of the nerve agent.

not necessarily increasing in such countries, economic vulnerabilities (and resulting losses) are expanding. However, even developing nations have concentrations of people and assets in capital cities or major metropolitan centers, meaning loss experience in at-risk areas can also be significant.

It is interesting to note just how many global urban centers are located in very high-risk areas: Kobe, Tokyo, Mexico City, Los Angeles, San Francisco (earthquake), Miami, Tokyo, Hong Kong, Taipei, Manila, Jakarta (hurricane/typhoon), Paris, London (windstorm), Amsterdam, Dhaka, Prague, Bangkok (flooding), and so on. It is also notable that half of the urban population of the world's 50 largest cities lives within 120 miles of fault lines capable of producing 6.9+ magnitude earthquakes. Centers of population and wealth are also clear targets of terrorist activities (to wit New York, Washington DC, London, Madrid, Tokyo, Moscow), and urban areas, particularly those forming parts of a broader megalopolis, are vulnerable from a crisis management perspective: it is often necessary to evacuate a large area in anticipation of, or response to, a disaster. If mass evacuation is required, the density of a megalopolis may prohibit easy departure, compounding problems and losses.

With background on identification of perils and vulnerabilities in hand, we turn our attention in the next chapter to the second element of the risk management process, the quantification of risk and potential losses.

4

Modeling Catastrophic Risk

The second stage of the risk management process introduced in Chapter 1 centers on quantification, or determination of the economic loss that might be sustained if an adverse event occurs. Quantification is the essential step that permits companies and sovereigns to make objective decisions based on risk of loss; it applies equally to high frequency/low severity risks and low frequency/high severity risks – though the technical approaches are often quite distinct, as we shall discover. In this chapter we consider the development and use of models, the goals of catastrophe modeling, general model construction, and specific catastrophe modeling challenges.

4.1 THE DEVELOPMENT AND USE OF MODELS

Quantitative models have been widely used in the banking, insurance, and corporate sectors for many decades to estimate the financial effects of high frequency/low severity risks. Indeed, stochastic processes (for financial risks) and actuarial processes (for insurable risks) are considered to be an elemental part of the risk management process.

Formalized quantification methods to cope with the unique characteristics of catastrophic risk are a more recent occurrence. Though catastrophe models date back to the 1970s and 1980s (based primarily on deterministic algorithms for estimating the potential impact of natural disasters on nuclear power plants, dams, and liquid natural gas plants), increased use did not commence until the 1990s, after insurers and reinsurers were impacted by a series of large disasters (e.g., Hurricane Andrew, Northridge earthquake, Typhoon Mireille). These events, which created losses that were much larger than expected, coincided with three other forces: implementation of increasingly sophisticated risk management processes within the financial/corporate sector, growing computing and networking power supporting simulation processes, and improved efforts in the collection and disaggregation of loss data. During this period various modeling companies began providing third-party clients with the tools necessary to estimate dimensions of catastrophic exposure (including pioneers Risk Management Solutions [RMS], Applied Insurance Research [AIR], and EQECat, which together remain at the forefront of model development in the millennium). Modeling continued progressing throughout the 1990s, gradually moving from a regime of deterministic assessment (i.e., the 'what has occurred' approach, based on applying historical disaster scenarios and limited simulations to current risk exposures to compute potential losses) to one of probabilistic assessment (i.e., the 'what could occur' approach, using a large number of simulations and physical/scientific algorithms to construct probability distributions for overlay on a portfolio of exposures).[1] This

---

[1] Consider, for instance, the deterministic approach to earthquake evaluation that was common from the 1970s through the early 1990s: earthquake faults posing a potential threat were identified; maximum earthquake magnitude was estimated based on the length of each fault; the severity of ground movement was estimated based on a rupture; ground movement for each fault was ranked; and the highest value became the benchmark for risk management or engineering design purposes. Even after raising individual fault experience to a statistical confidence level, this deterministic approach was flawed because of fixed occurrence/return periods (which indicated nothing about occurrence frequency).

fundamental change has allowed model users to move beyond past experience to speculate, under controlled circumstances, about what might happen in the future. Most modeling efforts of the millennium are based on probabilistic processes, which provide a far more realistic view of occurrence frequency and potential average and extreme losses.[2]

New generations of models continue to expand computation horizons. For instance, some models have been extended from relatively well-established areas such as earthquake, tropical cyclone, and extra-tropical cyclone into more complex areas such as terrorism, tornadoes, coastal surge/flooding, and hailstorm. Some physical models utilize stochastic elements rather than parameterized components to generate results (e.g., in modeling winter storms some models use data sets related to initial pressure in historical storms and then adjust them by space and time through differential equations to create a more realistic view of storm track and intensity). And some sophisticated (and 'user friendly') models allow input variables to be manipulated for sensitivity analyses; this is particularly useful in decision-making, especially as related to the mega-catastrophe/clash loss scenarios described in Chapter 2. Insurers/reinsurers and other financial intermediaries providing risk capacity remain the primary users of catastrophe models, though corporations with large amounts of property exposure and active risk retention/transfer programs now employ them to manage risk and ensure risk pricing is reasonable. Similarly, supranationals and governments have begun using them for government management purposes, as we shall note later in the chapter.

While commercial and in-house catastrophe models are driven primarily by a combination of scientific and statistical processes, they must also incorporate certain minimum standards established by regulators. This is particularly true for models used by insurers to establish premium rates and capital allocations. Rating agencies that evaluate insurers, reinsurers, and capital markets instruments (i.e., securitizations) exposed to catastrophe risk may also establish certain guidelines, including stress testing of model assumptions.[3]

Still, it is important to note that there is no single accepted standard for modeling catastrophic risks. Though many financial risks are quantified using standard processes (e.g., European exercise stock options are modeled through the Black–Scholes framework, American options via the binomial process, forward interest rates through derivation of the zero coupon yield curve, and so forth), wide variation continues to exist in the catastrophic risk sector. Key differences exist in the way in which model parameters are estimated and events are generated, the degree of probabilistic or deterministic implementation, the assumed distribution of perils, and so forth. Awareness of how these differences can affect output is critical prior to implementation.

4.2 THE GOALS OF CATASTROPHE MODELING

Before we consider the general construction of catastrophe models, it is useful to set the stage by examining goals related to the modeling effort. Specifically, we are interested in understanding what a model *can* and *cannot* be expected to do.

---

[2] Note that in some cases models measure hazard/peril probabilistically, but vulnerability/damage deterministically; this approach may be necessary when granular vulnerability data is lacking or cannot be updated frequently.

[3] For instance, insurers may be required to preserve a capital buffer capable of withstanding the probable maximum loss of a 100-year hurricane or some specified probability of ruin, such as 99.6% percentile aggregate for all retained catastrophic losses. AM Best, a credit rating agency specializing in insurance, requires insurers/reinsurers to demonstrate an ability to survive a 'reasonable' catastrophic loss, based on a probable maximum loss from a 250-year return period earthquake or a 100-year return period hurricane (except Florida, which is set at a 250-year return period level).

A properly constructed catastrophe model should allow corporate and sovereign users to:

- Estimate the probability of occurrence of a catastrophic event.
- Estimate the upper intensity limits of a particular occurrence.
- Estimate the financial loss that will result if an event of a particular intensity occurs.
- Evaluate the costs of retaining, transferring, or otherwise managing an exposure.
- Price each incremental exposure.
- Gauge accumulations/concentrations of risk, optimize the portfolio of risks, and provide a metric for acceptance/rejection of incremental risks.

A catastrophe model cannot be expected to:

- Predict when, or where, a catastrophic event will occur; modeling is a risk assessment exercise, not an event prediction exercise.
- Predict the precise intensity of an event in a particular location.
- Provide an exact assessment of the financial losses that may occur.
- Apply universally to all perils, regions, and locations, particularly those with unique characteristics.

By understanding these goals, financial surprises can be minimized. Since modeling is a time- and resource-intensive undertaking, realizable benefits, results, and limitations must be well understood in advance of development and implementation.

4.3   GENERAL MODEL CONSTRUCTION

Modeling catastrophe risk is a complex process that depends heavily on subjective and objective inputs related to natural and man-made forces. We begin our discussion with a brief review of alternative modeling approaches, and then provide detail on a typical multi-phase approach. Regardless of the specific techniques employed, the end goal is to generate useful information about expected catastrophic loss and the potential distribution of losses, so that rational pricing and risk decisions can be made.

- Under the first approach a probability distribution of future losses can be created based on historical loss data for a peril and an assumption of static vulnerabilities. While straight-forward, this method suffers from several flaws, including limited historical data for some perils (resulting in the creation of an incomplete/incorrect distribution) and potential understatement of vulnerabilities (particularly in fast growing regions). Lack of historical loss data is most apparent for perils such as earthquake and volcanic eruption, which may only occur in a given location every few decades or centuries; it is less problematic for tropical cyclones and extra-tropical cyclones.[4] As a result of these shortcomings, future losses might be significantly larger than those suggested through the loss distribution function (i.e., the 'fat tail' problem we describe later in the chapter).
- An improved version of this procedure adjusts data to reflect growth, inflation, and other material changes in vulnerability; this essentially means that historical catastrophe events are overlaid on more current vulnerability data. Nevertheless, this procedure can still be affected by limited sample size and the 'fat tail' problem.

---

[4] For instance, 160 hurricanes have made landfall in the USA over the past century, giving modelers an acceptable base from which to work.

- An alternative approach centers on making assumptions about the parameters used to construct the loss distribution. For instance, by assuming that the number of events occurring at a particular location and the parameters of each event are independent, 'synthetic events' can be created by sampling from distributions independently. This approach essentially combines historical information and parametric assumptions in an intensive simulation process. Probabilistic simulations of this type are common in modeling of earthquakes and tropical cyclones.
- In some cases it is possible to create a model of the physical process describing the catastrophic event, which can then be applied to vulnerability data to obtain loss estimates. This is a complex process that requires detailed scientific knowledge of the interaction between all of the variables that generate an event. Certain commercial models, including those related to extra-tropical cyclones, use this technique.

Though all four approaches can be found in practice, we shall focus our discussion and examples primarily on the latter two. It is necessary, in both cases, to consider two sources of uncertainty – the choice of the stochastic model, and the estimated value of the model parameters. In practice, models often use Poisson processes to determine the number of catastrophic events that can occur in a given period, and individual probability loss distributions for each event are then developed and combined.[5]

A multi-stage modeling process is common regardless of the specific approach used. The ultimate goal is to assess expected and unexpected losses, which are a function of hazard/peril, vulnerability and, for portfolios of exposures, contract characteristics. The process begins with the hazard/peril assessment phase, which generates a catastrophic event/probability function based on nature, frequency, and intensity (in practice, some modeling efforts divide the phase into two components, a hazard event generator and an intensity generator, but we shall review the process in combined format for ease). This result is then used in the vulnerability assessment phase, which estimates the potential for direct and indirect losses for an event of a given intensity based on the degree of damage to property and contents. A third contract assessment phase – commonly used by insurers, reinsurers, investors, and other financial institutions involved in supplying catastrophic risk capacity – centers on determining individual and portfolio losses generated during the vulnerability assessment stage based on insurance/reinsurance or derivative contracts that have been written to ceding or hedging parties. Thus, an insurer providing cedants with hurricane coverage first develops the specifics of a hurricane (e.g., wind speed, radius, storm track, central pressure, landfall zone) to obtain an event of a given intensity in a particular region, then identifies specific vulnerabilities (e.g. buildings, homes, contents) and computes potential economic losses; finally, it distills the losses to a net portfolio figure based on the specific contracts it has written (i.e., taking account of deductibles, coinsurance, policy caps, exclusions). We shall explore these phases in greater detail immediately below.

4.3.1   Phase one: Hazard/peril assessment

Hazard/peril assessment is the first step in any catastrophe model, and defines catastrophic events by physical characteristics (severity) and probabilities of occurrence (frequency). Risks

---

[5] If data is in the form of thousands of independent catastrophes, it is generally necessary to create separate frequency and severity curves. This can be done by applying certain assumptions (e.g., the sum of independent Poisson variables is itself Poisson, the severity distribution is discrete with probability equal to the Poisson frequency renormalized to 1) and allows practical computation of frequency and severity, e.g., in $x\%$ of years there will be 0, 1, 2, 3, 4, etc., events; if an event occurs, $x\%$ will be less than $\$x$ in size.

characterized by high frequency/low severity have a rich history of data, meaning construction of a statistical loss distribution is relatively straightforward. Since catastrophic events occur only rarely, the same breadth of historical loss data is typically not available for a given peril/location, suggesting an alternate process must be considered. In particular, using the third approach mentioned above, a probability distribution can be created from simulated events generated via random draws. The simulated events themselves may be based on historical data and scientific rules so that they resemble actual events (e.g., it is not particularly helpful if a hurricane model ignores scientific parameters and creates an event outside the natural boundaries for hurricanes). The hazard/peril simulation kernel generates event activity through repeated samplings until an entire catalog of potential activity – including events of a catastrophic nature – is created. Accurate hazard/peril modules, which should be flexible enough to allow for changing hazard conditions, ultimately allow annual loss amounts to be estimated with greater confidence.

Perils need to be modeled in light of their unique characteristics, including location, regional features, and seismic, geological, topographic, atmospheric, technological, urban, or geopolitical features. Natural disasters, in particular, may feature upper boundaries on potential losses due to the laws of nature, and these must be properly incorporated in the modeling process. For instance, the spatial location and intensity of a hurricane can be modeled through a combination of meteorological data, physical/numerical weather prediction, meteorological equations, and expert opinion. Atmospheric pressure build-up, peak, and subsidence can be developed through input parameters. The resulting hurricane path can then be supplemented by wind speed profile computations derived from meteorological data and local topography analysis. The spatial dimensions of earthquake events are based primarily on known fault lines, which are the source of most of the Earth's seismic activity (for reasons we have noted in Chapter 2). However, we have indicated that some intraplate regions also feature earthquake activity; determination of the spatial distribution of epicenters can be difficult, as there may be no visible surface expression. Some models attempt to overcome this challenge by allowing simulations to generate small probability events in areas not known to be earthquake prone.[6] Earthquake intensity can be modeled through regression, weighted by distance to the epicenter or hypocenter, or through attenuation functions and spectral ordinates (mathematical functions that describe a decrease in amplitude as seismic waves spread out from the rupture source). These processes may be supplemented by an examination of surrounding geological characteristics; soil composition, hydrological features, and potential for liquefaction can all influence the speed and dispersion patterns of seismic waves. Regardless of the specific methodology and peril, event intensity is obviously critical to the process as there is a high, though not perfect, degree of correlation between intensity and loss levels. This is particularly true in the region most immediately exposed to an event, as intensity tends to decline with dispersion or distance.[7]

The temporal aspects of an event can be estimated by understanding the effects of time on occurrence. For instance, we have indicated that Atlantic hurricanes occur from June to October, with a peak in August and September (the same is true for Pacific typhoons). This temporal relationship must be explicitly included in a hurricane hazard module. The temporal aspects of an earthquake can be modeled in one of two forms. Small or moderate events may

---

[6] The actual process of spatial analysis of historical data is very intensive and well beyond the scope of this work. It is sufficient for us to note that techniques exist by which to project, or simulate, possible events in areas where none have been recorded in the past.

[7] Indeed, certain sophisticated earthquake fault interaction (or stress interaction) models take account of activity in neighboring areas that are exposed to earthquake risk. This approach is based on stress theory, which indicates that when a fault breaks and produces a large earthquake, stress levels on the slipped plate decline and change the stress patterns in adjacent fault areas.

be treated as a random process, where the probability of a future event is not influenced by the location or time of a previous event (e.g., time-independent/Poisson variables). Large events can be modeled on a time-dependent basis, where the probability of an event is conditional on the time since the last event in the same region (this reverts to our point from Chapter 2, where we noted that certain earthquakes feature a time dependency, i.e., the probability of occurrence increases with the passage of time). Though historical seismicity is vital for all earthquake modeling efforts, it is absolutely essential for time-dependent events (and typically requires many decades of detailed seismic data, several centuries of anecdotal data, geodetic data on slip rates [average rate of fault displacement], and paleoseismic data based on liquefaction evidence).

Let us consider several simple conceptual examples. The characteristics of any earthquake – depth, rupture length, dip angle, rupture mechanism, location, seismic wave amplitude, and magnitude – are essential in determining frequency and locational intensity. The process of modeling an earthquake begins by fitting historical data and magnitude to an exponential distribution (e.g., Gutenberg–Richter), allowing a limited record of data to be used to estimate the affected area. The process is described by two key parameters, one related to the occurrence rate of an earthquake that is greater than, or equal to, a certain magnitude, another to the rate at which the log of the cumulative annual frequency of an earthquake declines as magnitude increases. For tropical cyclones the primary variables of interest include annual frequency, landfall location, minimum central pressure, maximum wind speed and radius, angle of landfall, and storm track. Historical parameter data can be used to construct the probability distribution, which can be supplemented via the simulation process (note that different distributions can be used for each variable, e.g., lognormal for forward speed, normal for radius of maximum wind, and so on).[8] Local wind speed can then be computed using meteorological equations. As noted earlier, extra-tropical cyclones are often modeled through physical model processes, including national weather prediction techniques that track storm evolution through small changes in atmospheric conditions; these relationships can be used to create 'synthetic' storms, which can then be applied to the development of probabilistic functions.[9] The physical model process uses sea surface temperatures, wind speed, and wind pressure in conjunction with physical law equations to model circulation patterns. These patterns define the state of the atmospheric variables, which are perturbed over time through differential equations to track evolution.

While the hazard/assessment module yields information about frequency and intensity for natural catastrophes and certain man-made disasters, it does not apply fully in the case of terrorist acts. Though certain aspects of the modeling effort parallel those used for natural disasters, two key differences exist: lack of historical data, and the influence of human behavior on location and frequency. The record of loss data related to terrorism is relatively sparse compared with natural disasters, and since few events can be publicly examined on an *ex post* basis to obtain additional detail, the ability to create probabilistic hazard models

---

[8] Consider a summarized process of hurricane simulation:

- A Poisson random variable generates an event occurrence time; this indicates the number of events occurring in one year (as noted, hurricane modeling must also take account of the fact that occurrence is not uniformly distributed throughout the year, but is actually bimodal).
- The time horizon is then increased and the process is repeated.
- A large number (x) of independent arrival times is created and ordered.
- For each of the x occurrences drawn from the distribution excesses over a particular magnitude threshold become the focus.
- The process is repeated until 100 000+ events of a given magnitude result; this becomes the probability of occurrence.

[9] For instance, in creating the Eurowind risk model, Swiss Re and EQECat reconstructed 180 historical storms from a database dating back to 1947, and supplemented the effort by using a physical model process to generate 8000 simulated storms.

is still constrained.[10] In addition, the dynamic and evolutionary nature of terrorist acts,[11] the covert nature of the groups, the extent of available resources,[12] and the ability for targets to be altered in response to countermeasures, complicate the analytic process significantly.[13] Terrorism hazard determination therefore remains a combination of objective assessment and subjective input. From an objective/quantitative perspective a terrorism model must weigh random human behavior against causal factors, including temporal patterns. Non-random factors also play a role; these include the availability of weaponry (explosives, weaponized nuclear, biological chemical, or radiological [NBCR]), degree of group centralization and decentralization,[14] presence of counter-terrorist measures, attack/defense patterns, and so forth. The subjective or judgmental dimension depends on input from global intelligence networks and expert judgment, and includes the logic, motives, and *modus operandi* of individual groups (this information is often highly sensitive and in some instances confidential). Most terrorism hazard models feature deterministic probability of occurrence. In fact, the hazard phase is intended to develop information related to the intensity of a named event, which can then be used within the vulnerability module. Naturally, once a sample act has been selected, such as a conventional explosion, or dispersion from weaponized NBCR agents, there is a large body of scientific and mathematical knowledge that can be applied to determine the extent of damage (e.g., blast and plume effects).

4.3.2   Phase two: Vulnerability assessment

Vulnerability assessment, the second phase of the quantification process, is designed to estimate the degree of local/regional damage and loss that can be caused to infrastructure, contents, and operating activities based on the events generated in the first phase; this stage essentially overlays a local event of a given intensity on an exposed region through a mathematical damage function. Though output can take different forms (as noted below), it essentially conveys the damage, loss, or loss ratio for each level of intensity, along with the variability of losses.

We have indicated in Chapter 1 that an event striking an area without vulnerabilities produces no losses, which is of little risk management interest. Areas with vulnerabilities, in contrast, are susceptible to losses, meaning specific details must be factored into the modeling process.

---

[10] The primary analytic focus is on urban terrorist catastrophe, so-called macro-terrorism, based on events causing $1b+ in damage and claiming more than 500 lives. Though many small terrorist events have occurred over the years, relatively few catastrophic events have taken place, meaning loss data is limited.

[11] Unlike natural hazards that are governed by forces of nature and tend to exhibit a range of well-understood behaviors across time and events, terrorist efforts may change, perhaps radically, as organizations learn from past failures and successes. This may require the introduction of statistical learning models, which allow for evolutionary development. For instance, a model may be based on a simulation process that is both a function of the probability that a new attack method will be selected and a complementary probability that an old method will be used; the relative likelihood that the old method will be used is an increasing function of previous use and success, and vice versa.

[12] Prior to 9/11 the hypothetical terrorism loss distribution was skewed heavily toward the right (e.g., fat tailed) as a result of a long planning horizon, accumulation of terrorist resources, and minimal defensive measures (e.g., very high vulnerabilities). Post-9/11 the loss distribution has become less skewed – at least temporarily: relative lack of terrorist resources, disruption in leadership, and imposition of defensive countermeasures have reduced the tail of the distribution; the possibility of a single large loss event has shifted in favor of a greater number of smaller events (e.g., more typical of the IRA activities evident from the 1970s through the 1990s).

[13] Considering different aspects of behavior is a challenging proposition. Some frameworks use complexity theory to reflect how organizations wage war and evolve spontaneously over time. Others opt for a two-state Markov process that features a 'normal' environment where an attack is possible and a 'heightened security' environment where an attack may be difficult or impossible to carry out. Still others are focused on the adaptability of an organization in the face of success or failure, while some are based on swarm intelligence and how individual members of an organization combine to adapt and solve a problem (instead of relying on a single leader); other approaches can also be introduced.

[14] For instance, a decentralized terrorist group is thought to be less vulnerable to counter-terrorism measures, while a centralized group is thought to be able to accumulate a greater amount of resources.

Losses can come from direct sources, such as damage to structure and contents, and indirect sources, such as loss of use and business interruption; in practice it is useful to determine expected losses and the variability of losses from both direct and indirect sources. The vulnerability phase is particularly important because, even though there is a strong correlation between intensity and loss, the relationship is not completely perfect: areas that feature strong construction, safety measures, and risk mitigants are less likely to suffer losses than those without them; *ex ante* knowledge of such features is thus essential.

Vulnerability assessments can be created by superimposing hazard/peril events generated in the first phase onto data related to property/infrastructure, building type (e.g., use, location), engineering/construction features (e.g., age, height, materials), and asset contents (e.g., occupancy, use). In practice, individual damage functions can be developed for different building types and construction methods, incorporating a spectrum of damage from total (i.e., replacement value) to partial (i.e., repairs, temporary loss of use/business interruption).

Since it is not always possible to analyze each individual property (unless robust data and computing resources are available), a workable alternative is to categorize property by general class such as residential building, commercial building, factory, or agricultural storage facility, where each class shares certain common structural features that allow for reasonable estimates. Hazard mapping of non-structural building codes is a valuable input, but is time- and resource-intensive and therefore not uniformly applied. If a locality uses zoning regulations, quantification by geographic zone becomes possible, allowing greater computational precision that improves the pricing of risk.[15] A similar process can be used when a locality has created standardized building codes that reflect safety characteristics based on engineering and construction methods.

Not surprisingly, accurate and granular data regarding structures and assets at risk is essential in attempting to model vulnerabilities. Indeed, the output that is generated for the third phase of the process is only as good as the input in the second phase. Though considerable strides have been made in some nations in compiling and coding structure-level data, the effort is not yet complete; in some countries no uniform data coding and collection exists or, where it does, the data elements are often erroneous. In some cases errors do not become apparent until a disaster occurs and post-loss financing commences. For instance, the poor quality of vulnerability data became very apparent in the aftermath of the Northridge earthquake; insurers and reinsurers were using incomplete and miscoded data that lacked specificity (often basing underwriting decisions on regional or ZIP code data, rather than building or neighborhood data). They also lacked detailed information on asset values, structure classes, and construction techniques. The result was a significant underpricing of risk coverage, causing insurers/reinsurers to sustain large losses. The lessons from Northridge led to the development of minimum acceptable standards, such as use of street address/construction type, and common data repositories. Similar processes must be enacted in other national systems.

Modeling of terrorism vulnerability again poses unique challenges. In general, attackers may favor targets with the greatest likelihood of destruction. But this can change as security or counter-terrorism measures are introduced. Game theory can be used to analyze choices between target sites by degree of protection; this helps determine the need for target substitution.[16] But it is important to note that rational dimensions of game theory need not necessarily

---

[15] Where zoning exists but zoning data is not accumulated, government sponsorship of a data-gathering framework may be desirable to ensure uniformity and precision.

[16] A body of work is developing related to game theory assessment of terrorist targets. For instance, given finite resources for both destruction and defense, the terrorist will attempt to maximize the expected loss of a physical target while the defender will attempt

apply in terrorist vulnerability modeling, as the goal of a terrorist group may not be to destroy the target with the greatest economic value, but the one that creates the greatest psychological impact. In practice, the vulnerability assessment may simply be a deterministic process based on the selection of a target. Once the target has been selected, and given the intensity of an attack from the hazard phase, actual direct and indirect damage can be assessed. While damage to physical property may be relatively easy to determine, the indirect effects may be more difficult to establish, and may ultimately require additional assumptions. For instance, an extremely large attack in an urban center may lead to significant indirect losses through curtailment/cancellation of tourist activities, retail purchasing activity, and so forth.[17]

Regardless of peril, the end result of the vulnerability assessment phase is an estimate of losses due to physical damage and interruption. For physical assets results can be measured through the replacement cost ratio (the ratio between repair cost and replacement cost), mean damage ratio (the ratio between total loss and value of insured objects), or mean damage degree (the ratio of total loss amount and total value of damaged insured objects). Some models also incorporate a contents damage ratio (also known as rate grade, or a multiplier that indicates the degree to which contents are damaged). Vulnerability curves, reflecting mean damage ratio as a function of structure type and intensity, are a common way of visualizing the information. The exceedance probability curve (illustrated in Figure 4.1) is an extension of the standard frequency/severity curve introduced in Chapter 1; it is a very common way of conveying loss information, depicting the probability of losing more than a particular amount on the vertical axis versus the amount of loss on the horizontal access (i.e., given a general loss distribution function $F(x) = P(\text{loss} \leq x)$, the exceedance probability $EP(x) = P(\text{loss} > x)$, or $(1 - F(x))$). The curve allows derivation of expected and worst-case losses, such as the likelihood that a loss of a given magnitude will be exceeded, and is particularly useful for insurers seeking to establish limits, reinsurers creating attachment points for layers of reinsurance, and capital markets investors evaluating the potential risks and returns on catastrophe-linked securities.

---

to minimize the loss. Not knowing which target will be selected, the defender should choose a strategy that results in the lowest possible worst case expected loss: more valuable targets should be defended more comprehensively until the expected loss declines; less valuable targets can remain undefended, as even if they are attacked they will not yield the greatest loss. Equilibrium is thus achieved. If a terrorist organization knows this, then it can choose among targets randomly; if it does not know this, it must weigh the probabilities among the defended targets to find the one that maximizes expected loss. Thus, the selection should be inversely proportional to the marginal effectiveness of defense.

[17] The three primary commercial modeling firms adapted their natural disaster models to develop terrorism-based quantification modules. For instance, AIR has created a loss estimate model for P&C, workers' compensation, life, accident, and disability insurance, built atop 300 000 potential targets. Estimates of frequency and attack method are computed for each landmark (in part through input from terrorism experts); the probability of attack for most targets is extremely small, though the probabilities for 'trophy targets' are somewhat greater. Conventional and NBCR attack events are modeled to create damage/fallout effects based on size, wind speed, direction, concentration; the combination of the hazard event and the target generates economic loss estimates by line of risk coverage. EQECat features a database of 10m possible terrorist events covering 250 000 targets, based on three different axes: power (New York, Washington DC), cultural/social (large cities, landmarks), and social instability (random locations). The model uses four weapons categories, including explosion, industrial chemicals, weaponized NBCR, and other. Attacks are assigned to targets based on expert opinion and relative probabilities are derived from a combination of game theory, decision theory, and Markov chains. Economic losses are then computed by taking account of blast damage (explosion) and plume dispersal (weaponized NBCR). The loss output is then applied to other catastrophe risks in the portfolio and existing insurance/reinsurance contracts to provide an overall portfolio view (similar to the third phase discussed below). The RMS model derives loss estimates for P&C, business interruption, workers' compensation, life, and health. The hazard database includes 200 000 targets, including 2400 high-risk targets (e.g., government buildings, stadiums, nuclear plants, central business districts, military installations, skyscrapers). One of four attack methods (weaponized NBCR, explosives, military weaponry, civilian weaponry) is applied to each target location based on expert opinion; plume and blast subroutines are added when computing damage effects. Using various combinations of location and attack methods, 100 000 individual attacks are simulated and resulting damage estimates are applied to a portfolio, which includes insurance and reinsurance contracts as well as government-sponsored programs (such as those we discuss in Chapter 9). Regardless of the specific modeling approach, some allowance must be made for the nature of the terrorist organization and its motivations; this requires expert opinion and thus introduces an element of subjectivity into the process.

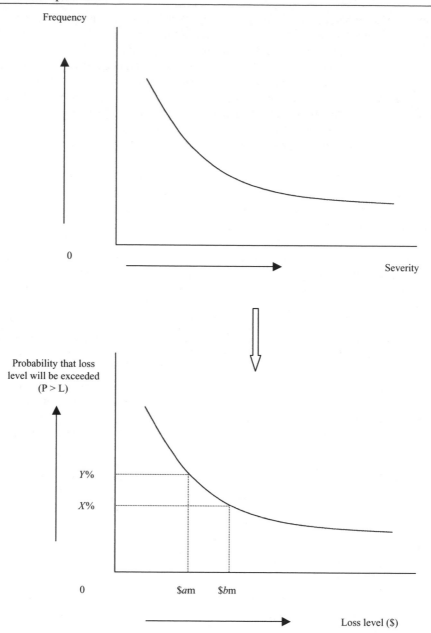

Figure 4.1   Exceedance probability curve

Output can also be used to construct a loss/return period curve (Figure 4.2), another version of the frequency/severity curve that reflects the size of loss on the vertical axis and the estimated return period on the horizontal axis. Consistent with our earlier discussion, this function reveals that larger loss events have longer return periods; the precise shape of the curve depends on specific model output. Note that estimates can also be derived for indirect losses, such as

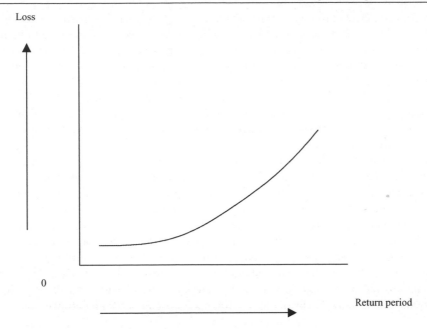

Figure 4.2   Loss return period curve

business interruption. Though various measures can be tabulated, vulnerability modules are typically based on replacement costs rather than insured value for ease of comparison and consistency (e.g., replacement costs are relatively standard across insurers, while insured value is often company/insurer-specific).

Three points are worth emphasizing. First, the more granular the vulnerability data, the more accurate the damage estimates; the more accurate the damage estimates, the more precise the pricing of risk capacity by insurers, reinsurers, and other financial intermediaries that offer risk cover – this ultimately yields an accurate metric that companies can use in the cost/benefit analysis process. Models that are populated by detailed structure data produce output that is more useful than those that are based only on broad ZIP/postal code or regional data; indeed, lack of detail can lead to wide variability between expected and realized results. Second, vulnerabilities are very dynamic: physical dimensions of property change constantly and population densities and commercial activities tend to increase steadily. This means data must be updated on a relatively frequent basis. Third, under any reasonable modeling framework expected and worst-case losses should decline as risk mitigants (which we consider in the next chapter) are introduced; safety controls, structural enhancements, and other forms of risk protection are designed to lower loss levels, and results must reflect this fact.

4.3.3   Phase three: Contract assessment

Institutions that are in the business of supplying catastrophic risk coverage or managing macro policies or portfolio exposures must add a third phase to the quantification process. Specifically, they must be able to distill, and then aggregate, the totality of their risks. By doing so, they obtain information that enables them to evaluate their portfolios/obligations in an accurate light, allowing them to increase or decrease risk levels as appropriate.

From an insurance/reinsurance perspective the damage estimates/dollar losses obtained in the vulnerability assessment phase[18] can be adjusted by specific policy conditions related to deductibles, coinsurance, exclusions, and caps in order to determine ultimate net losses. Deductibles and coinsurance are generally set as a percentage of the insured sum or loss, or they may be fixed; caps can also be set as a percentage or a constant, while exclusions can be expressed as a binary condition. Limits related to time (e.g., annual) or event (e.g., single occurrence), as well as the reinstatement of limits post-event, must also be considered. Risks that are hedged/covered through derivative contracts or transferred via securitization can be examined in the same manner.

Institutions with multiple catastrophic exposures (by peril, region, client) can use the contract phase to understand the effects of risk in isolation and, through correlation analysis, in a portfolio context; full analysis of the portfolio allows proper diversification/optimization routines to be incorporated (e.g., an insurer may simultaneously wish to minimize its exposure to the 250–500-year return period losses while maximizing premium income, subject to certain minimum loss/premium ratios). By examining each contract in the portfolio and its contribution to both return and risk, proper adjustments can be made to ensure that catastrophic risks are yielding the minimum required hurdle return. Figure 4.3 summarizes the process of combining separate exceedance loss curves by peril into a master curve and, using peril-based correlations, establishing the distribution of returns for use in portfolio optimization.

4.3.4   A general example

Let us consider the three-phase framework in the context of a simple earthquake model used by an insurer.

Hazard/peril assessment: the model computes earthquake events based on a common intensity metric (e.g., Mercalli intensity, maximum pulse ground-shaking), which is derived from the source, local conditions, and seismic attenuation. For each event the output includes earthquake size, distance from a particular location, amount of energy released (and how much reaches the specific location), and relative frequency.

Vulnerability assessment: potential damage for each earthquake of a given intensity is computed by considering the structural characteristics and use of buildings, by class. In this example the vulnerability module creates a mean damage ratio (MDR) for each of several classes (e.g., residential wood, residential brick, commercial steel high rise, commercial general, heavy industrial), and then determines a building MDR (based on year of construction, distance to event location, foundation surface, liquefaction potential, and so on); a contents damage ratio is also computed.

Contract assessment: using the results of the vulnerability assessment, the terms of individual earthquake policies in the target zone are evaluated in light of their specific exposure characteristics (e.g., deductible, caps, exclusions) to create a net loss per affected property. As noted, this stage of the process applies primarily to insurers/reinsurers providing coverage to numerous property owners in the area, though it can also be used by state/municipal government agencies and corporate property owners to determine the potential impact with and without coverage.

---

[18] Though the granularity of the data used in the vulnerability phase dictates the level of detail that can be computed in the contract phase, geographic zones or CRESTA zones have emerged as a minimum standard in various national systems; ZIP/postal codes and structure-specific data inject even greater accuracy into the process.

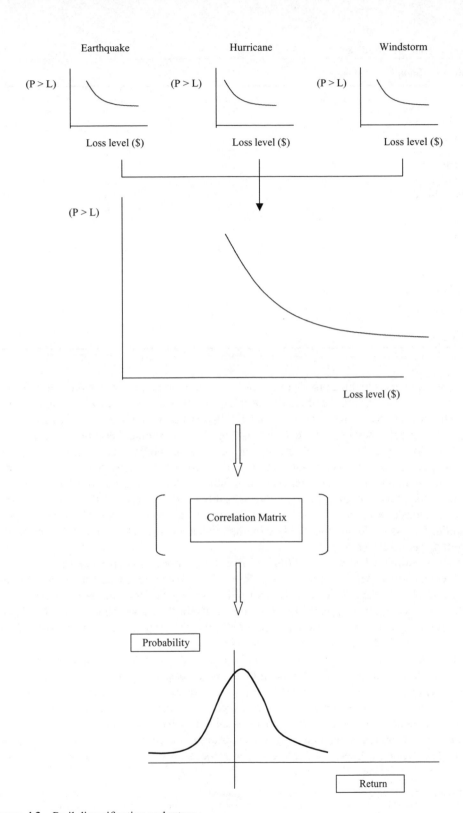

Figure 4.3 Peril diversification and return

Table 4.1   Sample model output

	Event 1	Event 2	Event 3	Event 4
Intensity	Eq-4	Eq-2	Eq-5	Eq-1
Building 1				
Value	$100m	$100m	$100m	$100m
MDR	5%	4%	8%	2%
Total loss	$5m	$4m	$8m	$2m
Deductible	$1m	$1m	$1m	$1m
Net loss	$4m	$3m	$7m	$1m
Building 2				
Value	↓	↓	↓	↓
MDR				
Total loss				
Deductible				
Net los				
Building 3				
...				
Building 10				

We can now use the three phases to create a basic numerical example. Consider an insurer that is writing catastrophic earthquake coverage on 10 buildings with an insured value of $1b. The insurer models 10 events covering a 200-year period in the hazard/peril assessment stage. The model generates earthquake intensities for each event and building, and creates an MDR and loss exceedance curve for each one in the vulnerability assessment phase. It then applies specific insurance conditions in the contract assessment phase to determine net loss. The model then repeats the entire process for all other buildings under the same event in order to generate a total event loss; similarly, it repeats the process for each of the remaining events to create a master event loss list. Using all event losses, an expected annual loss is computed by adding across the losses and dividing by the model years (this is commonly expressed in percent or per mille per year).

Assume Building 1 is worth $100m and Event 1 produces an earthquake of intensity 4, which equates to an MDR of 5%; the total loss is $5m. If the insurance conditions contain a deductible of $1m, then the net loss to the insurer on the policy for Building 1 under Event 1 is $4m. The cycle is then repeated for Buildings 2–10 for the same Event 1, which yields the insurer's total event loss. It is also repeated for all other events to create an event loss list. The output assumes the form denoted in Table 4.1.

Although this is a very simplified example, it provides insight into the types of assessments that can be made through the quantification process. The process is especially useful for institutions that need to understand the profile and dynamics of an entire portfolio. For instance, the largest result obtained via the exceedance curve is a representation of an extreme loss scenario, commonly referred to as an estimated maximum loss (simply a loss from a large event in an area with high concentration in the portfolio) or probable maximum loss (a loss from the largest possible event in a location with the highest value).[19] It also

---

[19] Insurers and reinsurers commonly use probable maximum loss (PML) measures to establish coverage limits and manage their portfolios. In practice PMLs for a peril are added across locations, although lack of correlation between the regional components means conservatism is injected into the portfolio management process, e.g., if PML(Cal EQ) is not correlated with PML(NMSZ EQ), then PML(Cal EQ + NMSZ EQ) < PML(Cal EQ) + PML(NMSZ EQ).

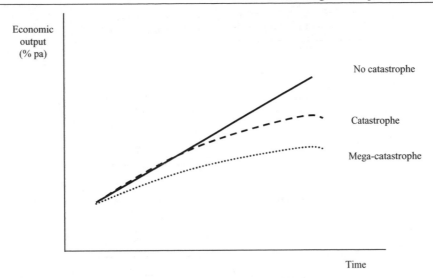

Figure 4.4   Impact of catastrophe on gross domestic product output

allows an institution to price and risk manage its own portfolio of catastrophic risk coverage. For instance, by aggregating all event losses and dividing by the projected number of model years, the insurer obtains information about the amount of premium needed to cover losses over the long term. Different stages of the modeling process can provide users with different views of important risk management information. While the net loss information generated through phase three contract assessment is often the most practical manifestation of user results, it is not the only useful model output. For example, algorithms can be developed to provide the number of potential catastrophic threats, the economic losses with and without different levels of insurance (or other protection), the changing loss profile for events of particular intensities, the changing loss profile for slight variations in location or path, and so forth. Indeed, the modeling process can become a useful tool in the scenario analysis framework.

Standard models can be extended to consider the effects of disaster on an entire economy, and how national programs may be affected (e.g., grants, subsidies, post-loss financing, government-sponsored reinsurance programs, and so forth). To be effective, a macro model relies on assumptions about essential and non-essential replacement of infrastructure, costs related to reconstruction and emergency management/relief efforts, changes in trade balance and tax revenue accounts, diverting of government funds from planned investments, external borrowing requirements, access to foreign aid, and so forth. The ultimate goal is to determine how a catastrophe can affect a country's gross domestic product; this is particularly critical for nations that are in an early stage of economic development. For instance, a severe event with a 250-year return period striking a developing nation can deplete economic resources, force external borrowing, and lead to a slowdown in economic growth over time. *Ex ante* knowledge of this possibility can provide valuable information for use in risk and financing decisions. Figure 4.4 highlights the effects of moderate and mega-catastrophes on economic output over time.

4.3.5   Other perils

While our discussion has centered on a general quantification approach for perils such as earthquake, hurricane, and terrorism, the same framework is applicable to other catastrophic events

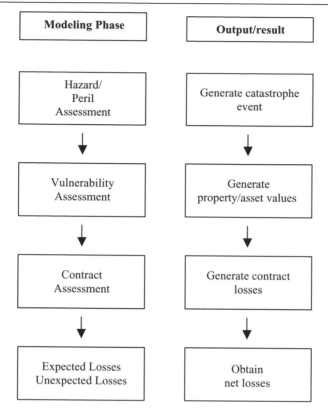

Figure 4.5   General construction of a catastrophic risk model

we have described in Chapter 2, including flood, industrial contamination, technological fail-ure, financial dislocation, and so forth. Every model must focus on the defining characteristics of the hazard/peril (e.g., frequency, intensity, location) and how these interact with vulner-abilities to produce damage/losses. Where applicable, contract assessments can be applied to determine net exposures and losses. When events give rise to employee health, safety, and life issues, the analysis of insurance/reinsurance contract conditions must extend beyond the tra-ditional domain of property and casualty exposure to include workers' compensation, health, and life coverage. Consider, for instance, a scenario based on extreme financial dislocation. Historical and simulated events related to micro- and macro-events can be used to construct dimensions of hazard (e.g., gross domestic product, interest rates, inflation rates, systemic leverage, money supply, key market references, trade deficit). The intensity of the financial hazard can then be applied to vulnerable assets to determine financial losses, and net losses can be computed in the contract phase by considering hedges.

Figure 4.5 summarizes the general steps involved in constructing a catastrophic risk model and the resulting output.

4.4   CHALLENGES

Quantifying catastrophic risk is a challenging process that must be regarded as an 'impre-cise' science; indeed, there is a great deal of subjectivity, qualitative input, experience, and judgment involved in the creation of a workable model – which is still only a best estimate of possible losses. In this section we highlight some of these key challenges, including model characteristics and assumptions, model validation, tail risks, and data quality and granularity.

4.4.1   Model characteristics and assumptions

Modeling sophistication varies by institution, and resources, exposures, and goals. As a result, each institution must define precisely the scope of its model coverage: models that are extremely comprehensive are very time- and resource-intensive and may be driven/influenced by a larger number of assumptions; those that are more basic may lack the depth to provide a realistic assessment of potential damage.[20] Trade-offs must be evaluated in light of specific needs.

Other characteristics must be considered. For instance:

- Events that are potentially subject to changing climatic factors (e.g., warming ocean temperatures, ENSO events) must be explicitly treated in the model.
- Events that have a degree of time dependence, such as earthquakes in particular fault zones, must be distinguished from those that are time-independent.
- Non-linear relationships between physical process intensity and damage must be evaluated (e.g., a hurricane that is two times stronger than a second hurricane may do more than twice the damage).
- Scientific, structural, and engineering assumptions must be examined closely to determine their accuracy (e.g., the strength of steel reinforcement beams and their ability to withstand stresses of particular levels).[21]
- Post-event price inflation measures that can impact reconstruction costs may have to be incorporated.

Ultimately, probabilistic models are susceptible to errors that can arise in the hazard/peril phase (frequency, intensity, physical event parameters, correlations), the vulnerability phase (value and characteristics of the subject property, structural weakness, physical force impact), and the contract phase (nature of policy conditions), meaning due care must be taken when calibrating the model and interpreting/using results. Institutions relying on third-party models must understand how specific parameters are treated and how sensitive a model is to assumptions.

Since models are tools based partly on assumptions, it is important that they not be overly simplified just to create an analytically tractable process. In addition, some account must be made of situations where historical experience and/or data are lacking; this is an epistemic problem that can only be resolved by acquiring additional experience and data, a process that may take time to complete. If key information is missing or flawed, the model may collapse in the face of a significant event.[22]

If models are constructed incorrectly, or if the parameters are flawed, output errors will result; more importantly, risk management decisions based on the output will lead to mispricing of risk exposure and erroneous cost/benefit decisions – including risk underpricing. Since a sustainable level of profit is an essential requirement for sustainable risk capacity, continuous mispricing

---

[20] For instance, an earthquake damage model may lack the ability to model damage from post-event fire, a hurricane damage model may not reflect the post-hurricane storm surge, a terrorism model may make overly simplistic assumptions above human behaviors – any of these can lead to an underestimate of potential losses.

[21] For instance, in the Northridge earthquake, assumptions regarding the ability of steel supports to withstand particular types of shocks proved flawed, resulting in greater than expected building/structure failure and associated losses.

[22] For instance, though models became more sophisticated after Andrew, they still underestimated the potential for damage in certain other perils – such as in the Northridge earthquake, which went undetected because it occurred on an unknown fault line. Hypothesizing on the unknown is an important part of the modeling exercise.

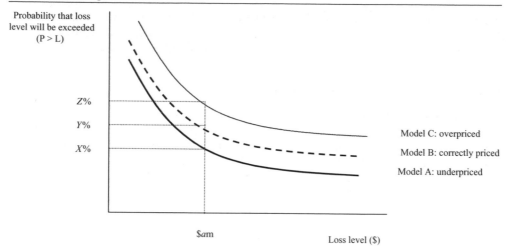

Figure 4.6   Exceedance curves and underpricing/overpricing

as a result of flawed model assumptions will eventually lead to greater than expected losses and contraction of risk capacity. Consider the simple illustration in Figure 4.6, which depicts three loss exceedance curves: a 'correct' curve (Model B) based on an accurate model, and two 'flawed curves' (Models A and C) which contain model errors. It is easy to see how model flaws can lead to overpricing or underpricing of risk – and overly aggressive or conservative decisions.

4.4.2   Model validation

Financial models are typically validated or benchmarked so that the accuracy of the results can be verified and any biases identified and corrected (including underestimates of event frequency or magnitude, miscalculation of event correlations, assumptions of long-term stability in low-risk regions). This is especially vital when model output is being used for mark-to-model pricing purposes or other elements of the risk management process. In fact, it is generally simple to validate results in markets involving high frequency/low severity risks as there is a rich history of price/market data and strong secondary liquidity. Even financial instruments that are not traded frequently can be benchmarked to certain tolerance levels through extrapolation and other accepted techniques.

Lack of historical data or actively traded markets makes this approach more complicated for catastrophe models. In practice, validation is generally limited to obtaining the parameters of known historical events and applying them to a portfolio of exposures to construct an *ex post* simulation. For instance, model-determined annual hurricane events must fall within the intensity scale and landfall characteristics suggested by history and/or science; model output can be benchmarked against this reference. An alternate version of this applies near real-time damage data obtained shortly after the onset of an event to the portfolio of exposures to verify estimates against realized losses; this, however, is an *ex post* exercise. Ultimately, each new catastrophe provides additional information that modelers can use to test, validate, and refine their models.

4.4.3   Tail risks

The tail of a statistical distribution (i.e., the extreme right-hand portion) can be difficult to measure with precision and may, in some instances, lead to an underestimate of losses. Since construction of loss distributions is central to catastrophe modeling, the accuracy of the construction has a direct bearing on the result of the output. If the tail of the realized distribution is larger than the tail of the modeled distribution (i.e., the 'fat tail' problem), then an exposure of a particular severity will occur with greater frequency than expected, or an exposure of a given frequency will be larger than expected. Either situation can create unexpected losses and possible financial distress. For instance, losses attributable to windstorm are typically much larger than those for hurricanes on an average annual basis, but the variance of hurricane losses is much greater (e.g., probability of a \$10b loss from windstorm in any one year is less than 1%, but increases to 8–10% for hurricanes); the hurricane loss distribution features a fatter tail, creating greater quantification challenges. To help overcome this problem, non-encounter probabilities close to zero (such as hurricane wind speeds in excess of 200 mph or an intraplate earthquake above 8.0) must be supplemented by extreme value tests that provide sensitivity detail in the tail of the distribution.

4.4.4   Data quality and granularity

It is clear that modeling exercises in general, and catastrophic ones in particular, are strengthened through good data. The more dependable and granular the information, the more accurate the loss distribution functions, and the more meaningful the decision-making process. Obtaining high-quality, granular data, and updating it frequently, is therefore vital. We have already mentioned the limitations that exist regarding hazard/peril data insufficiency. When direct data is lacking, inferences can sometimes be drawn from contingent data, though this can influence the quality of the model. Greater possibilities exist regarding the accumulation of vulnerability data; when information can be obtained at a building/structure level, loss estimates improve dramatically. That said, obtaining detailed data is still a non-trivial task. Estimates of commercial structures can be difficult to accumulate as buildings and infrastructure come in many sizes, types, and uses, each with unique structural and engineering qualities (houses/dwellings, in contrast, are relatively more homogenous). Over the medium term it is incumbent upon those dealing with disaster risks to champion the use of central data repositories, particularly those that have cross-border interest and use (and which are therefore more likely to be funded and maintained). Supranational organizations and industry groups, for instance, should consider development of databases with information related to casualties, damage, replacement costs, and so forth. As part of such an exercise, data standardization is desirable, so that inputs across countries are consistent; in fact, it is not difficult to imagine the confusion that might arise regarding repair value, replacement value, premises and structure type, and so forth. Importantly, such a repository must be based on a true assessment or estimate of findings, and not subject to manipulation for political or economic purposes.

Quantification is a vital element of catastrophe risk management, but it is also a complex area that is dependent on simplifying assumptions and may be prone to errors. A model should always be regarded as a limited view of the world. In practice the end goal should not be to create a perfectly accurate model – indeed, this has to be viewed as an impossibility – but a workable one that allows exposed parties to determine how best to manage expected and unexpected losses. We re-emphasize that catastrophe modeling is not an attempt to predict when a disaster might occur, but a process that allows users to create a meaningful distribution of future events so that associated expected and extreme loss patterns can be developed. This allows exposed parties to gain an understanding of their risks and how they may be financially impacted under different scenarios; by incorporating a sufficient degree of realism and a margin of error, the output can be used with confidence in the management stage of the risk process.

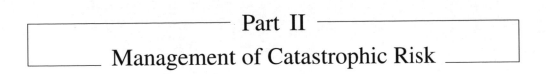

Part II
Management of Catastrophic Risk

5
Catastrophe and the Risk Management Framework

We recall from Chapter 1 that the financial toll of a disaster is a function of both the peril and the vulnerability of the exposed area; the interaction of the two dictates the degree of gross loss. This is equivalent to saying that the probability of loss due to a catastrophe is a function of the probability of a catastrophe occurring, and the conditional distribution of loss severity given an occurrence. Since risk management is concerned with minimizing losses, it follows that peril and vulnerability must be managed. In practice peril can only be managed to a limited degree: an earthquake or hurricane will occur regardless of attempts at intervention and cannot therefore be managed; an industrial accident or terrorist act can, in some instances, be minimized or delayed – though perhaps never completely eliminated – through intervention.[1] Accordingly, the main focus turns to the management of vulnerabilities and the transfer/reduction of losses arising from the interaction of peril/vulnerability.

In Part II we consider techniques for managing the potential losses associated with catastrophe risk. In this chapter we discuss the general elements of the risk management framework as related to catastrophic risk, with an emphasis on overarching corporate/sovereign goals. In Chapter 6 we analyze the insurance/reinsurance mechanism, which plays a dominant role in the transfer of disaster risks. In Chapter 7 we examine the nature of alternative capital markets structures that are increasingly used to manage low frequency/high severity risks, including insurance-linked securities (catastrophe bonds) and contingent capital; we extend the discussion in Chapter 8 by considering the role of exchange-traded and over-the-counter catastrophe derivatives. In Chapter 9 we shift our focus to the analysis of risk management solutions offered by national and local governments, and conclude with a review of future risk management challenges in Chapter 10.

5.1 ACTIVE RISK MANAGEMENT

The primary goal of a private- or public-sector risk management program is to permit active management of exposures that have been identified and quantified, so that losses can be minimized or eliminated. In designing an analytical framework for decisions it is important to consider the nature of the risk exposures, expected/worst-case losses, expected frequency, and expected cost of management. These are all necessary in order to generate a reasonable program of action. We commence our discussion of active risk management with an overview of enterprise value, liquidity, and solvency, and then consider techniques that can be employed to manage exposures, including loss control, loss financing, and risk reduction (some of which we shall revisit in detail in Chapters 6 through 9). We then discuss issues associated with

---

[1] Within the broad category of natural disasters, the only notable exceptions related to management possibilities include emission controls to limit greenhouse effects and global warming (which can affect certain storm patterns) and land development controls that reduce erosion into riverbeds (which might otherwise increase flood risk). Other attempts at peril modification, such as influencing tropical cyclones through cloud seeding, or inducing small earthquakes through drilling and conventional/nuclear detonations, have not yielded satisfactory results.

risk monitoring, the essential fourth stage of the risk framework, and briefly highlight points related to public- and private-sector efforts and sources of risk capacity. Though the active risk management process applies generically to all risks, we shall focus specifically on catastrophic exposure.

5.1.1 Enterprise value, liquidity, and solvency

An institution manages its risks for three primary reasons: to increase the value of the firm, ensure sufficient liquidity, and remain solvent. The specific nature of the risks is not relevant when considering these goals, as any risk exposure that has the potential of creating a loss that can reduce enterprise value and/or jeopardize liquidity and solvency must be managed. However, catastrophic risks, particularly those that are deemed to be so highly unlikely that they are effectively 'ignored' in the management process, can quickly destroy enterprise value and create financial distress; accordingly, they deserve special focus.

A typical joint stock company receives capital from investors and uses the resources to create and sell products and services. In exchange for the use of capital, the firm attempts to maximize the value of the enterprise so that investors can receive a fair return on capital supplied, typically in the form of dividends and/or capital gains. Maximizing enterprise value – where enterprise value is defined as the discounted value of net cash flow – is therefore an important corporate goal.[2] Techniques of catastrophic risk management that allow a firm to protect, and ultimately increase, enterprise value must therefore be analyzed as part of the management process.

Consider, for instance, a manufacturing company with its sole factory located in an earthquake fault zone. Its only ability to produce goods that create revenues, and shareholder returns, is vested in that facility. To protect against the possibility of business interruption or destruction from a non-catastrophic peril, such as fire, the company purchases a standard property and casualty (P&C) insurance policy. The cost of the policy detracts from revenues and, therefore, shareholder returns (e.g., the insurance premium is a cost to the company), meaning that it may not be a value-maximizing strategy. However, the policy provides assurance that if a fire occurs the plant will be rebuilt (direct loss coverage) and any loss of use will be reimbursed (indirect loss coverage). The benefits obtained are therefore considerable – but only if a fire actually occurs. *Ex post*, a firm that has insurance coverage can restart its operations and resume enterprise value creation and maximization, while one without coverage will be forced to fund reconstruction from its own resources, detracting from enterprise value. The decision on whether to purchase the insurance coverage is part of the cost/benefit evaluation associated with the risk management decision process and will depend on the estimated costs and perceived benefits of purchasing/not purchasing the insurance.

A similar evaluation can be applied to the earthquake risk the company faces; if an earthquake strikes and destroys the property, the company cannot generate revenues. The issue again centers on the purchase of an earthquake policy, and whether the firm believes that the cost involved is justifiable in light of the probability of occurrence and potential damage. If the premium on the fire insurance policy with 100% replacement value coverage is $1m and the probability of occurrence is 10%, while the premium on the earthquake policy is $500 000 and the probability of occurrence is only 1%, the company may believe that it is not worth purchasing earthquake coverage. Alternatively, if the price of the earthquake coverage is only

---

[2] Government/quasi-government institutions, which are not in business to generate profits, are unlikely to be interested in maximizing value, but in operating efficiently and prudently.

$100 000, the firm may feel that it is a fair deal. Though it recognizes that the assumed probability is only 1%, the premium charged is consistent with one that it believes is 'fair.' Importantly, it has protected itself against a disaster that might otherwise damage enterprise value – though the full benefits are only realizable if an earthquake occurs.[3]

While this example is simplified, it illustrates the type of decision that a firm must make when evaluating strategies designed to protect and maximize enterprise value. The fundamental cost/benefit decision, and how this can impact the value of the firm, is thus critical (note also that it is applicable across all products/mechanisms, not just insurance).

While enterprise value maximization is the ultimate goal for joint stock companies operating in a free market system with mobile capital, two other goals must always be satisfied as a matter of course – ensuring adequate liquidity and solvency. Liquidity is defined as access to sufficient cash to meet current obligations (i.e., unsecured funding, unencumbered assets that can be pledged as collateral, or outright asset sales). Solvency is defined as the excess of asset value over liability value (generally contained within the paid-in capital/retained earnings accounts) to meet unexpected losses. A company that is unable to preserve access to liquid resources and/or an adequate level of capital is likely to enter into a phase of financial distress where ongoing survivability becomes questionable. Since equity capital investors often suffer considerable losses if a company migrates from financial distress to outright bankruptcy, a sensible risk management program must ensure preservation of prudent levels of liquidity and capitalization. Indeed, liquidity/solvency can be regarded as primary goals and enterprise value maximization as a secondary goal. Not surprisingly, liquidity and solvency can be threatened in the event financial and operating risks lead to excessively large losses; while this is unlikely to happen with high frequency/low severity risks, unless management repeatedly ignores the lessons of many small loss events or fails entirely to identify a particular source of risk, it can occur with catastrophic risk. In fact, a single catastrophic event that has not been properly considered in the risk management framework can lead to instantaneous financial distress and insolvency.

Let us return to the example of the earthquake-prone manufacturing company. While enterprise value maximization may be the firm's stated objective, it must first ensure that it can preserve sufficient liquidity and capital. In the normal course of affairs the company will arrange its liquidity program so that its current assets and unsecured funding adequately meet current liabilities (plus any surprise payments). In addition, it will ensure that its capital account (i.e., the net of assets over liabilities) is large enough to withstand unexpected losses to a particular magnitude, probability, and/or statistical confidence level. Since the firm is located in an earthquake fault zone, it must take account of the fact that a high severity/low probability event may occur. If an earthquake strikes and destroys the factory, the firm will no longer be concerned with maximizing enterprise value, but surviving as a going concern. If it has not made *ex ante* risk management arrangements, such as the purchase of insurance or a capital markets hedge, then it will sustain significant losses; the lack of production facilities will eliminate its ability to generate revenues and essential operating cash flows. In addition, the replacement factory will have to be funded from internal reserves. This means that in meeting its current liabilities, which will continue to be due and payable, the firm will have to access any remaining unencumbered assets or unused funding sources; if these are insufficient to meet cash outflows, it will suffer a liquidity squeeze – perhaps one that is so great that it

---

[3] In some instances the market value of a company may actually increase with the purchase of risk protection such as insurance; investors may view the action favorably, despite the fact that it involves a cash expense at $t = 0$.

sustains large losses by sourcing new funding at higher rates, or selling remaining assets at a deep discount. The financial impact of the catastrophe on the liquidity profile of the firm may therefore be significant. Similarly, if the value of the unprotected (and now worthless) assets is less than its liabilities (e.g., the factory, which accounts for 75% of total assets, is now largely without value), then the firm will record negative net worth and become technically insolvent. Again, the financial impact of the disaster on the solvency of the firm is clear. Obviously, if the firm protects itself on an *ex ante* basis it can minimize or avoid the prospect of illiquidity and insolvency. As we have already noted, the risk protection subtracts initially from enterprise value, but dramatically increases the likelihood of survivability in the event of a disaster. The risk management program must examine this choice in detail.

One of the greatest barriers to active risk management in the catastrophe sector relates to the relative infrequency of damaging events. The low probability associated with disasters makes it difficult for management to perceive the potential for damage, and can alter behavioral attitudes towards risk management applications; lack of direct loss experience compounds the problem, meaning that risk management efforts may not be analyzed in the correct light. One short-term solution to this hurdle is to consider the implications of not taking conscious steps to protect against disaster, and highlighting the potential impact on enterprise value, liquidity, and solvency (i.e., extreme scenario analysis assuming no risk mitigants are in place).

5.1.2   Loss control, loss financing, and risk reduction

In order for a company to attempt to maximize enterprise value and ensure sufficient liquidity and solvency it must create a risk management program that centers on one or more of three broad techniques: loss control, loss financing, and risk reduction. We shall consider each in general terms, and in the context of catastrophic risks.

5.1.2.1   Loss control

Loss control, also known as risk mitigation, is one of the most elemental components of risk management. The process centers on taking *ex ante* actions that can help minimize the level of vulnerability and reduce the chance that a loss event will impact operations. Loss control is typically based on rules, regulations, education, and safety measures, and can be divided into two general categories: avoidance and resistance. Avoidance reduces the financial impact of a hazard by prohibiting expansion in at-risk areas (e.g., no development or construction in certain zones). Resistance, in contrast, tries to reduce the effects of a hazard through safety precautions or rules/standards in at-risk areas (e.g., minimum strength and reinforcement standards for particular buildings, use of high-resistance building materials and construction techniques). Long-term risk mitigation plans that are based on avoidance or resistance techniques typically require input from the science/engineering community and safety experts, and should ideally be a core part of sustainable development plans at the micro and national levels. A government authority may coordinate mandatory rules or best practice recommendations; we shall discuss this point in Chapter 9. Note that a key element of focus is on the ability to control a hazard/peril. We have noted that some catastrophic events can be reduced or eliminated through loss control measures, while many others cannot; this means that some catastrophic losses can be prevented and others cannot. For instance, some mass movements can be avoided by ensuring that zoning, development, and construction do not promote erosion. Similarly, by improving screening and security and enforcing various other safety protocols, some terrorist acts can be avoided or delayed. Obviously, many perils cannot be reduced or eliminated at all – the occurrence of an earthquake or hurricane, for example, cannot be influenced by loss control measures – meaning the focus of loss control must turn toward vulnerabilities.

Education about the potential for damage is an important part of loss control as it focuses attention on what might occur if a disaster strikes. The education process is often most effective when it conveys information on actual events that have occurred and those that are seemingly 'unthinkable,' and how these can shape economic and social forces; indeed, it is important to stress that the 'unthinkable' periodically occurs (e.g., the 9/11 collapse of the World Trade Center towers, the 2004 Indonesian tsunami). The power of education should not be underestimated in the successful application of vulnerability reduction.

Let us consider a company that wants to reduce the likelihood that it will sustain a loss from a fire in its warehouse. It can enact certain loss control measures that include banning placement of flammable materials within the structure, installing an automated sprinkler system,[4] and conducting regular fire inspection drills. These mechanisms reduce hazards, which can reduce the likelihood of a peril and potential loss. All involve some type of investment (e.g., the sprinkler system is a capital investment that must be funded at $t = 0$ and maintained annually thereafter, the fire inspection drills have to be performed by a professional at a cost, and so on), and must therefore be considered in the cost/benefit framework to determine potential impact on enterprise value. Generally speaking, however, such activities are seen as beneficial and advisable; indeed, insurers often credit a portion of a cedant's premium when these types of measures are implemented.

We can also consider an example of loss control of a catastrophic risk. A company attempting to control losses may willingly adopt minimum construction standards for a warehouse located in an earthquake-prone area; alternatively, municipal or regional government authorities may mandate such use. By adhering to urban planning standards, non-structural building codes (e.g., restricted building zones in floodplains, coastal areas, fault zones), and structural building codes (e.g., building materials, protective devices, extra structural supports, elimination of 'soft' first floors), the company is taking steps to minimize the likelihood of damage and loss; note, however, that it is not reducing or eliminating the risk of hazard or peril, as in the example immediately above – the earthquake will occur regardless of what the company does.

Loss control is so important that considerable efforts are now applied in structural engineering processes to consider the effects of catastrophic damage and associated mitigants on structures; indeed, each new disaster provides information on how best to enhance design and materials.[5] Of course, adherence to loss control measures does not mean that losses will not occur in the event of disaster, simply that such losses will be minimized in light of the best available standards. For instance, adhering to minimum structural building codes (either initially or through retrofitting) is considered to be one of the most effective catastrophe risk mitigants: some studies have shown that investing 1% of a structure's value on safety measures can reduce the probable maximum loss by up to 33%. Creation of a new steel structure on a commercial building that costs just under 3% of a building's value can reduce the probable maximum loss created by a Category 3 hurricane by 50%; a retrofit of an existing building, costing approximately 4%, can yield the same loss reduction. Thus, a company owning a commercial

---

[4] Automated sprinkler systems, which are quite common in many commercial buildings around the world, are a very limited form of loss control, intended only to prevent fires from becoming significant; once a particular threshold is reached, the sprinklers are quite ineffective. Limitations in loss control systems must be well understood in order not to be lulled into a false state of comfort.

[5] For example, in the aftermath of the Kobe earthquake, engineers altered their focus from methods designed to resist force to those designed to absorb and convert force.

warehouse with a probable maximum loss of $10m in the event a Category 3 hurricane strikes can reduce the loss to $5m by investing $400 000 in a steel retrofit.[6] The amount of insurance coverage it requires declines commensurately. Consider the effects of proper structural controls in the face of earthquakes: in late 1988 a 6.9 earthquake struck Armenia, killing 25 000 as residential structures collapsed due to poor construction materials and structural supports; one year later a 7.1 earthquake struck Loma Pietro, California, killing only 25, as reinforced structures remained standing.

Similar loss controls can be developed to minimize losses from terrorist threats (e.g., extra security staff, concrete barriers in sensitive access locations), industrial contamination (e.g., outer shields, hulls, or barriers to prevent leakage should the primary containment facility rupture, emergency clean-up equipment for spills), and other perils we have described in Chapter 2. These measures are similar to those taken to prevent fire, i.e., reduction, though not necessarily elimination, of the hazard/peril, which is possible to varying degrees. *Ex ante* and *ex post* measures such as warning systems, evacuation plans, security coordination, and emergency response can also be viewed as forms of loss control that help reduce the impact of indirect losses and social costs in the aftermath of a disaster. As before, these mitigants require an initial and/or ongoing capital outlay that must be considered within the context of costs, benefits, and corporate/national goals. There is little doubt, however, that broad-based application of loss control measures across risk-prone regions can lead to a meaningful reduction in the financial burden that arises in the wake of a catastrophe; this is particularly true in developing nations that lack a robust insurance mechanism. There is general concurrence within the disaster management community that a strong regimen of loss controls, while sometimes costly to implement (and enforce), is almost certain to be cheaper than the *ex post* costs associated with repair, replacement, and lost opportunity. Ultimately, the success of loss control is based on a combination of education, select regulation, and appropriate incentives/enforcement.[7]

5.1.2.2   Loss financing

Loss financing, the single largest class of risk management mechanisms, centers on risk retention, risk transfer, and hedging; the majority of the discussion which follows in subsequent chapters is focused primarily on these techniques. Under the overall umbrella of loss financing we can distinguish between pre-loss and post-loss financing. Pre-loss, or anticipatory, financing includes all techniques/mechanisms arranged in advance of a loss, and generally involves an *ex ante* cost (e.g., premium, fee); insurance, catastrophe bonds, contingent capital, and derivatives are all examples of pre-loss structures. Post-loss financing, or financing arranged in response to a loss event, includes cash/reserve access, short- and long-term debt issuance, and equity issuance. Though post-loss financing does not involve an *ex ante* cost, it may feature an *ex post* cost in the form of a higher cost of capital, particularly if an exposed company has suffered a large loss and has become less creditworthy.

Risk retention, the first loss financing technique, can be passive or active. Passive risk retention occurs when a firm preserves more exposure than it wants because it has failed to properly identify the nature and magnitude of its risks. This is a potentially troublesome issue,

---

[6] Loss of roofing is a major cause of economic damage in hurricanes, windstorm, tornadoes, and earthquakes, and a relatively inexpensive element to fix or reinforce.

[7] Such as tax credits or financial assistance for those adhering to voluntary avoidance/resistance schemes, penalties for those violating rules or choosing not to follow recommendations.

as it may indicate a flawed risk management process. For example, a company that operates a factory in a politically unstable emerging nation may not realize that it is exposed to sovereign risk (the risk of loss should the local government impose capital controls or expropriate private assets); it may not actually become aware of its exposure until a sovereign act has led to the loss of its local assets. Active risk retention, in contrast, occurs when a company knowingly preserves certain risk exposures (i.e., classes and/or magnitudes), generally those that have the possibility of producing only small losses, and which appear on a very frequent, or statistically predictable, basis. For instance, a large company with many employees may choose to retain a certain amount of employee health benefit exposure as it may be able to estimate the net claims outlay with enough precision to finance its own self-insurance fund (thereby eliminating the need to pay insurance premiums). In general, catastrophic risks are not considered to be good candidates for active retention as they occur infrequently (i.e., they are statistically unpredictable, particularly in the tail of the distribution) and have the potential of being very severe. Some companies, however, choose to retain them since the likelihood of occurrence is very small. That said, there is empirical evidence to suggest that in the aftermath of a major disaster retention of catastrophe risk exposure declines as more risk is transferred (though sometimes at the expense of low severity risk transfer).

Risk transfer, a second form of loss financing we consider in Chapter 6, shifts risks via the insurance/reinsurance mechanism. Insurance effectively transfers the cost of financing from the cedant (or insured) to the insurer; in exchange for a premium from the cedant, the insurer agrees to provide the cedant with a compensatory payment if a specified loss-making event occurs. The compensation provides the ceding company with the earnings stability, liquidity, and solvency it requires in the aftermath of an event. The risk transfer mechanism functions primarily because of risk pooling by the insurer: by grouping together a large number of independent (uncorrelated) risk units (e.g., policies) an insurer can reduce the overall level of risk and the possibility of extreme outcomes. According to the statistical principle known as the Law of Large Numbers, when a large number of statistically independent loss events are observed, the average loss is predictable, meaning that the probability of an actual observed loss deviating from the expected loss by a significant amount is very small. (Note that pooling is essentially a form of risk reduction that applies equally to the portfolio diversification scheme discussed below.)[8]

For instance, a firm seeking to protect against fire damage can purchase a fire insurance policy from an insurer by paying a premium. If a fire occurs, the firm will receive a compensatory payment that will allow damaged inventory, plant, or equipment to be replaced. The insurer, if it is managing its own risk process correctly, will group the policy with its other fire policies into a diversified portfolio that reduces its expected loss level.[9] The same approach can theoretically apply with certain catastrophic risks: a firm can purchase flood insurance from a private sector insurer or public sector agency, paying an *ex ante* premium for an *ex post* settlement should a flood occur and create damages. Again, the insurer or public agency providing the cover can pool the policy with others located in different areas in order to lower the overall level of flood risk exposure. However, if the pool cannot be constructed with a sufficient number of statistically independent events (e.g., all the policies are located in the same floodplain), the Law of Large Numbers does not apply and an accurate assessment of potential losses becomes very challenging and correct pricing may be difficult to estimate. This effectively means an insurer

---

[8] Risk transfer and pooling are not necessarily mutually dependent; that is, a cedant can transfer a risk by paying an insurer a premium, while the insurer can choose to retain the risk, pool it with others, or transfer the risk to a reinsurer.

[9] Alternatively, it may reinsure the exposure in the reinsurance market.

or public agency providing cover is in the same position as the entities requiring protection – risk is shifted, but not reduced.

Hedging is a third form of loss financing, and is often associated with unique or uninsurable risks that cannot be handled through a standard contractual insurance arrangement. While risk transfer via insurance can lead to a net reduction of exposure as a result of diversification and pooling, hedging simply shifts an exposure from one party (hedger) to a second party (generally a financial intermediary), which then preserves the exposure or hedges it with yet another party. For instance, a company that relies on oil as a manufacturing input is exposed to rising oil prices; as prices rise the cost of goods detracts from revenues and results in a smaller amount of operating income. To protect against this eventuality the company can hedge the risk by entering into a contract with a second party, which provides a compensatory payment if the price of oil rises. In practice, this type of hedging is generally arranged through derivatives, or financial contracts that derive their value from other references such as oil prices. Hedging can also be arranged for catastrophic risks: a firm that is exposed to risk of loss from windstorm can purchase a hedge that provides a payment if a windstorm occurs and creates damage. In fact, this is similar to an insurance contract covering windstorm, though subtle differences exist regarding pricing, documentation, taxes, legal treatment, and portfolio diversification. Certain hedging, transfer, and financing techniques between financial institutions and insurers/reinsurers have converged in recent years, meaning that a strict distinction between the business of managing catastrophic exposures has become increasingly blurred. Indeed, growth in alternative risk transfer and hedging mechanisms is a central element of catastrophic risk management; we shall consider the issue more fully in Chapters 7 and 8.

5.1.2.3   Risk reduction

Risk reduction, a third general risk management strategy available to institutions managing exposures, can be split into two components, withdrawal and diversification. Withdrawal, as the name suggests, refers to the partial or complete abandonment of a business, activity, or location that gives rise to a particular risk exposure; in fact, complete withdrawal is the only risk management strategy that ensures there can be no possibility of loss. For instance, if a firm is exposed to the movement in the dollar/yen foreign exchange rate by virtue of its sales activity in the Japanese market, it can lower or eliminate its exposure by reducing or eliminating its activities. Alternatively, if a company is exposed to potential environmental liability risk by operating a factory with antiquated equipment that does not comply with current safety standards, it can eliminate the risk by permanently closing the factory. The same applies to catastrophic risk: if a firm's manufacturing facilities are located on an active fault line, it can eliminate the threat of loss from earthquake by closing down the facility and relocating it to another area (in practice a company seeking to maximize enterprise value is unlikely to close down a functional facility to avoid the possibility of catastrophic loss; however, it might consider doing so if the facility is fully depreciated and needs to be replaced in the short term).

The second form of risk reduction relates to portfolio diversification, which is an extension of the pooling concept noted above. Portfolio management theory indicates that combining uncorrelated assets produces a superior return without a commensurate increase in risk; assets that are negatively correlated can actually lead to a reduction in risk. More formally, a diversified pool can be created by assembling a large portfolio of independent (e.g., uncorrelated) and identically distributed assets (risks) so that the variance of the average expected return in the portfolio increases (or the losses decline); the mean of the expected returns (losses) of the pool is greater (smaller) than the individual assets (risks) in the portfolio. For instance, a common risk management strategy is to diversify a portfolio of assets across uncorrelated risk classes. An investment manager holding a portfolio of technology stocks (highly corre-lated with one another) can reduce the risk of the portfolio by adding financial or industrial stocks (less correlated, though still correlated with the general stock market); to further reduce risk the manager can then add agency securities or government bonds (which are even less correlated with the stock market), and so on. Depending on the construction of the portfolio, the end result will be a lower amount of risk exposure for a given level of return. The same principle applies to physical or financial assets exposed to catastrophe. A company that pro-duces 100% of its goods in a factory located in a coastal area exposed to hurricane can reduce its exposure if it shifts 50% of its production to an inland facility that is not exposed to the same peril. Alternatively, an investment manager holding a portfolio of catastrophe bonds that reference Japanese earthquake events can reduce the risk of the portfolio by adding bonds referencing California earthquake, French windstorm, or Florida hurricane (all uncorrelated perils). Naturally, risk reduction involves costs and benefits that must be weighed in an analyt-ical framework. Closing down a factory or diversifying a portfolio involves certain one-time or ongoing charges that must be balanced against perceived or actual gains (e.g., not having to fund a new facility in the event of a disaster, not having to purchase insurance/derivative protection).

In practice, the mitigation and minimization of catastrophic losses is typically an amalgam of the solutions we have outlined. For generic catastrophic risk in any geographic location, a company might therefore take the following steps:

- Obtain crisis/disaster management information on local hazards/perils (*ex ante*).
- Adhere to voluntary or mandatory building/engineering codes (*ex ante*).
- Reduce or eliminate non-essential activities in the hazard/peril zone (*ex ante*).
- Arrange private-sector and public loss financing solutions (*ex ante*).
- Arrange supplemental post-loss capital (*ex post*).

It is possible, of course, that a party with a catastrophic exposure will choose to take no risk management actions. An assessment of costs, benefits, and likelihood of occurrence may indicate that preserving the status quo is valid, i.e., choosing not to create safety measures or structural mitigants, purchase insurance or a hedge, or reduce/diversify the core risk exposure. In such instances the party will be forced to bear the costs of repair and replacement should an event strike and create partial/complete destruction – as we have noted, this can impact liquidity, solvency, and enterprise value maximization. While it is unusual for a firm exposed to catastrophic risk not to take any protective action, it is an option that must be considered.

We have briefly mentioned some of the general risk management mechanisms that a com-pany (or sovereign entity) can use to manage exposures; we shall explore them in greater detail in the coming chapters. For now we simply note that loss control/safety programs, portfolio diversification techniques, insurance/reinsurance mechanisms, capital markets solutions, and government-sponsored programs are in different states of readiness within specific market-places; some of the mechanisms we discuss in the next chapters are not available to all parties within all countries/regions, though growing capital availability/mobility is expanding access. Until the process is complete, however, management solutions must typically be tailored to the specifics of the local marketplace. For instance, loss control solutions are widely used in

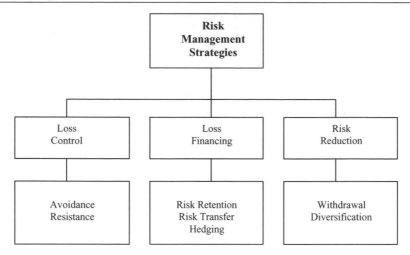

Figure 5.1   Common risk management strategies

many industrialized nations, and are becoming more apparent in certain emerging nations. Penetration of loss financing varies considerably: catastrophe insurance and reinsurance are very common in North America, Western Europe, and selected parts of industrialized Asia, but far less prevalent in emerging nations, which often lack insurance mechanisms to deal with all but the most essential elements of health and life coverage. Capital markets solutions (bonds, contingent capital, and derivatives), which feature considerable potential, are still in a relatively nascent stage and limited to the most advanced markets, including the USA, Western Europe, and Japan. Government-sponsored programs are used to varying degrees throughout the world; they are quite popular in emerging nations (particularly when supplemented by supranational or donor relief), as well as hazard-prone areas of industrialized nations (e.g., Florida, California, Hawaii).

Figure 5.1 summarizes the common risk management strategies described above.

It is important to stress that total elimination of risk, which reduces the probability of loss to zero, is not generally a practical or desirable goal. The marginal returns from each dollar invested in loss control, loss financing, and risk reduction decline, sometimes rapidly, as risk elimination moves towards 100%. This means each exposed party must find an optimal solution. Since absolute protection against loss can never be guaranteed without 100% elimination of risk, some level of 'acceptable' loss – expressed in the form of a loss tolerance or loss threshold level – must be established. This may be defined by society or the economy in a macro sense, or by individuals and companies in a micro sense. Tolerance levels, which can vary widely, are based on knowledge of exposures and risk management solutions, and on available resources. There is no single 'correct' solution regarding optimal catastrophe risk management techniques – a great deal depends on the specific goals of each company, its operating environment, the totality of risks that must be managed, individual pricing dynamics during different market cycles, and so forth. That said, a conventional risk management 'rule of thumb' suggests that low frequency/low severity risks should be managed via risk retention, high frequency/low severity risks via loss control and risk retention, and high severity/low frequency through a combination of loss control, risk retention, risk transfer, and hedging; high frequency/high severity risks must be eliminated entirely. Figure 5.2 summarizes these general rules.

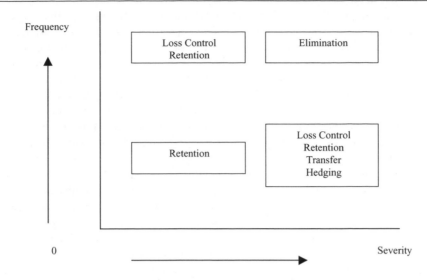

Figure 5.2   General risk management approaches by frequency/severity

5.2   RISK MONITORING

Regardless of the specific techniques a firm or sovereign entity uses to manage its catastrophic risks, the fourth stage of the risk management framework culminates in monitoring. An entity with a single catastrophic risk exposure or an entire portfolio must have mechanisms in place to track the size and location of its risk. A company with a single risk exposure can monitor the risk on a monthly or quarterly basis; unlike other high frequency/low severity financial and operating risks that change continuously, the exposure is likely to remain relatively static from quarter to quarter, meaning periodic monitoring is generally sufficient. Companies with entire portfolios of catastrophic risk must be able to monitor exposures daily. The dynamic nature of risks written, ceded, retroceded, purchased, and sold, means that the monitoring effort must be able to report an accurate profile on a regular basis. In-house technology platforms and modeling packages developed by third parties generally feature comprehensive reporting modules that can provide portfolio- and contract-level detail by country, peril, frequency/return period, loss exceedance, probable maximum loss, mean damage ratios, and so forth.

Scenario analysis should form part of the monitoring process. Those operating in a conventional environment where high frequency/low severity risks (and losses) are the norm typically have a strong appreciation of the small variabilities that can occur as a result of these exposures. Those exposed to catastrophic risks may lack first-hand knowledge of the degree of financial damage that can be wrought by a single event; indeed, the relative infrequency of events (and losses) may force greater attention on daily matters. Lack of loss data and complex modeling efforts make matters even more difficult to grasp. Accordingly, those formulating risk management strategy must ensure they have access to scenario analyses that describe the possible financial losses that might occur under a range of disasters, from 'moderate' single-event catastrophes up to mega-catastrophes. While the main focus of scenario analysis is rightly on single catastrophic events that have the potential of producing losses ranging from $100m to $5–20b, those that can lead to damages of $50b to $100b must also be considered; the

Kobe earthquake, events of 9/11, and Indonesian tsunami have demonstrated that large events can, and do, occur. Extreme scenarios may include a devastating 7.5+ urban earthquake followed by widespread fire, a Category 5 hurricane followed by significant tornadoes and storm surge flooding, or a terrorist release of weaponized NBCR followed by mass evacuation; these types of events, with an infinitesimally small probability of occurrence but potentially large economic impact, should form part of the scenario analysis monitoring process.

From a governance perspective, any risk that a company assumes should be reported on a regular monthly or quarterly basis to members of executive management and the board of directors. Indeed, in industrialized systems it is increasingly common for risk and financial reporting to be part of the regular communication and decision-making process. Similar reporting must often be prepared for regulators, rating agencies, and other external stakeholders, who may need to be aware of a company's general risk profile and catastrophe exposures/concentrations. Monitoring ultimately serves two purposes: adding transparency to a firm's overall operations and risk profile by detailing the specific nature/magnitude of exposure and the potential losses that might be sustained; and providing a mechanism by which ongoing risk decisions can be made (including cost/benefit, risk/return, concentration, diversification).

5.3   PRIVATE AND PUBLIC SECTOR EFFORTS

Since catastrophic events can be financially devastating, comprehensive risk management often involves efforts and resources of both the private and public sectors. From a private perspective, we have briefly mentioned the loss-financing techniques that are available in certain national systems to help protect against losses and financial distress. The availability of private sector capital, conveyed through insurance, reinsurance, and capital market instruments, makes it possible for companies to obtain indemnification or funding at competitive rates. Loss-financing mechanisms and risk capacity are gradually spreading around the world, and more institutions in more countries now have access to leading edge solutions. As this process continues, efficiencies should increase and pricing should become transparent and equitable. Unfortunately, resource insufficiencies, technical inadequacies, and regulations mean that some national systems cannot offer the necessary private sector solutions. Furthermore, some exposures are so large and concentrated that they cannot be managed solely through private sector institutions. This means that public efforts – at the national, regional, state, or local level – must form part of the total solution.

Public efforts are generally non-financial (i.e., creating and guiding disaster and emergency programs, loss control regulations, civil protections) as well as financial (i.e., supplying capital/funding). In practice these can be divided into *ex ante* and *ex post* mechanisms; both are essential, and lack of either means greater potential for losses. For instance, some aspects of the public sector effort are based on *ex ante* safety and coordination programs, with government authorities establishing minimum safety measures and risk mitigants in order to help reduce vulnerabilities. These, as we shall discuss in greater detail in Chapter 9, may include building codes, zoning, and other structural and non-structural rules designed to ensure a safer environment, as well as warning systems, emergency/crisis protocols, and public safety education and guidance – the very processes that provide individuals, companies, and communities with the information they require in order to cope with a disaster. Certain other aspects of the public sector effort are based on *ex post* relief and recovery, which can often be coordinated and implemented most efficiently at a local or national level. Measures such as emergency response, business recovery, social/humanitarian relief, and direct loans, grants, and subsidies, are an essential component of social and economic management, and can reduce financial pressures and speed recovery. They can, unfortunately, lead to a unique set of problems, including adverse incentives and moral hazard. In addition, *ex post* legislative efforts regarding new/revised loss controls to protect against future losses, while theoretically worthwhile, may proceed slowly in practice – sometimes so slowly that memories regarding the disaster fade before implementation occurs. This leads to an almost continuous cycle where development in vulnerable areas outpaces risk protection initiatives. Breaking the cycle may only be possible when the loss level from catastrophes is so significant that society demands change.

Given the unique qualities of catastrophic risk – particularly the potential (and realizable) severity – no single risk management solution can cover every eventuality; the scope and magnitude are simply too large. In fact, as vulnerabilities continue to expand, the private/public partnership will become increasingly important. That said, balancing public and private initiatives is an important element of overall risk management. Excessive public intervention may become intrusive, rigid, or irrelevant, and may ultimately be ignored or abused. Similarly, excessive reliance on the private sector may result in lack of coordination or inadequate financing. In the aftermath of a major catastrophe it is vital that public stability be reinforced, or the overall social framework may be threatened (leading to even greater loss of confidence and economic damage). Effective mitigation and loss control, based on clear responsibilities and coordination, must ultimately lead to sustainable and equitable development.

5.4 SOURCES OF CAPITAL

Risk capital permits risk transfer and hedging; without debt and equity capital, intermediaries that are in the business of creating risk management solutions and risk capacity cannot operate. Accordingly, it is important to understand sources of capital and how they can be allocated in support of risk-taking activities. Though capital can come from both retail and institutional sources, we focus our comments on three major institutional classes: insurers/reinsurers, investment funds, and financial institutions. We exclude from our discussion any outright grants of capital made available by government or supranational organizations; though these constitute a legitimate form of post-loss financing, they are not return-driven risk capital allocations that expand and contract with market cycles.

5.4.1 Insurers/reinsurers

Insurers and reinsurers are central to the supply of catastrophic risk capacity.[10] Indeed, linkages between insurance/reinsurance cycles, mitigation, exceedance probabilities, and ruin probabilities (as well as alternatives from other markets) ultimately dictate the amount of capital available to support catastrophe risk.

Insurers and reinsurers are sensitive to the returns they can earn on their risk exposures. When an insurance market features limited supply and excess demand (i.e., a 'hard market' cycle), the price of risk capacity increases and insurers/reinsurers earn greater returns on the business they write. These excess returns attract new capital – typically through new reinsurers

---

[10] An insurer can be viewed as a leveraged investment fund that generates liabilities by issuing policies (rather than debt) and using the proceeds to invest in a portfolio of assets. The insurer enjoys no tax efficiency from its investments (i.e., gains are taxed at the level of the insurer and investors are taxed on dividends), but obtains a relative advantage in raising liabilities via the insurance market, which is relatively inefficient (i.e., it is possible to sell policies for more than their economic worth); by doing so insurers are able to generate enterprise value and attract capital.

formed expressly to take advantage of the market cycle – until supply expands and returns weaken. A hard market cycle can occur in the aftermath of a disaster, when large claims lead to insurer/reinsurer losses, a depletion of capital, and curtailment of business. A poor investment environment can compound the cycle, as interest income and equity returns from insurer investment portfolios decline. When an insurance market features excess supply and stable or decreasing demand (i.e., a 'soft market' cycle), the price of risk capacity declines and insurers/reinsurers earn lower returns on their business. Though catastrophic (and non-catastrophic) covers are still written, the overall pace of expansion remains relatively stable and may continue until a disaster strikes and excess losses result. This can lead to a contraction in business and the start of the hard market cycle. Accordingly, it is important to consider the general state of the insurance/reinsurance markets when determining the availability of risk capacity in support of catastrophic risks; we shall consider this point at greater length in the next chapter. When insurer/reinsurer capital is in short supply, as in the aftermath of a poor underwriting cycle or in the midst of a weak investment market, cedants seeking risk cover generally, and catastrophic cover specifically, may be unable to do so. In such cases they may have to employ additional loss control measures or seek coverage from alternate sources (such as the capital markets or government-sponsored programs); in the extreme, they may even decide to relocate their activities away from a vulnerable area. We shall consider market cycles in greater detail in Chapter 6.

An insurer employing its own risk mitigants, including reinsurance and portfolio diversification, lowers its exceedance probability curves. If the business it writes is driven by a probable maximum loss measure, it can expand its risk capacity while remaining within a target probability of ruin; in fact, we can consider a probable maximum loss rule where an insurer limits its business to a level where the exceedance probability is just below a target ruin probability. The insurer therefore has every incentive to actively manage its portfolio. Naturally, if an insurer lowers its own target ruin probability, the coverage it can write will decline by a corresponding amount. Similarly, if the cost of reinsurance rises, coverage will decline. Ultimately, an insurer (reinsurer) must determine how much coverage to write, retain, and reinsure (retrocede); the decision will be a function of its own capital and target ratios and the state of the market cycle.

5.4.2 Investment funds

Mutual funds and hedge funds control very substantial amounts of investable capital and support the catastrophic risk process directly and indirectly. In fact, their role in capacity supply is critical: when fund managers are in search of excess returns they expand the base of capital available to cover risks; when they become risk-averse, such as in times of excessive financial volatility or economic instability, they withdraw capital, including resources allocated to catastrophe exposures. Although the relative lack of correlation between catastrophe-based risk capital and traditional asset classes can produce attractive returns in poor markets, the lack of liquidity and volatile pricing associated with catastrophe assets can still be too risky. Fund managers can supply capital in support of catastrophic risk management directly by investing in the equity of insurers/reinsurers that specialize in providing catastrophic cover or purchasing catastrophe bonds linked to specific regions. Or, they can supply capital indirectly by investing in the equity of insurers/reinsurers that write a broad range of non-catastrophic and catastrophic policies; however, investors seeking a pure catastrophe-related return may find this approach sub-optimal, as it involves investing in the non-catastrophic element of the business, which is driven by different dynamics.

5.4.3   Financial institutions

Banks and securities firms, like funds, supply catastrophe risk capital directly and indirectly. In a direct sense, they can lend to insurers and reinsurers that specialize in writing catastrophe risk insurance, invest in the equity of insurers/reinsurers, or purchase catastrophe bonds. Indirectly, they can invest in the capital of insurers that run diversified portfolios of non-catastrophic and catastrophic risk. The amount of capital banks may be willing to supply in support of catastrophe risk depends on the returns they can earn and the relative riskiness of their own operations. It is also worth noting that financial institutions play a vital intermediation function. Though by no means equivalent to acting as direct suppliers of capital, banks and securities firms routinely raise funds for insurers, reinsurers, and funds in the public and private capital markets; the capital that is ultimately raised is then used to support catastrophic and non-catastrophic business. Similarly, financial institutions may help insurers, reinsurers, and funds arrange over-the-counter derivative transactions that result in the exchange of different types of catastrophic exposures.

5.5   TOWARD ACTIVE RISK MANAGEMENT

Active risk management is an essential element of proper governance and management. And, while the process is accepted for high frequency/low severity financial and operating risks, it is not as widely used in the context of catastrophe risk. The process of formally reviewing the relative costs and benefits of catastrophe loss control, loss financing, and risk reduction is not well established in the corporate and sovereign sectors; some of the efforts are ad hoc, and in some instances the process is viewed as a secondary priority. While this behavior may be a function of various factors, one issue is especially notable: the low probability of occurrence and, by extension, the long return periods associated with catastrophes. Directors, managers, executives, and government officials contending with many pressing issues and scarce resources often focus their risk management efforts on the small, but frequent, risk problems that can affect daily operations.[11] Those lacking first-hand experience with catastrophe losses may not fully appreciate the financial distress that can arise with a disaster, and those contemplating a 10- or 20-year career in a company or industry may not be particularly concerned about events with a return period of 100 or 200 years. As a result, active management of catastrophe risk is not yet uniform across companies, industries, or countries. This will become a more significant problem as vulnerabilities grow, and will ultimately demand detailed examination and use of risk management solutions – including the instruments and programs we consider in the next chapters.

---

[11] In addition, in a world of finite economic resources, processes requiring considerable analytic efforts and those dependent on sometimes scarce information may not be given top priority.

6

Catastrophe Insurance and Reinsurance

Global insurance and reinsurance are the most important mechanisms for financing catastrophic losses. The two sectors are very well established in many countries, and have proven effective over time in facilitating the transfer of various classes of catastrophic risk. Indeed, institutions that actively manage their catastrophe exposures generally turn directly to the insurance/reinsurance markets once they have implemented loss control measures. In this chapter we commence our discussion with a brief review of general elements of insurance, insurable risk, and reinsurance.[1] We then explore the unique features of catastrophic insurance and reinsurance, as well as market cycles, internal risk management processes, and general challenges.

6.1 INSURABLE RISK AND INSURANCE

In order for a risk transfer contract to qualify as insurance it must feature certain characteristics, including:

- The contract must cover an insurable risk with respect to some fortuitous event – one that is unforeseen, unexpected, or accidental.
- A sufficiently large number of homogenous exposure units must exist in order to make the losses predictable and measurable.
- The cedant must have an insurable interest and be able to demonstrate an actual economic loss.
- The risk of loss must be specifically transferred under a contract providing indemnity and involve appropriate consideration (i.e., exchange of risk for upfront premium payment).
- All dealing must be *uberimae fidei*, in 'utmost good faith,' through the conveyance of material representations.
- The right of subrogation, or the transfer of loss recovery rights from cedant to insurer, must exist.

In order for an insurance contract to be binding it must include offer/acceptance and be executed with knowledge and legal purpose. The contract itself is aleatory rather than commutative, meaning that values exchanged are unequal and uncertain. In fact, they are almost invariably different, as the premium paid for an insurance contract is unlikely to match precisely any loss experience (which will in virtually all cases be smaller or larger than, but not equal to, the premium). Insurance therefore represents the transfer of fortuitous losses from the cedant, which pays an economically fair premium, to the insurer, who agrees to provide relevant indemnification (i.e., settlement of a claim that occurs as a result of a named peril or event).[2]

---

[1] Aspects of the introductory section are adapted from Banks (2003); those seeking additional detail on the broader alternative risk transfer market may wish to consult the text.

[2] Claims that occur in a given year are not all paid in the same year; those not settled are reserved, meaning that claims occurring in previous years are paid from reserves.

Insurers generally only cover pure risks that are based on a large number of non-catastrophic exposure policies. There are, of course, some exceptions to this: some insurers, for instance, underwrite risks where the expected loss is difficult to estimate or the potential for a catastrophic outcome exists, or where the risk characteristics are so unique that a large number of homogenous policies cannot be written. Within the general category of risk retention/transfer we note a spectrum of transferability that moves from minimum (e.g., significant retention via structural features in standard contracts, dedicated risk financing products, captives) to maximum (e.g., full transfer via structural features in standard products).

6.1.1   Full insurance

Full insurance is a maximum risk transfer contract designed to shift as much exposure as possible from cedant to insurer in exchange for a fair premium. A traditional contract is based on an upfront premium payment for one year of cover. Full insurance is generally characterized by a small deductible, large policy cap, limited (or no) copay/coinsurance, and limited exclusions. A cedant creating a full insurance maximizes its premium payment (cost) in exchange for what it perceives to be greater risk transfer advantages (benefit). Thus, a company with $1m of exposure to a particular risk that prefers minimal risk retention can purchase a policy with no deductible or exclusions and a $1m cap. This ensures it will receive a compensatory payment of any losses up to $1m if the named event occurs.

6.1.2   Partial insurance

Partial insurance is a standard insurance contract that is altered so that the cedant retains more, and thus transfers less, exposure.[3] This results in a lower premium payment from the cedant to the insurer, consistent with the cedant's desired cost/benefit trade-off. In practice, full insurance can be converted to partial insurance by changing deductibles, policy caps, coinsurance, and/or exclusions.

A deductible, which is the cedant's first loss retention, can be set on an individual loss basis or in aggregate (i.e., the sum of all loss events occurring during the coverage period); the greater the deductible, the greater the retention and the smaller the transfer. For instance, a standard insurance policy for a risk-adverse company seeking to transfer a significant amount of catastrophic or non-catastrophic exposure might feature a $1m policy cap and a $100 000 aggregate deductible. After the first $100 000 of losses (which may come from a single event or many smaller ones), the next $900 000 of losses is fully covered by the insurer. A risk-taking company seeking to retain more risk might increase the deductible to $400 000 and thus be liable for the first $400 000 of losses; the insurer de facto provides $600 000 of loss coverage as a second layer.[4]

Policy caps can also be used to define a level of risk retention by limiting the insurer's settlement liability to the cedant: the smaller the cap, the greater the ultimate retention and the lower the transfer. For instance, a company might purchase a policy with a $1m cap; if an insurable event occurs and generates $2m of losses, the insurer bears the first $1m (assuming no

---

[3] Customization is conveyed through a manuscript, or non-standard, policy.

[4] In fact, while this may be precisely what the risk-taking company wants, insurers tend not to favor high deductible policies since pricing the fair premium is difficult; this reverts to our point in Chapter 4 related to the difficulties involved in determining, with reasonable precision, the magnitude of the tail of the distribution. In addition, the insurer loses incremental investment income from a smaller amount of reinvested premium.

deductible) and the company the second $1m. Through this mechanism the company increases its risk retention by accepting any potential losses greater than $1m; importantly, it retains the upper layer losses, while the insurer bears the first loss. Caps therefore force the cedant to accept risk of loss in excess of the cap, meaning the amounts may be unpredictable and potentially large. In fact, by using a cap the company remains uninsured in the tail of the distribution, which is precisely where coverage is most often needed – particularly against catastrophic events that might precipitate financial distress. Insurers favor policy caps because they need not be as precise in estimating the tail of the curve and can cap their liabilities.

Risk transfer can also be limited through coinsurance/copay features, where the cedant and insurer share in a certain amount of losses. The greater the cedant's coinsurance percentage, the greater its retention, and the lower the transfer. Coinsurance payments can be determined in various ways. For instance, the insurer might agree to pay a set proportion of the actual cash value of the loss, with the cedant bearing the balance. Alternatively, the amount a cedant can recover from the insurer might be set as a function of the amount of insurance carried relative to the amount required, multiplied by the actual loss experience. The insurer and cedant thus share in each loss on a predetermined percentage basis; the premium payable to the insurer is a function of both the full premium and the proportion of risk retained.

Policy coverage/exclusions are another form of risk retention. By specifically defining the scope of desired coverage the cedant indicates which risks it is willing to retain and which it prefers to transfer. As the number of exclusions increases – either as broad categories of risk (e.g., catastrophic P&C), or specific events (e.g., European windstorm) – the implicit level of risk retention increases and the amount of risk transfer decreases. In some policies all risks within a category might be covered unless they are specifically excluded; the cedant is responsible for identifying and specifically removing exposures that it wants to retain. In some cases, of course, the insurer will exclude coverage, including risk deemed to be temporarily/permanently uninsurable or excessively uncertain (e.g., terrorist risk, nuclear accident risk); the cedant is therefore forced to retain the exposure or seek alternate solutions.

6.1.3   Captives

A captive is a special purpose entity established as an insurer or reinsurer that companies use for purposes of self-insurance – a basic form of risk retention. Rather than contracting with a third-party insurer, a company pays the captive a premium in exchange for the necessary protection. The captive may be wholly or jointly owned by the company; in practice many captives are solely owned, though companies in a common industry often band together to create joint/association captives to manage risks on a consolidated basis, particularly when risk coverage is in short supply and/or premiums are deemed to be too high. Captives are used primarily for high frequency/low severity risks because they involve exposures that are statistically predictable, meaning expected loss levels can be determined *ex ante* with reasonable precision. However, captives are occasionally used for catastrophic coverages (as certain industries have done with regard to terrorism risk, for example).

6.2   CATASTROPHE INSURANCE

Catastrophe insurance is available for firms seeking to transfer their low frequency/high severity exposures. In the normal course of business a firm may distinguish between risks with a known probability of loss and expected size of loss (e.g., fire), risks with an uncertain probability/size of loss (e.g., earthquake), and risks with an unknown probability/size of loss (e.g., nuclear accident or terrorist attack). Companies exposed to the latter two may seek catastrophe insurance coverage; note coincidentally, these are the most challenging ones for insurers to price and manage.

Common areas of catastrophic coverage include P&C, liability, business interruption, workers' compensation, life, and health (of course, these elements of coverage are available for non-catastrophic risks as well, but we focus our discussion on the catastrophic dimension). A policy may be deemed to provide catastrophic cover if it provides for indemnification when a specific named catastrophe event occurs, or when an insurable event occurs and creates large losses for the cedant, e.g., when amounts exceed a large deductible and the policy features a large cap – this is equivalent to the insurance providing the cedant with upper layer coverage. Not all elements of coverage are available to all parties at all times; only the most comprehensive (and expensive) full insurance policies provide protection against economic losses sustained from all factors.

- *P&C*: P&C coverage is intended to provide post-loss financing for any physical property that is damaged or destroyed by a catastrophic peril. Under many P&C contracts insurers use actual cash value (replacement less depreciation) rather than replacement cost to determine post-loss settlement if property is destroyed and not rebuilt or replaced. Most P&C contracts are written on an occurrence basis, where the full limits granted apply to each catastrophic event, without a maximum aggregate; any deviation from this practice must be specifically noted in the policy through the establishment of aggregate loss limits.
- *Liability*: liability coverage provides economic restitution from losses or injury sustained as a result of inadequate safety or protection measures that become evident in the aftermath of a disaster; building owners (e.g., third-party property owners) are often required to provide tenant companies with liability coverage.
- *Business interruption*: business interruption coverage is intended to provide compensation for revenues lost as a result of an inability to operate business in a normal fashion after a catastrophe strikes. In most policies the coverage is written on the basis of 'actual losses sustained,' meaning that cedants and insurers must mutually agree on amounts lost.
- *Workers' compensation*: workers' compensation coverage relates to economic restitution for workers who are unable to continue working as a result of a catastrophe-induced interruption that prohibits normal functions from being carried out, or injury that prevents workers from completing their assigned duties. Coverage can be seen as a replacement of lost income.
- *Life*: life coverage provides economic restitution to the beneficiaries of any individual that has lost his/her life as a result of a particular catastrophic peril. Though insurers write such policies on an individual basis, they may also do so for an entire company on a group-wide basis; to minimize large losses from a single incident, an insurer may avoid writing group life cover for a single company that occupies a single at-risk location.
- *Health*: health coverage provides financial payments for any health-related injury or illness caused by a disaster; coverage often extends to medical consultations, hospitalization, and prescriptions.

Full catastrophe insurance coverage for disasters can be reduced through the mechanisms described immediately above, which results in only a partial transfer of risk. Most insurance policies feature deductibles, coinsurance, caps, and/or exclusions to reduce instances of moral hazard, divide the loss burden, and reduce premium costs. For instance, in some jurisdictions, earthquake deductibles range from 5% to 15% of the insured value, while hurricane deductibles may range from 2% to 5%. Some policies feature coinsurance clauses requiring cedants to bear a portion of every loss on a percentage basis once any deductible has been met (e.g., 10% coinsurance, where the insurer pays 90% and the cedant 10% of any loss up to the defined cap). Some policies have specific exclusions that limit payout on certain claims (e.g., a commercial earthquake contract may only provide restitution for direct damage to property, meaning losses due to business interruption are not covered). Insurance contracts always feature policy caps that limit the insurer's liability for losses. Caps may be set as an aggregate across multiple events, or on a per occurrence basis (e.g., an annual hurricane policy may provide $1m of P&C loss coverage for each hurricane event, or $3m of coverage for all hurricane events, where each 'named' hurricane constitutes a discrete event). Policies may include reinstatement clauses that allow cedants to renew their limits in the aftermath of a disaster with the payment of a new premium. Note that in some cases insurers may be unwilling to provide any coverage at all, or they may choose to shorten terms or increase exclusions; this can happen when the catastrophic exposure is classified as temporarily or permanently uninsurable, reinsurance coverage is insufficient, or planned premium increases are rejected by regulators. The supply of catastrophe insurance is therefore dependent on overall market conditions.

Insurers commonly write catastrophe policies related to a range of perils, including earthquake, tropical cyclone, extra-tropical cyclone, industrial contamination (ex-nuclear), sovereign political/financial events, and engineering/mechanical failure. Some write cover related to risks that are only partly insurable (or occasionally uninsurable), such as terrorism and flood. Insurers writing earthquake risk policies often provide cover as an endorsement rather than a standard feature; for instance, in the US market earthquake coverage is supplemental, and generally includes a deductible set as a percentage of pre-loss value.

Coverage of terrorist events presents a unique challenge for the private insurance sector. Prior to 9/11 terrorism was routinely included in most all-risk policies for free (though most policies contained war exclusions); after 9/11 many insurers cancelled their coverage. In fact, private coverage was particularly scarce in the aftermath of the attack, and though some capacity eventually returned, government-sponsored programs are likely to be a permanent feature of the sector henceforth.[5] Indeed, there is every expectation that private insurance coverage will contract again in the aftermath of the next major terrorist act, particularly if pricing has not been estimated properly.[6]

Pricing of catastrophe insurance requires high-quality data so that loss distributions can be created. In such cases expected losses can be regarded as the fair value benchmark – but only if catastrophe risks can be diversified to some degree and exposure computations are unbiased; this reverts to our point from the last chapter, where we indicated that the Law of Large Numbers allows expected loss levels to be used with confidence when a large number of statistically independent events are included in the portfolio. In such instances an insurer can

---

[5] The ability for insurers to provide terrorism coverage is dependent in part on the availability of reinsurance. Post-9/11 it became very difficult for insurers to obtain the reinsurance they needed, meaning clients of insurers faced policy cancellations as well (those that were able to obtain coverage from reinsurers paid a steep price, e.g., pre-9/11 Chicago O'Hare Airport's $750m of terrorism coverage cost $125 000; post-9/11 a mere $150m of coverage cost $7m).

[6] We have noted in Chapter 4 the importance of having a strong base of loss data in order to compute expected losses. Terrorism risk in general, and US terrorism risk in particular, suffers from a relatively sparse data set, meaning that fair pricing of insurance coverage becomes very complicated – and perhaps overly subjective. While the modeling efforts put forth by major analytics firms provide some guidance, the industry has little experience in knowing how much premium should be charged and how much price elasticity of demand exists (and how that might change in the intervening period between incidents). Agents and brokers attempting to create risk management solutions for corporate clients lack the base of information that is available for other perils and may be unable to offer proper guidance. In the absence of compelling data, modeling efforts are likely to be more, rather than less, conservative; this means there is a greater likelihood that insurers and reinsurers willing to provide cover will charge high premiums – possibly driving some cedants away, and leaving them uninsured.

examine the probability of an industry-wide catastrophe of a certain minimum magnitude by estimating frequency/severity distributions across perils and regions. It can then use distribution information and market share to derive the probability distribution for a single contract, and then estimate expected losses. Final pricing must also include a profit load factor. As we shall note later in the chapter, pricing of catastrophe insurance (and reinsurance) is rarely this straightforward. When a catastrophe insurance portfolio is not diversified enough, statistical assumptions break down, making it difficult to relate the variability of losses to the expected loss level. The variance of losses in the portfolio is much higher than in a non-catastrophic risk portfolio, meaning insurers may charge premiums that are a multiple of the expected loss benchmark in order to protect their operations.

6.3 REINSURANCE

Reinsurance contracts are central to the effective management of insurance risks and the creation of risk capacity. Reinsurance is insurance cover written by a reinsurer for a primary insurer, while retrocession is insurance cover written by a reinsurer for another reinsurer. A primary insurer seeking to lower its risk will transfer the exposure to a reinsurer, obtaining a cover known as a cession. The reinsurer, as retrocedant, will itself pass any unwanted exposure to the retrocessionaire in the form of a retrocession. Reinsurance and retrocession are popular risk management tools in advanced markets; for instance, in the USA approximately 50% of exposures are reinsured in a given year, and nearly 20% of those are retroceded. Reinsurers can therefore create well-diversified portfolios of non-catastrophic and catastrophic risks (across perils, time, and regions) by virtue of their business and operational breadth. However, their ability to do so depends on the state of reinsurance and retrocession capacity, as discussed below.

Insurers need reinsurance to balance their portfolios. An insurer transferring selective risks by entering into a reinsurance contract diversifies its exposure, thus lowering its risk profile. For example, an insurer might have certain constraints related to large line capacity (a large loss exposure on a single policy) or premium capacity (a large volume of policies written on the same line of cover); by using reinsurance it can reduce concentrations and achieve a more balanced portfolio. Since reinsurance cover allows insurers to reduce their unearned premium reserves (i.e., a reduction of reserves increases the insurer's capital/surplus position), the process permits more insurance to be written in a particular sector. Reinsurance cover can also create profit stability and reduce the probability of financial distress. Risks can be ceded and accepted as facultative or treaty reinsurance, and as quota share, surplus share, or excess of loss arrangements. We consider each one in brief.

6.3.1 Facultative and treaty reinsurance

Reinsurance contracts can be written on a facultative or treaty basis. Facultative reinsurance is the term applied to any transaction that involves a case-by-case review of risks. Under a facultative contract, which is highly customizable, the primary insurer is not obligated to cede a particular risk, nor is the reinsurer required to accept it. Each risk that is ceded and accepted is analyzed on its own merits and governed by a separately negotiated contract (reflecting the bespoke nature of the process). Not surprisingly, a facultative agreement is often used when risks are very large and unique, or require special analysis and consideration. Facultative reinsurance is widely used to cover various risks in the P&C sector (including those with catastrophe characteristics). For instance, standard insurance lines in the property sector may be reinsured through a facultative agreement based on analysis of probable maximum loss and maximum foreseeable loss; a similar arrangement can be concluded in the casualty sector to cover general liability, automobile, workers' compensation, excess liability or umbrella covers. In general, the ceding insurer gives the reinsurer information on the specific exposure it seeks to cover. If the reinsurer agrees to accept the risk, it provides a quote and written confirmation; if the insurer accepts the quote, the reinsurer then forwards confirmation of binder and receives a policy from the insurer, which it uses to prepare the final certificate of reinsurance.

Though facultative business gives both parties greater ability to specifically examine risks prior to commitment, it also means that there is no *ex ante* guarantee of cession or coverage. Thus, if the reinsurer believes that a particular exposure generated by the primary insurer is inconsistent with its own risk tolerance, it can decline to write the cover. Or, if an insurer generates an especially profitable risk, it may choose to retain the entire exposure.

Treaty reinsurance, in contrast, is a contract where risks are automatically ceded and accepted (for that reason it is sometimes referred to as obligatory reinsurance). The primary insurer agrees to cede a portion of all risks conforming to pre-agreed guidelines under a treaty agreement; the reinsurer is similarly bound to accept all conforming risks. Underwriting criteria in the treaty must be delineated with enough specificity that there can be no doubt about the nature of risks to be ceded and accepted. Those that conform to established guidelines are automatically transferred; those that do not conform fall outside the scope of the treaty and must then be considered on a facultative basis. While the treaty process is efficient and economical (i.e., less expensive on a 'per risk' basis than facultative cover), and provides comfort that coverage will be available when needed, it also reduces the reinsurer's 'underwriting power;' that is, the reinsurer agrees to absorb all conforming risks, up to a limit, without being able to inspect each one individually. In addition, some of the risks assumed by the reinsurer through the treaty may ultimately be unprofitable (though in the long run the reinsurer expects the relationship to be profitable). Similarly, while the ceding insurer gains comfort from having automatic capacity for conforming risks, it can no longer choose to retain selective exposures for its own book (i.e., very profitable ones, or those that help with its portfolio diversification efforts). A great deal of catastrophic and non-catastrophic reinsurance is written on a treaty basis.

6.3.2   Proportional and excess of loss agreements

Reinsurance risks, returns, and losses can be divided between the primary insurer and the reinsurer on a proportional (or pro rata) basis or an excess of loss basis. This is true for both facultative and treaty risks.

Proportional agreements, such as the quota share and surplus share arrangements discussed immediately following, require the insurer and reinsurer to share premiums, exposures, losses, and loss adjustment expenses (LAEs) on the basis of a pre-defined formula, such as a fixed or variable percentage of policy limits. Such agreements adhere to the proportionality principle, where the insurer and reinsurer are involved in a risk exposure under the same terms and conditions. Proportional treaty agreements always result in some amount of cession and allocation of losses, while proportional facultative agreements result in cession and allocation of losses once an exposure has been agreed and accepted. The advantages to the insurer of using a proportional agreement include recovery on small losses, protection of net retentions on a 'first dollar lost' basis, and protection against both frequent and severe events.

By way of contrast, excess of loss (XOL) agreements (sometimes known as non-proportional reinsurance agreements) call for the insurer and reinsurer to allocate risks and returns in specific horizontal or vertical layers; depending on the magnitude of losses and the sequence and level of attachment, a reinsurer may or may not face some cession and allocation of losses. The advantages to the insurer of using an XOL mechanism include greater protection against frequency or severity (though this depends on retention), increased retention of net premiums, and improved efficiencies in administration and premium allocation; XOL agreements also allow insurers to reduce peak exposures to retention levels they feel are more manageable. XOL protection can be arranged separately for each loss (e.g., loss per risk cover) or for each event (e.g., loss per event cover), and is generally designed to cover only a few large losses; if too many claims arise, the pricing may not be economical.[7]

Under the proportional quota share (QS) structure the insurer and reinsurer agree to split premiums, risk, losses, and LAEs as a fixed percentage of the policy limit. The reinsurer thus pays the primary insurer a ceding commission for a share of the exposure and premium. A QS permits the ceding insurer to reduce its unearned premium reserves (through premiums ceded to the reinsurer) and increase its surplus (through commissions received from the reinsurer). The assets of the ceding insurer are reduced by the premium paid to the reinsurer, while liabilities (reserves) are reduced by the lower unearned premium reserve. Since the decrease in liabilities is greater than the decrease in assets (by the amount of ceding commission received), the ceding insurer's surplus increases. The QS can also strengthen other financial ratios, such as premium to surplus; the more capital an insurer has on hand to support the premiums it is writing, the stronger its financial condition. A QS written with a creditworthy reinsurer provides the insurer with credit for reinsurance ceded, helping decrease the premium to surplus ratio.

Through a proportional surplus share (SS) structure the reinsurer agrees to accept risk on a variable percentage basis above the insurer's retention limit, up to a defined maximum (known as a line), and pays the insurer a ceding commission for a share in the premium. Once the insurer's retention limit has been exceeded, the reinsurer assumes the additional exposure, and resulting premiums, losses, and LAEs are shared between the two on a fractional basis. Since a separate dollar retention is set for each policy (or certain groups of policies), the sharing is variable in percentage terms across an entire portfolio. An SS can help an insurance company improve its surplus account, reduce the possibility of large losses from catastrophic events, and provide an increased level of underwriting capacity. It is worth noting that even though the ceding insurer must transfer a portion of risk and premium to the reinsurer, it has flexibility in selecting the retention level on each policy (or group of policies); this means that adverse selection can still occur. For instance, the insurer might choose higher retention (lower cession) on all low-risk policies and lower retention (higher cession) on high-risk policies.

While QSs and SSs allocate risks and returns on a fixed/variable basis, the XOL agreement creates risk allocations in non-proportional layers. Through an XOL the reinsurer agrees to pay any losses above a specified retention (attachment) level, up to a maximum limit. Coverage can be set for a single occurrence or in aggregate over a defined time period, typically one year. For example, a reinsurer might agree to '$10m XOL $5m,' meaning that it will cover losses above $5m (i.e., it attaches at $5m) up to a maximum level of $10m, implying net loss coverage of $5m (i.e., $10m − $5m). Since there is no longer any equal sharing of risk as with proportional QS and SS agreements, the premium charged by the reinsurer is not based on a fractional portion

---

[7] From a practical perspective, XOL contracts are often arranged by reinsurance brokers, who work with insurers to design the desired coverage based on requirements and costs/benefits and then contact reinsurers to obtain the best possible deal.

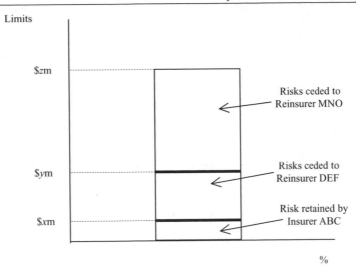

Figure 6.1   Vertical reinsurance layering

of the amount charged by the primary insurer to its own clients; rather, it becomes a function of general underwriting factors, including the nature of the exposure, concentration, prior loss experience, and portfolio composition. The XOL gives the primary insurer capacity to write large lines and protects against high severity/low frequency events; while XOL arrangements are used in a range of P&C covers, they are often applied to catastrophic exposures.

In some cases several reinsurers might participate simultaneously in an XOL agreement, each taking a preferred layer of exposure; this is known as vertical layering. For instance, Insurer ABC might retain $2m of a $20m P&C cover and cede $5m to Reinsurer DEF (who attaches at $2m and caps at $7m), and cede $13m to Reinsurer MNO (who attaches at $7m and caps at $20m). If an $8m loss occurs under this scenario, ABC bears the first $2m, DEF assumes responsibility for the next $5m, and MNO the last $1m (see Figure 6.1). XOLs may also be structured with horizontal layering, where different reinsurers take pieces of the same loss layer. For instance, in the preceding example MNO might only take 50% of the vertical layer between $7m and $20m, while Reinsurer TUV might take the other 50%. If the same $8m loss occurs, MNO and TUV split the $1m of excess layer losses on the agreed 50%–50% basis (see Figure 6.2). XOL layering works in practice because different reinsurers often have different risk/geographic expertise, portfolios, and tolerance levels; one reinsurer (e.g., DEF) might find that a 'closer to the mean' first loss layer is better for its business, while a second reinsurer (e.g., MNO) might find that a 'farther from the mean' second loss layer is better, and so forth. Willingness and ability to participate in different layers can change over time, as a reinsurer's portfolio or profit and capital targets change.

6.4   CATASTROPHE REINSURANCE

If insurers could freely raise their premiums without requiring approval from state or national regulators, their need for reinsurance generally, and catastrophe reinsurance specifically, would diminish considerably (or the attachment levels selected would increase dramatically). Insurers

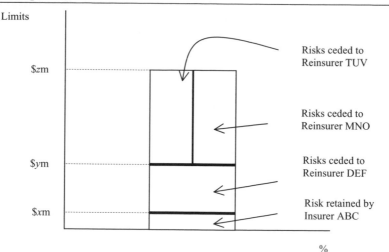

Figure 6.2   Horizontal reinsurance layering

would simply increase premiums to compensate for the increased risk of loss, particularly in the aftermath of an event. In practice, however, premiums cannot be increased at will, meaning catastrophe reinsurance remains an essential risk management tool.

Insurers view catastrophe as an event that can create financial distress – the ambiguity in the tail of the loss distribution means that reinsurance is necessary in order to reduce the probability of a liquidity squeeze or insolvency. In fact, insurers are cognizant of the need to reduce the probability of financial distress, as any evidence of financial weakness can lead to an immediate loss of business. Studies suggest that insurers facing a greater probability of financial distress (e.g., those with higher leverage, lower liquidity, and lower credit ratings) are more willing to pay for catastrophic reinsurance; similarly, those with larger exposures are more likely to demand incremental coverage (interestingly, large insurers, who value the liquidity rather than the solvency features of catastrophic reinsurance, are also likely to demand more coverage). Reinsurers, viewing a catastrophe as a single large event that produces a loss for one or more insurers or many smaller events that produce losses for a large number of insurers, are willing to supply cover to protect insurers from financial distress if they can obtain a fair return.

An insurer can use various methods to determine optimal catastrophe retention and cession levels. For instance, it may find a point where the marginal benefit of reduced reinsurance cost is outweighed by the marginal increase in retained losses. Or, it may establish a minimum solvency target (e.g., net loss + LAE [after catastrophe reinsurance] must be less than 50% of surplus at the 100-year return period). Alternatively, an insurer may set retention/cession based on risk-adjusted returns (e.g., the marginal return of retaining a particular layer of catastrophic risk may be a function of a change in the catastrophe premium less a change in the recoverable, divided by the change in required capital). The decision becomes particularly complex when catastrophe premiums are high; an insurer can create significant enterprise value by retaining, rather than ceding, risks, but it increases its likelihood of encountering financial distress.

Though the reinsurance contracts we have described above can be applied to any insurable risk some, including proportional covers, catastrophic XOL agreements, and second event reinsurance, are commonly used to manage catastrophic risks. Catastrophic XOL agreements, functioning as upper layer risk protection, are particularly popular with insurers as they cover 100% of aggregate claims above the retention (generally in the year of occurrence), with a cost based on an assessment of the degree to which a ceding insurer's aggregate expected loss will exceed established limits. XOL cover can essentially be viewed as a bet, providing the insurer with full liability coverage once the retention is exceeded, but no protection until that occurs – a large loss, such as might be experienced with a catastrophe, can quickly exceed the retention and trigger cover. If the ceding insurer sets its retention too high it may encounter a significant liability, and must therefore balance the relevant costs and benefits. Some insurers use the stop loss XOL reinsurance variant, which limits the claims burden from retained exposure for any given year. Second event reinsurance, also known as a reinstatement contract, is also widely used by ceding insurers. Under this structure capacity limits are available once during a single contract period (generally one year); if they are used, however, they can be reinstated to the original level through the payment of an additional premium (the second premium payment is generally cheaper to arrange in advance of a loss event). Such contracts may be useful in active catastrophe zones, which can be impacted by multiple events during a single annual season (e.g., hurricanes, extra-tropical storms, tornadoes).

Proportional and XOL agreements covering a catastrophic peril are not, of course, mutually exclusive. Insurers can combine different elements of retention and transfer in unique ways to achieve specific results. For instance, after an initial deductible an insurer might seek to transfer 70% of its exposure to Japanese typhoon through a QS agreement (meaning it still retains 30% of each new typhoon risk originated). Or, it may reduce the de facto QS retention in half by introducing a 15% catastrophic XOL layer that comes into effect for particularly large losses. An extension of the examples illustrated above is given in Figure 6.3 (note that many other variations are possible).

Reinsurance is used to protect against a range of perils. The most significant reinsurance markets, in order of amount of risk transferred, include US earthquake, US hurricane, and

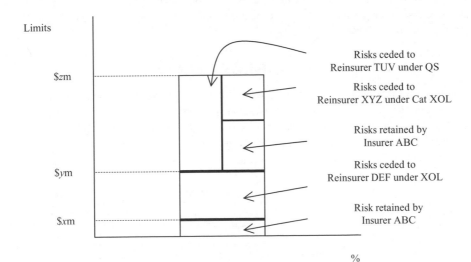

Figure 6.3   Quota share and catastrophic XOL reinsurance structure

European windstorm,[8] but other perils, including Japanese and NMSZ earthquake, are also routinely reinsured. Most of these perils are transferred through treaty arrangements; more complex risks, including nuclear contamination, terrorism, flood, and tornado, are often reinsured on a facultative basis.

Reinsurers must operate with care and diligence, as the potential for adverse selection and moral hazard exists. An insurer will always have more information about a particular catastrophic risk policy than the reinsurer as a result of thorough underwriting work and actual experience with the policy; it can thus adversely select from its portfolio (particularly when facultative arrangements are being used),[9] leaving a reinsurer without adequate protection. The problem is intensified by the potentially large severity of the risks. Moral hazard is another potential problem, as the negotiation of a reinsurance arrangement may cause the ceding insurer to be less diligent in its own underwriting process.

In order to guard against these potential problems, reinsurers generally require insurers to supply extensive underwriting details and may demand use of treaty agreements (particularly proportional agreements, where both parties share in the risks on a percentage basis). Ultimately, there is some belief within the industry that moral hazard and adverse selection issues may actually be relatively minor. Insurers and reinsurers dealing in catastrophe risks enjoy a mutually beneficial relationship – provision of risk capacity in exchange for ceded premiums – and they conduct their business on a temporal basis, meaning a great deal of weight is accorded to long-term views and relationships; while spatial management is also important, and leads to proper portfolio diversification, the temporal elements of risk generally, and catastrophe risks specifically, play to the strengths of the reinsurance industry. Accordingly, it is in the best interests of insurers to minimize instances of adverse selection and moral hazard.

The role of reinsurance in the risk management process is vital, and if reinsurers cannot provide adequate cover (or claims payments), systemic imbalances can arise. In fact, the reinsurance market cannot supply all of the required catastrophe protection on its own; several large disasters occurring within a span of several months, coupled with claims arising from non-catastrophic business, would severely impact the financial standing of the reinsurance industry. Reinsurance must therefore be considered as only one of several elements of the total catastrophe risk management solution, to be supplemented by capital markets programs and government-sponsored mechanisms.[10]

6.5   MARKET CYCLES

As noted in the last chapter, insurance and reinsurance markets experience regular cycles driven by supply of, and demand for, insurance protection; the cycles are heavily related to both insurance loss experience (which impacts insurer/reinsurer profitability, capital, and risk capacity) and general investment market experience (which affects investment earnings, capital, and risk capacity). As we have indicated, insurance/reinsurance can be described as

---

[8] There is some evidence to suggest that insurers and reinsurers have historically underpriced their risk capacity with regard to European windstorm or have actually purchased insufficient reinsurance or retrocession cover. Indeed, the Lothar and Martin storms of 1999 placed a number of insurers in danger of insolvency as a result of reinsurance inadequacies; similarly, a number of reinsurers sustained large losses as a result of underpricing. With models suggesting that a 100-year return period loss of $30–35b is possible, insurers and reinsurers must reassess pricing and risk management strategies.

[9] There are rare instances where a reinsurer has superior information and can adversely select the insurer's portfolio via a facultative process; this, however, is a less common problem.

[10] Indeed, it is important to note that many of the public sector loss-financing programs we discuss in Chapter 9 are simply government versions of the insurance or reinsurance mechanisms mentioned above; though they are offered by government authorities with taxing authority and debt capacity sufficient to mobilize necessary resources, the basic structures are similar.

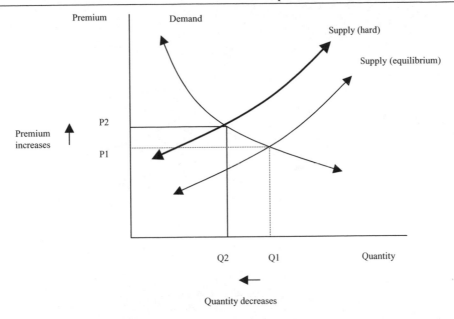

Figure 6.4 Hard market cycle, constant demand

being in a 'hard market' state, or a 'soft market' state; this is particularly true of non-life insurance, which is highly cyclical (featuring average cycles of 5–7 years and peak to trough price and volume changes of up to 40%).

A hard market occurs when supply of risk capacity declines. The insurance/reinsurance supply curve illustrated in Figure 6.4 shifts to the left, causing supply to contract and prices to rise, assuming constant demand (e.g., post-Andrew, risk supply declined by approximately 20%). In some instance this may be compounded by an increase in demand, which forces premiums to rise even higher, as in Figure 6.5.[11] A hard market occurs when insurers and/or reinsurers have experienced a series of large losses that erode capital; as capital declines the ability and willingness to write new cover decreases, causing a contraction in supply.[12] This may be supplemented by a weak investment market, which fails to generate the additional income insurers and reinsurers require in order to supplement their operations.

Naturally, as supply declines and premiums rise (e.g., to levels that may be 3–5× higher than the expected loss benchmark), potential future profit opportunities begin to appear attractive and draw in new sources of capital (e.g., new reinsurance companies may be formed, investors may be willing to purchase new tranches of equity issued by existing insurers/reinsurers). This gradually leads to an excess supply of capital capable of supporting new risk exposures, and the

---

[11] Studies by Froot and O'Connell (see Froot, 1999) suggest that supply shifts, rather than demand shifts, have the greatest impact on prices and quantity; the authors have found little evidence of demand adjustment in the aftermath of a catastrophe, e.g., a $10b catastrophe can raise prices by 19–40% and reduce quantity purchased by 5–15%. While this result might be expected across catastrophes in general (e.g., hurricane, earthquake, terrorism), the study has found that it is true within perils, e.g., hurricane losses do not appear to cause any meaningful increase in hurricane coverage by parties that have become nervous about the prospect of future losses. The authors thus conclude that the driving force in reinsurance pricing is based on supply, rather than demand.

[12] Note that the full effects of large losses on supply may be somewhat dampened by *ex post* government intervention/financing, which can ease some of the demand pressures that might otherwise arise; for instance, the US government provides $8–10b in disaster financing during a typical year, which would otherwise need to come from the insurance sector.

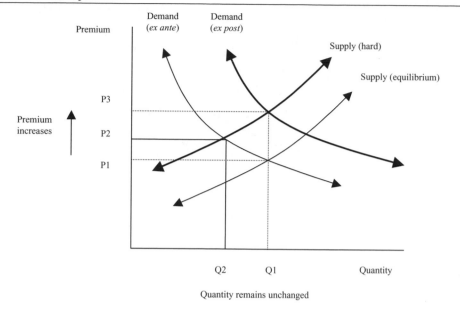

Figure 6.5   Hard market cycle, increasing demand

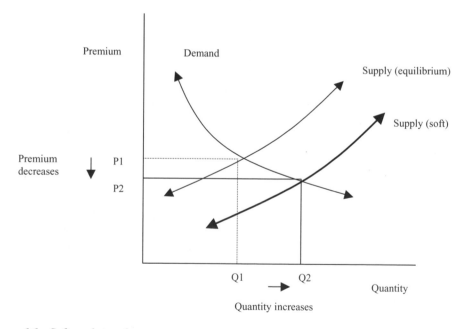

Figure 6.6   Soft market cycle

beginnings of a soft market cycle start to appear. A soft market occurs when the supply of risk capacity expands; the supply curve shifts to the right, causing premiums to decrease, as in Figure 6.6. Importantly, during soft market cycles when excess capital attempts to take advantage of profit opportunities, underwriting standards can loosen – sometimes dramatically. In order to win or retain market share, insurers and reinsurers lower their underwriting criteria and may accept marginal risks, liberalize policy conditions (e.g., offer flexible terms, reinstatement clauses), or fail to price exposures according to their true loss characteristics.[13] This sets the stage for greater underwriting losses when the cycle turns.

Hard markets appear every few years, as in the mid-1990s (the result of losses from Andrew and Northridge) and in the early part of the millennium (losses from Lothar and Martin, Taiwanese and Turkish earthquakes, the 9/11 attacks). Over the past decade catastrophic insurance/reinsurance cover has increased by approximately 10% per year, which is on a par with the general increase in catastrophic exposures. However, evidence from the large losses before and after the millennium suggests that covers purchased may have been insufficient to cover potential losses (e.g., an underestimate of risks). Considerable fluctuations in insurance/reinsurance prices have appeared over the past two decades, driven to a great degree by the onset of catastrophic events.

6.6 INTERNAL RISK MANAGEMENT

Catastrophic insurance/reinsurance coverage is only available to third parties if insurers and reinsurers providing risk capacity are managing their own risk profiles prudently. An insurer that writes a great deal of catastrophic coverage must pay its cedants in the event of losses and claims; if it is not managing its portfolio properly and encounters financial distress as a result of an excess of claims, cedants may not receive the sums they are rightly due. The same applies to reinsurance. For this reason, global insurers and reinsurers must generally adhere to minimum internal and external standards of risk management and regulation.

Prior to events such as Andrew and Northridge, insurers were generally unsophisticated in their analysis of catastrophic risk concentrations and probable maximum losses. For instance, in managing earthquake risk many insurers simply reported exposure accumulations by broad earthquake zone and loss ratios by construction class, using certain deterministic relationships to arrive at potential losses. In fact, the exercise was more of a regulatory reporting task than a dynamic risk management process, and inadequate given the growing size of both exposures and vulnerabilities.

Major loss events forced a change in thinking,[14] and the industry began developing more sophisticated and dynamic approaches to the process. Considerable focus has been placed in recent years on the capital used to support catastrophic insurance and reinsurance, and diligent management of scarce resources is now a primary goal for the entire industry. Insurers/reinsurers must establish internal solvency requirements and earnings targets in order to determine how much revenue each line of risk can generate and how much capital is needed to support the exposure. Part of the process involves determining whether specific lines of business, such as catastrophe risk, add to enterprise value, and how the resulting risks can be managed. The impact of incremental exposures must also be considered (i.e., whether each additional risk compounds or reduces overall portfolio risk). When analyzing portfolio composition, insurers and reinsurers must ensure that diversified exposures across perils, regions, and time are properly understood. Failure to properly isolate the specific drivers of a portfolio can lead to misallocation of capital and mispricing of risks. For instance,

---

[13] Some insurers and reinsurers write risks on a speculative basis, with little relation to actuarial pricing; this is particularly true when the market cycle is softening and new business opportunities are being sought. The intent in such instances is to build a large portfolio of single risks, including catastrophic risks, with the expectation that most will be profitable and only a few will result in claims. Such an approach to business is highly correlated with market cycles; during hard markets, when the industry as a whole has sustained large losses, special risk underwriting is likely to be curtailed.

[14] For instance, the claims settlements for Northridge were equal to $28\times$ aggregate earthquake premiums collected the year before the event.

grouping all earthquake exposure under a single portfolio may be misleading, as California, Japan, and NMSZ earthquake are uncorrelated. However, segregating French extra-tropical cyclones and French flooding may also be misleading, as there is at least some degree of correlation between the two. A defined risk strategy that relates capital, earnings, and management solutions to overall composition and magnitude of risk should be the end result of the evaluation process.

Prudent, best-practice procedures, coupled with regular external inspections, can help ensure that management of risks is proceeding as required. In the context of insurable risks generally, and catastrophic risk specifically, this can be accomplished through various mechanisms, including:

- Formalized risk governance process, with a clear expression of risk tolerance, priority markets, and target returns.
- Centralized risk limits, including minimum levels of diversification and maximum levels of concentration.
- Comprehensive hedging and risk transfer programs.[15]
- Minimum standards of solvency (capital) and reserves.[16]
- Minimum standards of liquidity.[17]
- Formalized management of counterparty credit risk (including reinsurer credit risk).[18]
- Rigorous financial and actuarial modeling processes.
- Continuous monitoring and evaluation of portfolio risks.
- Robust internal and external audit controls.

Insurers and reinsurers are more likely to remain in a financially healthy state by following these basic rules, providing cedants with the coverage they require. Naturally, the process must be dynamic, and enhanced as the market cycle changes (e.g., an insurer should transfer risk to a reinsurer when the market cycle indicates that the cost of doing so is less than the cost of preserving the risk). Though the internal risk management framework is generally accepted and practiced in industrialized nations, it is not uniformly prevalent in emerging nations that feature relatively immature insurance systems. To achieve these minimum best-practice standards, technical assistance from established insurers and insurance regulators is required – particularly in the area of pricing and portfolio diversification, where errors in either sector can have costly consequences that can impact liquidity, solvency, and client coverage. It is important to stress that internal risk management procedures, such as those above, apply equally to all other financial intermediaries providing risk capital, including banks, securities firms, and funds; the process of risk governance and management is universal across industries that supply capacity.

---

[15] Apart from reinsurance and retrocession, insurers and reinsurers can develop additional risk transfer and hedging mechanisms. For instance, the systemic risks in insurance liabilities can be hedged through offsetting positions in the asset portfolio, complex market risks can be hedged via derivatives, catastrophic exposures can be transferred via securitizations, and so forth.

[16] Insurer and reinsurer capital comes from multiple sources, including equity, debt, hybrids, and contingent capital. Since policy liabilities must generally rank senior in the event of default, most debt capital is subordinated, e.g., higher cost.

[17] Insurers generally have enough liquidity in their core operations to be able to invest in higher-yielding, and less liquid, assets, which helps boost returns.

[18] In purchasing reinsurance, insurers assume the risk that the reinsurer will perform as contractually required in the event of loss and claim; an element of credit risk therefore exists. In practice, insurers tend to diversify their reinsurance relationships across various institutions in order to mitigate the potential effects of credit risk, so that default by any single reinsurer is unlikely to pose a threat (the top five reinsurers hold approximately 50% of all cessions). Reinsurers themselves actively manage their portfolios, avoiding undue concentrations to large claim situations such as disasters. The sector credit profile is generally sound: only 24 reinsurers have failed over the past two decades, and more than 90% of technical reserves are held by reinsurers rated AA or AAA.

6.7 CHALLENGES

Insurance and reinsurance are critically important to proper management of catastrophic risks. However, the sector faces certain challenges, including those related to pricing difficulties, earnings and capital volatility, concentrations, limits of insurability/uninsurability, lack of penetration, capacity constraints, and contagion effects.

6.7.1 Pricing difficulties

An insurer/reinsurer assuming a catastrophic risk must be able to estimate expected losses of an exposure or portfolio; this is an essential element in determining a fair premium (e.g., pure premium plus premium loading). It must also be able to estimate extreme, or unexpected, losses in order to prevent capital depletion. We know that non-catastrophic risks, when pooled together, allow for rather precise estimates of both expected and extreme losses, meaning fair pricing of risk can be determined with considerable accuracy. We recall from our discussion in Chapter 4 that challenges can arise in modeling low frequency/high severity events; the statistical distributions that are created may not be indicative of possible experience, meaning pricing may not be accurate. Relative lack of data is a key problem, and even efforts to supplement the process via simulation cannot provide complete assurance of accuracy. These difficulties can lead to instances of mispricing. In fact, empirical studies have revealed pricing aberrations with specific perils occurring during specific market cycles. In many instances historical premiums appear to have been priced well above actuarially fair value, ranging from 1.5 to 5× expected losses for a given layer (the higher premiums are especially evident for upper layers of catastrophe cover). The 'justification' in such cases is that statistical ambiguity causes actuaries to favor higher (conservative) premiums. The high premiums may also be justified by the high cost of capital (particularly during a post-disaster hard market) and friction costs (illiquidity, brokerage costs, reinsurance collateral costs, moral hazard/adverse selection costs, and other agency costs). On other occasions risks seem to have been substantially underpriced. In fact, the industry appears to have regularly underpriced premiums when a catastrophic event has failed to appear for a period of time;[19] this may relate to lack of large losses/claims and a relatively healthy amount of capital available in support of claims. Accurate catastrophe pricing is a persistent challenge that will only be overcome through the accumulation of a greater quantity of detailed loss data related to specific locations and perils; expected and unexpected losses cannot be accurately determined through limited data sets.

Not surprisingly, there is a certain elasticity of demand built into reinsurance pricing. Empirical studies have shown that as catastrophe reinsurance prices rise, insurers increase their retentions, decrease their limits, and increase their coinsurance levels.[20] Though demand for reinsurance can remain strong in the wake of a large disaster (which almost invariably leads to short-term price increases), it can wane over the medium term if pricing is not perceived as equitable; this is consistent with the results of various empirical studies. Reinsurers must therefore strike a balance between the pricing they believe to be commensurate with the risks they are assuming (along with normal profit loads) and the pricing they believe will be palatable to

---

[19] For instance, European flood risk, European windstorm risk, Japanese typhoon risk, California earthquake risk, and Florida hurricane risk have all been underpriced during specific cycles.

[20] The expected value of an insurer's retention depends on the frequency with which the insurer expects losses in a particular range to occur, which is a function of the underlying exposure; demand is thus a function of relative retention, relative limits, and coinsurance levels.

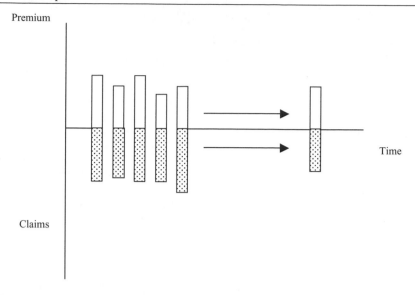

Figure 6.7 Non-catastrophic cash flows

insurers. In practice reinsurance pricing tends to be much more volatile than primary insurance pricing, adding to the risk management challenges of the insurance industry.

6.7.2 Earnings and capital volatility

The catastrophe insurance and reinsurance business is susceptible to earnings and capital volatility as a result of the erratic nature of payment inflows and outflows. A single large catastrophe can result in settlements that are many multiples of the normal experience attributable to non-catastrophic risks. Indeed, it is possible to view a catastrophic risk as an intertemporal financial problem rather than a single 'point in time' financial problem, with a balancing of a continuous stream of premium inflows against relatively infrequent, but large, outflows. With standard high frequency/low severity risks, which have an approximately equal pattern of inflows and outflows over time (see Figure 6.7), premiums can be established to cover a targeted loss ratio that is well behaved – meaning that it is theoretically possible to pay current losses from current premiums (with only a small reserve to cover slight excesses and investment income from the asset portfolio available to generate shareholder returns).[21]

The same framework does not apply to catastrophic risks; loss ratios can vary widely from year to year, meaning it is not possible to match current premium inflows with outflows (see Figure 6.8). Ultimately an insurer needs access to a large pool of capital/reserves to meet occasionally large outflows. The obvious answer might be to establish an *ex ante* reserve by redirecting a portion of each premium into a buffer account. In practice, however, some national

---

[21] The goal of many insurers is to create a replicating portfolio with assets and income that match expected cash outflows on policies. While this cannot always be done with complete precision, the predictable nature of a well-diversified portfolio of high frequency/low severity risks helps considerably. Insurers wanting to boost returns may willingly deviate from the replicating portfolio; this can be accomplished by varying the nature of the policies or the riskiness of the asset portfolio (e.g., taking greater credit risk, call risk, subordination risk, liquidity risk). Ideally, insurance underwriting activities should be viewed as separate and distinct from the investment activities; that is, insurance operations should not serve as a loss leader or subsidy provider for the investment management operations through mispricing.

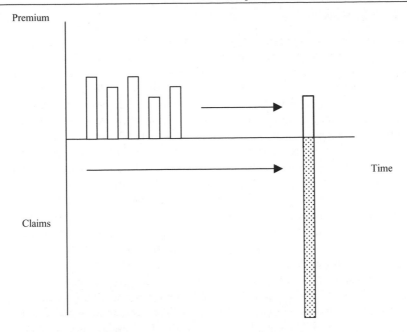

Figure 6.8   Catastrophic cash flows

accounting systems prohibit the accumulation of reserves in P&C lines for losses that have not occurred (e.g., in the USA Financial Accounting Standards No. 5 for contingencies bars this practice); attempts to circumvent this rule by creating retrospectively rated policies may also be disallowed.

Though some amount of reserves can be accumulated, they often cannot be earmarked for specific purposes. In addition, even when a reserve buffer can legally be created, it is likely to be tax-inefficient (e.g., reserves are often taxed as income in the year they are established, and any interest income generated by the reserves is also taxed).[22] Furthermore, insurers holding excess cash balances (even if permissible and tax-neutral) are almost certain to face criticism from investors for not maximizing enterprise value (in the extreme they might even become takeover targets); using capital to fund potential, though perhaps not realized, catastrophic losses is an expensive process that ultimately reduces shareholder returns. Reinsurance/retrocession is only a partial solution as post-loss capital is not committed and can easily be withdrawn – it can more readily be viewed as a form of contingent capital. In fact, there is no optimal solution from a pure profit and capital management perspective, though a greater linkage to the structures of the capital markets, which can provide committed *ex post* funding on a relatively quick basis if arranged in advance, surfaces as a solution (this presumes, of course, that transactions can be floated at economically reasonable levels). Apart from this solution, however, insurers and reinsurers actively writing catastrophic risks are likely to continue to experience earnings and capital volatility.

---

[22] International reinsurers incorporated in certain offshore jurisdictions do not necessarily face the same hurdles in establishing reserves; in fact, some jurisdictions grant favorable tax treatment to reserves. Whether these are sufficient to cover potential catastrophes losses, and whether such reserving represents an optimal use of capital is, of course, another matter.

6.7.3 Concentrations

Insurers and reinsurers writing coverage need to be aware of the accumulation of concentrations; while this is true for all risks accepted, it is especially important for catastrophic risks. Any meaningful accumulation of a catastrophic exposure can lead to instances of financial distress if a disaster occurs. In practice a catastrophe risk portfolio cannot be diversified to the same extent as a non-catastrophe risk portfolio. An insurer writing automobile insurance can diversify across age, geography, automobile type, and so forth, writing a large number of individual policies that will ensure proper diffusion of risk. The same is not true with catastrophe risk coverage; an insurer can only write a small number of low frequency/high severity events on a particular region/peril, meaning diversification benefits are difficult to obtain and concentrations can build. The Law of Large Numbers and Central Limit Theorem that allow an insurer to properly diversify and price a portfolio are severely restricted.

An insurer/reinsurer that experiences large losses as a result of concentrations is likely to curtail the risk capacity offered to cedants or ceding insurers, leading to hard market conditions; this represents a cost for clients attempting to manage their own catastrophic exposures. In order to manage concentrations, insurers and reinsurers must follow a rigorous internal risk management process (based on the steps highlighted above) that properly identifies and transfers any excess exposures and those that fail to meet total or marginal return hurdles. Fortunately, the classes of catastrophic risk we have discussed in this book tend to be uncorrelated with one another; thus, a stress event in the hurricane portfolio will not impact the earthquake portfolio, or a Japanese earthquake exposure will not affect a NMSZ earthquake exposure. However, where correlations exist or might appear (e.g., Florida hurricane and flood), care must be taken that risks do not become excessively large.

6.7.4 Limits to insurability/uninsurable risks

The essence of insurance relates to the insurability of a risk. If a risk is deemed to be uninsurable then the traditional mechanisms of insurance/reinsurance cannot be used and alternate solutions, such as those provided by national or local governments or the capital markets, must be sought. Though differences exist across perils and national systems, available evidence suggests that catastrophe risks are insurable to varying degrees during most market cycles. That said, temporary limitations on insurability (and outright instances of uninsurability) appear more often than with standard low severity/high frequency exposures. Insurers and reinsurers that willingly or forcibly absorb significant catastrophe risks have the potential of creating systemic instability, as large claims are unlikely to be met through pricing adjustments alone – meaning that capital depletion and instances of financial distress may follow.

In general, exposures associated with terrorism, flood, and nuclear risk, among others, are often classified as partially insurable, temporarily uninsurable, or permanently uninsurable, meaning that they must be supported by alternate solutions. For instance, in the wake of 9/11, insurers covering airline hull and liability faced $4b of claims; they cancelled certain elements of war hazard/terrorism coverage and established new third-party liability risk retention group covers with $50m caps. Since this was inadequate under terms of airplane lease agreements, several national governments had to provide additional third-party liability coverage under the programs described above. In essence, aspects of airline coverage had become temporarily uninsurable and required an alternate solution from the public sector; this process lasted approximately two years, after which insurers were more willing to write hull and liability cover at relatively reasonable rates. Whether private sector insurance will be available in the aftermath of a future terrorist strike is, of course, uncertain. Flood risk is generally regarded as uninsurable through the private sector as a result of high correlation of losses in a given region (e.g., little ability to diversify risks within a particular market); in many national systems flood risk insurance is provided by government, rather than private, sources. Nuclear risk is only partly insurable via the private sector and public involvement appears to be a permanent characteristic of the market. The failure of Reactor 4 at Chernobyl in 1986 made very apparent the social and financial dangers of nuclear contamination and led eventually to the creation of special liability structures for insurers and operators. Since radioactive contamination is essentially uninsurable in a conventional sense, nuclear risks are generally excluded from standard P&C policies and are insured via special national pools. Pool members keep their share in the pool as a retention without any recourse on amounts above the retention; most pools also provide third-party liability insurance for operators.

6.7.5   Lack of insurance/reinsurance penetration

In some national systems private sector catastrophe insurance and reinsurance penetration is very limited. In most instances this is a result of lack of education, lack of income, lack of information/data related to perils and vulnerabilities,[23] and a belief that the government will provide post-loss restitution as necessary. As a result, the theoretical and actual benefits that can be obtained from the insurance/reinsurance mechanism do not exist, meaning that resources may not be used optimally and excessive burdens may accrue to government authorities. Injecting pricing transparency, providing education, and sharing data related to losses and vulnerabilities can help improve penetration levels; naturally, these efforts need to be supplemented by mobilization of financial resources, which may involve short-term cross subsidies. A special focus is likely to be required on individual/private policies; business and commercial penetration is generally much higher as a result of greater risk awareness and larger financial resources to cover premiums.

6.7.6   Capacity constraints

There is legitimate concern within the insurance/reinsurance and corporate sectors that capacity for catastrophic risks will become constrained in the future, particularly if vulnerabilities continue to expand at a rapid rate (and there is little evidence to suggest any slowdown in growth will occur). The capital access of the insurance/reinsurance markets is finite, and may affect the risk management options of companies and sovereigns. In fact, the concerns are so significant that they have led to the creation of the alternative solutions we consider in the next chapters.

   Capacity constraints present themselves every few years as part of the cyclical process; the onset of a few large claims and a decline in investment markets can reduce available capital and squeeze capacity. For instance, after Andrew and Northridge risk capacity declined by 25% to 40% in specific sectors (and led ultimately to the creation of various government-sponsored

---

[23] There is some evidence suggesting that the relative lack of information/data, and the considerable efforts that must go into the modeling effort, act as barriers to participation in the insurance/reinsurance market; this is a particular problem in developing nations that lack the intellectual property and financial resources to create the proper infrastructure. This does not suggest that new competitors cannot enter, simply that the speed at which they can establish an operation and the level of risk coverage they can actually offer are likely to be limited.

programs and the establishment of eight new Bermuda reinsurers with $3b in combined capital, which eventually gained a 25% share of the global reinsurance market). In the aftermath of 9/11 and the sharp decline in the global equity markets, reinsurance capital contracted by 25%, leading to a noticeable reduction in risk capacity. The gradual issuance of catastrophe bonds/contingent capital facilities and the creation of various public risk management programs emerged to meet shortfalls, and additional capital was eventually injected via the establishment of new Bermuda-based reinsurers. Thus, capacity was temporarily curtailed and prices rose. In both examples the effects of the cycle lasted approximately two years, and illustrate the larger concern – namely, whether future catastrophes will create an even greater capacity constraint, and whether alternative mechanisms will be prepared to absorb the excess demand. If they are not, those seeking protection may be unable to do so at economically reasonable prices, which may ultimately have an impact on business activities and economic growth. Any cataclysmic event, e.g., a mega-catastrophe of the scale that modelers believe is quite possible, is likely to overwhelm available capacity from the insurance/reinsurance sector. With capital markets solutions (and capacity access) in a developing state, government involvement is almost certain to be required.

6.7.7   Contagion effects and systemic concerns

An insurer/reinsurer holding a large portfolio of unprotected low frequency/high severity exposures that does not follow basic internal risk management procedures is susceptible to financial distress, including direct economic losses and indirect financial damage related to reputation, franchise value, personnel, and financing/dealing terms.[24]

If an insurer or reinsurer is required to pay on a large number/amount of claims, those providing funding (e.g., in the form of short-term optionable facilities, short-term guaranteed investment contracts, and so forth) may withdraw their capital. This can create a liquidity crisis that is similar to a bank run, where depositors withdraw funds, causing more depositors to do the same, and so forth, until the institution is left without sufficient liquid resources to meet its obligations. Failure by an insurer/reinsurer can create widespread losses for policyholders submitting claims on unrelated non-catastrophic coverage. This is one primary reason why global insurers and reinsurers must adhere to certain minimum standards of regulation regarding solvency, liquidity, and diversification. Nevertheless, the specter of large losses and financial distress is present.

Systemic concerns can also arise from within the reinsurance sector, which remains rather opaque; low transparency and minimal regulation mean stakeholders may not have a true picture of portfolio risks. Any excessive concentrations or large exposures within the portfolio that are subject to claim could lead to significant losses and systemic disruption, particularly if a retrocession spiral is invoked.[25] At a minimum such a disruption might curtail industry-wide risk capacity, including capacity normally intended to support catastrophic risks; in more serious instances it could impact the financial health of one or more insurers, causing a broader spillover effect. Despite the existence of potential systemic dislocations, it is important

---

[24] Several small reinsurers have failed as a result of exposure to excessive natural disaster claims, e.g. the UK's Charter Re (1993) and Singapore's ICS Re and RMCA Re (1991).

[25] A retrocession spiral occurs when XOL reinsurers underwrite each other's XOL layers rather than dispersing them more broadly; this means losses are concentrated within a very small number of institutions, and can lead to financial distress if a very large insurable event/claim occurs. Since the XOL events are not less likely to occur than lower layer events under this process, and since premiums earned are much smaller, the risk/return profile is severely skewed. Retrocession spirals appear on occasion, e.g., UK windstorm 87J, Hurricane Hugo, and the Piper Alpha explosion.

to note that this concept is still largely theoretical. The insurance and reinsurance sectors have successfully navigated many crises over the past decades and have not yet been at the center of any significant systemic problems.

The insurance/reinsurance market will continue to be a vital element of the catastrophe risk management process, and as the challenges noted above are overcome, it will become an even more robust mechanism. It is clear, however, that insurance and reinsurance will need to work in concert with the alternative risk management solutions and public sector mechanisms we consider in the next chapters.

7

Catastrophe Bonds and Contingent Capital

The global capital markets, comprised of investable funds allocated across a large number of asset classes, regions, industries, and obligors, is generally defined to include equity, debt, and hybrid capital (in both direct and securitized form), along with associated instruments such as derivatives. The markets represent the central conduit for mobilization of capital and creation of risk management solutions and capacity. In this chapter we consider the nature and function of securitization and catastrophe-related capital markets instruments, including catastrophe bonds and contingent capital, and extend the discussion in the next chapter by examining catastrophe derivatives. We will illustrate how these instruments are becoming an increasingly important element of overall risk management, supplementing the private sector loss-financing capabilities available through the insurance/reinsurance mechanism.

Before commencing our discussion, it is important to note that the insurance/reinsurance market and the capital markets are gradually converging, with institutions from the two sectors becoming increasingly involved in each other's business lines. Financial intermediaries are actively involved in insurable risks and markets, while insurers/reinsurers routinely participate in financial risks. This convergence generates important benefits for end-users, including efficiency and cost savings. In fact, any holistic view of catastrophe risk management requires a focus on both sectors, and how they can be used jointly to create optimal solutions. Catastrophe bonds and other structures of the capital markets are designed to work in concert with, rather than as replacements for, catastrophe insurance/reinsurance; the availability of alternative solutions reduces the price volatility that can arise from capacity constraints (particularly those appearing in the wake of a major disaster), creating greater stability for those trying to actively manage their risks. This process is expected to continue as deregulation permits convergence to spread even further.

7.1 OVERVIEW OF SECURITIZATION

Securitization, which is the process of removing assets, liabilities, or cash flows from the corporate balance sheet and conveying them to third parties through tradable securities, has been an established feature of the capital markets since the late 1970s, when financial institutions began repackaging assets in trusts and issuing tranches of securities to fund the resulting risk portfolios. Securitization efforts started with mortgage backed securities (MBS, pools of residential mortgages), collateralized mortgage obligations (CMOs, pools of MBS), commercial MBS, and asset-backed securities (ABS, pools of receivables, leases, and so forth), and then extended to the credit markets through the creation of collateralized loan obligations (CLOs, pools of loans), and collateralized bond obligations (CBOs, pools of corporate bonds) – together comprising the broad class of collateralized debt obligations (CDOs). More recently, the same structures have been applied successfully in the insurance sector, creating a vital link between the financial and insurance markets. Though the market for insurance-linked securities

(ILS) is very broad and includes catastrophe bonds, weather bonds, life securitization bonds, and residual value securities, we shall confine our focus to catastrophe bonds.

Under a generic financial securitization, an issuing trust is structured as an independent, bankruptcy-remote entity that is responsible for acquiring assets, issuing liabilities, managing cash flows, administering receivables and payables, and arranging swap hedges. In order to generate the desired risk and return profiles for each tranche, the trust redirects cash flows from the underlying asset, repaying investors principal and interest (P&I) in order of priority. Thus, the most senior (i.e., lowest return, lowest risk) investors are repaid first, and the most junior (i.e., highest return, highest risk) investors last. In most instances the issues are supported by a highly subordinated 'equity-like' tranche, known as a residual, that carries equity returns and risks. In some instances arrangers credit-enhance certain tranches through letters of credit, over-collateralization, financial guarantees or insurance wraps, thus creating higher ratings (including so-called 'super AAA' tranches, where the risk of default is infinitesimal). Ultimately, the securitization is intended to transfer risk to investors in customized tranches so that balance sheet and capital are released and new business can be generated.

7.2   CATASTROPHE BONDS

Catastrophe bonds have become an increasingly important, if not yet dominant, part of the loss-financing market, supplementing solutions from the insurance/reinsurance and public sectors. Since the launch of the first catastrophe bond by USAA/Residential Re in 1997 (see footnote 4 for details),[1] more than 60 issues covering $8b of risk have been arranged. Annual issuance has been steady, averaging approximately 5–10 new deals with transfer capacity of $1–1.5b; $3–4b of securities are typically outstanding at any point in the cycle, which is approximately equal to 5% of the catastrophe reinsurance market. Though early estimates of $5b of annual issuance have not yet materialized, the securities have gained a critical mass of acceptance among a growing base of issuers (who find them to be a cost-competitive alternative during certain market cycles) and investors (who find the bonds carry attractive returns that are uncorrelated with other financial assets).[2] In this section we examine standard structures, innovations, and market focus and direction; later in the chapter we will also consider some of the challenges facing the market.

7.2.1   Standard structures

Catastrophe bonds allow an issuing institution to transfer catastrophic exposures to investors, thereby creating capital relief and additional risk capacity. The standard catastrophe bond is similar to the other securitized capital markets structures mentioned above. A special purpose entity (SPE) trust or a special purpose reinsurer (SPR) acts as issuance vehicle, selling notes to investors, passing proceeds to the trustee for further reinvestment, and providing an indemnity contract to the issuing company. The return generated through reinvestment and the premium payment from the issuing company form the investor coupon that becomes due and payable on a periodic basis; the invested proceeds held in the trust account are used to repay principal

---

[1] The California Earthquake Authority (CEA), which we discuss in Chapter 9, was originally meant to be the first issuer of a catastrophe bond, covering California earthquake. Ultimately, however, Berkshire Hathaway's National Indemnity unit undercut the pricing on $1b of earthquake coverage (e.g., 4-year reinsurance with an expected loss of 170 bps and premium of $113m), causing CEA to suspend its planned bond.

[2] Although the very high yields of early issues (e.g., 200 bps above comparably rated corporate bonds) have given way to some compression, the returns continue to be very attractive, and are generally insensitive to events in other markets.

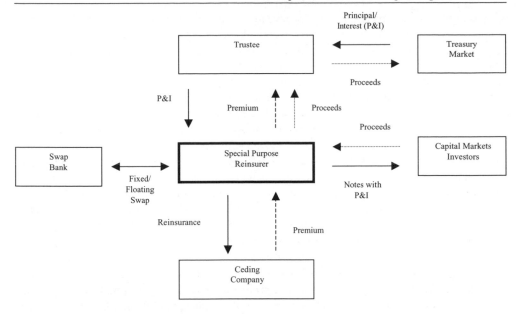

Figure 7.1 Standard castastrophe bond structure

at maturity. If a named catastrophic event occurs the trustee withholds interest and/or principal payments temporarily or permanently.[3] Since the issuing company will be exposed to losses on its underlying catastrophe risk but will no longer need to provide payments to investors, it has effectively used the capital markets investor base to hedge its risk.

Figure 7.1 summarizes the standard structure using the SPR.[4]

A catastrophe bond can be viewed as a standard bond with an embedded contingent option giving the issuer the right to delay, or permanently withhold, principal and/or interest upon the

---

[3] In some cases investors will only receive restitution after all claims and contingent liabilities arising from the insurable event have been paid.

[4] To provide an example of structural details, we briefly review the market's inaugural transaction, a 1997 hurricane bond launched by USAA, a mutually owned insurance company providing auto, homeowners, dwelling, and personal liability risk coverage to US military personnel and their families. After Hurricane Andrew, in which USAA experienced a disproportionate loss of $620m due to its risk concentrations in Florida, the insurer began examining alternate mechanisms to reduce a portion of its excess layer P&C risk in at-risk states such as Texas, Florida, and California. After engaging in preliminary work during 1994, USAA sent out requests for proposals in 1995 to nine investment banks and eventually awarded the mandate to Merrill Lynch in 1996; AIR was given the mandate to create the analytics. Much of 1996 was spent resolving structural, legal, and regulatory issues, and addressing the concerns of potential investors and credit rating agencies. The realizable benefits of the bond remained uncertain for much of the year, and USAA continued to evaluate other options, including traditional reinsurance, exchange-traded catastrophe derivatives, and contingent surplus notes. However, by early 1997 transaction details began to solidify; USAA added Goldman Sachs and Lehman Brothers to the underwriting syndicate and the team prepared for launch. The bond was structured to give the insurer coverage of the XOL layer above $1b, to a maximum of $500m at an 80% rate (e.g., 20% coinsurance) – this was equal to $400m of reinsurance cover. A Cayman SPR, Residential Re, was established to write the reinsurance contract to USAA and issue notes to investors in two classes of three tranches: Class A-1, rated AAA, featuring $77m of principal protected notes and $87m of principal variable notes, and Class A-2, rated BB, featuring $313m of principal variable notes. The transaction was based on a single occurrence of a Class 3, 4, or 5 hurricane, with ultimate net loss defined under USAA's portfolio parameters (e.g., cover under existing policies/renewals and new policies, in 21 listed states). The bond was thus a multi-tranche, single-event bond with an indemnity trigger. One of the important elements of this pioneering transaction was convincing regulatory authorities that investors would be purchasing bonds and not writing reinsurance contracts (which most were not authorized to do); regulators ultimately agreed to give investors capital markets treatment. With details resolved and pre-marketing completed, the three-bank syndicate issued the bonds on a 'best-efforts' basis, placing the entire targeted amount with institutional investors. In fact, pricing was purposely made attractive (e.g., priced at a wide spread) in order to ensure successful placement. This inaugural hurricane bond thus set the stage for many others to follow (some using the very same mechanics). USAA, convinced of the efficacy of the structure as a risk management tool, has issued similar bonds on a regular basis since 1997.

triggering of a defined event (which may have indemnity, parametric, or index characteristics, as noted below). Most bonds are issued on a private placement basis, which limits the base of potential buyers to sophisticated institutional investors, including mutual and pension funds, financial intermediaries, and companies; retail participation is confined to indirect investment via a small number of catastrophe bond funds. Bonds generally have short claims periods of less than two years, meaning all claims must be submitted and evaluated during the valid period or they may be dismissed. The relatively quick claim/settlement timeframe stands in contrast to that of reinsurance contracts, which often have open-ended periods to deal with late claims.

Securitization of catastrophe risk generates benefits for various parties, including issuing companies, investors, and intermediaries. The issuing company (often an insurer or reinsurer) can manage risk through an alternative loss-financing mechanism; this might be an attractive option during a hard insurance/reinsurance market when insurance prices are high. The issuer also reduces its credit exposure to individual insurers/reinsurers; since the risk is repackaged into notes and sold to investors via the SPE or SPR, the issuer no longer needs to be concerned about the credit performance of the insurer/reinsurer. In addition, since the marketplace is bespoke, the issuer can design its preferred note structure: absorbing greater basis risk but eliminating moral hazard, bearing the incremental cost of moral hazard but reducing basis risk, issuing single-year or multi-year cover, protecting against single or multiple perils, and so forth (we consider some of the innovations that have appeared in the marketplace in recent years in the section below). Investors can benefit by purchasing securities that have little, or no, correlation with other financial risk assets in their portfolios. This is appealing to investment managers eager to find opportunities to earn extra yield without taking more risk. In addition, and assuming no trigger event occurs, investors can generate good returns. Most deals of the past few years have featured spread premiums of 50–100 basis points over comparably rated corporate bonds to compensate investors for both the 'novelty' aspects of the transactions (and the resulting difficulties in analyzing the risks) and the general illiquidity of the bonds. Though margins have compressed, as investors have grown more familiar with potential risks, they remain attractive. Intermediaries benefit from new sources of business, earning fees from structuring the securities and commissions from selling the bonds. There are, of course, certain costs and disadvantages, including expenses associated with establishing issuance vehicles/programs and floating securities (deals must generally be at least $100m in size to be economically justifiable), the analytic work that must be performed in assessing and pricing the securities, the illiquidity of the marketplace (e.g., it is largely 'buy and hold'), and the lack of hedging instruments that might otherwise allow intermediaries to make markets and add liquidity.

To expand on certain aspects of the standard structure, we consider additional details on issuing vehicles, triggers, perils, ratings and tranches, and pricing.

7.2.1.1 Issuing vehicles

Corporate issuers of catastrophe bonds can float securities through a standard SPE. Insurers and reinsurers, in contrast, must use an SPR: a pure securitization of risk does not help a ceding insurer meet its statutory capital surplus requirements, so some amount of risk must be reinsured to the SPR. This permits the risk to be reinsured, and then securitized, allowing for the necessary capital relief. Using the insurer/reinsurer issuer as an example, the bankruptcy-remote SPR is responsible for writing a reinsurance contract to the ceding issuer in exchange

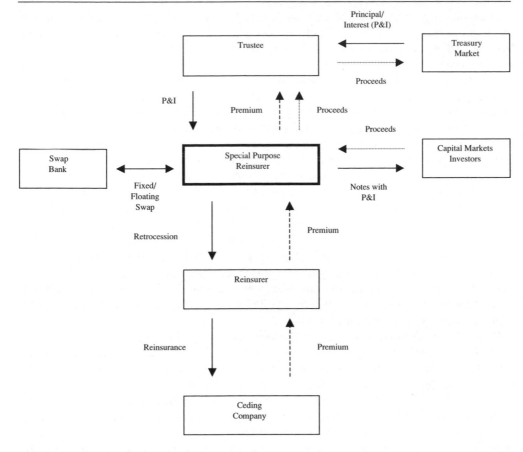

Figure 7.2   Catastrophe bond with interposed SPR

for premium. Since the protection provided is a reinsurance contract rather than a derivative, the SPR must be established as a licensed reinsurance company. In order for the insurer to receive the benefit of ceded exposure, risk must be transferred, meaning the ceding issuer cannot directly own the SPR; charitable foundations sponsor most SPRs to fulfill this 'independence' requirement. In some instances another reinsurer is interposed between the ceding issuer and the SPR, meaning that the contract becomes one of retrocession rather than reinsurance; this structure, depicted in Figure 7.2, permits the reinsurer to accept indemnity risk and hedge with index contracts so that the ceding issuer does not have to bear basis risk.

7.2.1.2   Triggers

Catastrophe bonds can be structured with indemnity, parametric, or index triggers that reference single or multiple events; each version has its own characteristics, advantages, and disadvantages. Regardless of the trigger type, most bonds are structured with initial deductibles (e.g., first loss retention by the issuer) and caps (e.g., maximum 'payout' or protection by investors to the issuer).

Indemnity triggers are based on an issuer's actual exposure to a particular catastrophe (or series of catastrophes); investors absorb any losses that occur as a result of a specified event by relinquishing principal/interest (after taking account of initial retentions and a maximum event loss cap). As a result of this 'perfect match,' the issuer eliminates any instance of basis risk. Naturally, a precise contract of coverage gives rise to moral hazard risk (i.e., the issuer, knowing that coverage is available through the securitization mechanism, will be less diligent in its underwriting standards or corporate behavior). While most of the earliest bonds in the market featured indemnity triggers, a gradual shift towards parametric and index triggers has occurred since the turn of the millennium – partly as a result of the lack of transparency surrounding portfolios of risk, which some investors find difficult to analyze.

Parametric triggers are based on one or more physical parameters associated with a peril, such as location and intensity (e.g., for an earthquake this can be the location of the epicenter and the magnitude of the event, for a hurricane it may be the location of landfall and the minimum central pressure or average sustained wind speed). Parametric structures focus primarily on event location and intensity rather than structural vulnerabilities (the vulnerabilities must still be evaluated, but only as a secondary step). If an event that meets the criteria defined by the parametric trigger occurs and generates losses, principal and/or interest payments are suspended. Since the match between an issuer's exposure and the parametric characteristics is not perfect, basis risk exists; however, moral hazard decreases and analytics need not be calibrated to the issuer's specific portfolio.[5]

Index triggers are based on a recognized industry loss index. In practice industry losses can be derived from granular property databases (e.g., to the level of a ZIP code/postal code, which, depending on locale, corresponds to approximately 2000 households/business operations), including number of risks, value by type, occupancy, coverage, and business.

A survey firm is typically responsible for conducting post-catastrophe surveys to obtain the estimates needed for loss index compilation.[6] Like parametric issues, index-based structures eliminate the need for an issuer to disclose the nature of its business, which reduces concerns about proprietary information and protects investors against moral hazard; they do, however, introduce basis risk. While a detailed correlation analysis between an issuer's actual book of business and the proposed index can help minimize basis risk, the exposure cannot be eliminated. In addition, index structures generally involve a lag in determination of payouts to investors, as there is often a delay between the onset of a disaster and the completion of an index-based survey.

As noted, the market in recent years has shifted from a majority of indemnity deals (e.g., 70%+ in the late 1990s) to a majority of parametric and index transactions (e.g., 70%+ in the millennium, by both dollar value and volume). This is consistent with investor preferences; many favor index transactions because they add transparency and do not require a full evaluation of the cedant's underlying risk portfolio. In addition, securities are slightly more tradable, as they are based on metrics that all investors can evaluate (that said, the securities are still quite illiquid, certainly when compared to similarly rated corporate securities).

---

[5] The 2000 issue of Prime Capital by Munich Re serves as a good example of a multiple peril parametric structure. The $300m, 3-year bond was based on California earthquake, Miami hurricane, New York hurricane, and European windstorm. The Californian peril was divided into eight seismic zones (four in Los Angeles, four in San Francisco) with principal suspension set as a function of the moment magnitude reported by the US Geological Survey. Similarly, principal suspension on the hurricane peril was set as a function of a specific landfall zone and central barometric pressure defined by the National Hurricane Center, while principal suspension on the European windstorm was based on weighted wind speed at defined weather stations located across portions of the continent.

[6] Determining the value of a catastrophe index commences with a catastrophic event that produces losses for the entire insurance industry. The market share of individual insurer losses is then adjusted for underwriting quality, to yield a 'per insurer' index value.

Table 7.1   Catastrophe bond references

Peril	Region
Earthquake	California, NMSZ, Japan, Taiwan, Monaco
Hurricane/typhoon	Florida, North Atlantic, Hawaii, Japan
Windstorm/extra-tropical cyclone	Europe, Atlantic
Hailstorm	Europe
Event cancellation (e.g., terrorism)	Europe

7.2.1.3   Perils

Though catastrophe bonds can theoretically be issued on many of the perils described in Chapter 2, in practice most activity is centered on earthquake, tropical cyclone, and windstorm (from extra-tropical cyclones). US hurricane and earthquake were the first perils to be securitized, because of the financial losses created by Andrew and Northridge and the generally advanced state of earthquake and hurricane analytics needed to structure and price the securities. Since then bonds have been structured on perils such as hailstorm, windstorm, and terror-related events, while regional coverage has expanded to countries such as Japan, France, Germany, and Taiwan. Standard catastrophe bonds generally reference single perils; however, some structures incorporate multiple peril events per tranche, or multiple peril events in a single tranche, as we discuss below. Common catastrophe bond peril and region references are summarized in Table 7.1.

Hurricane bonds entered the market in 1997 and have been issued steadily since that time. Most hurricane peril covers are written on the US Northeast/Atlantic, Gulf Coast/Caribbean, and Hawaii, as well as typhoon equivalents in Japan. Expansion into other regions of Asia, including Taiwan and India, is expected in the medium term. Earthquake bonds have also emerged as important corporate risk management tools; deals have been structured to cover earthquakes in California, NMSZ, and Japan (with a modest amount also on earthquake risk in Taiwan and Monaco). Bonds referencing other seismically active zones, such as Mexico and Turkey, are expected over the medium term, once issues related to sovereign risk and data are resolved. Bond issuance related to windstorm risk has increased steadily in recent years, providing issuers with coverage against P&C damage from very strong winds and rain arising from extra-tropical cyclone activity. Such deals have been written primarily on European references (either the entire European continent, including the UK, or individual countries, such as France).

Terrorism-related bonds are beginning to enter the market. Interestingly, such bonds did not appear in the immediate aftermath of 9/11, despite the obvious shortage of terrorism-related risk capacity. Several fundamental reasons have been posited for the lack of activity, including reputational concerns associated with issuing a security linked to potentially tragic human events, strong correlation between a terrorist act and the global equity markets (removing some of the diversification benefits that make catastrophe bonds so appealing), pricing uncertainties/modeling challenges (including many of those we have noted in Chapter 4), and potential moral hazard problems. The first terrorism-related bond did not appear until late 2003, when FIFA issued a security to protect its investment in the 2006 World Cup;[7]

---

[7] FIFA did not originally intend to issue the pioneering bond ($260m Golden Goal), but when insurer AXA withdrew its cover of the 2006 World Cup in the post-9/11 environment, the association was left with little choice if it wanted to retain its sponsors. In fact, risk coverage for the 2002 Japan/Korea World Cup was also extremely difficult to obtain as it happened directly after the terrorist acts, and was only possible through an 'eleventh hour' policy written by Berkshire Hathaway at a very high premium.

Table 7.2   Sample catastrophe bond tranches

Tranche	Economic impact of trigger
Tranche A (enhanced)	No loss of principal/interest
Tranche B	Loss of interest
Tranche C	Delay in principal
Tranche D	Partial loss of principal
Tranche E	Total loss of principal
Residual	Total loss of principal and interest

the bond was broad in scope, however, and intended to cover any disaster that could lead to cancellation of the tournament, including natural disaster or terrorism. More terrorism-related bonds (some under the guise of 'event cancellation' risk) are likely to appear in the medium term, particularly as modeling processes improve (indeed, if insurers are pricing terrorism coverage into their policies then the next logical step, securitization, should follow in due course).

7.2.1.4   Ratings and tranches

Catastrophe bonds are often issued with two or more tranches, allowing investors to select the level of risk and return participation they deem most suitable. For instance, hedge funds often prefer purchasing low-rated/high-risk tranches, while investment funds and bank/insurance company investment accounts tend to prefer higher-rated pieces. Tranches can be structured in combinations that reflect different levels of interest and/or principal delay or forfeiture. Some tranches result only in a delay, rather than permanent forfeiture, of principal; these typically repay investors a portion of the principal as scheduled and the balance over a period of time through a funded zero coupon position. Other tranches result in permanent loss of principal and interest, suggesting they are riskiest. Though every unsecured tranche is at risk (i.e., there are no principal and interest-protected securities unless specifically enhanced by a third party), expected losses can range from modest to extreme.

Principal-at-risk securities typically carry sub-investment grade ratings. Assuming that the risk of issuer default is negligible (which is a fair assumption since most underlying issuers are rated investment grade), the risk premium investors receive for the pure catastrophe risk exposure is similar to that of a BB corporate bond (e.g., 1–2% probability of loss per year).[8]

Tranches that are structured with multiple trigger events (as discussed below) can often achieve ratings in the A/AA ranges since the probability of loss under a multiple event scenario is very small. Those that are specifically supported by third parties can also achieve strong investment grade ratings.

Table 7.2 illustrates sample tranches of a typical catastrophe bond. Tranche A, enhanced through a guarantee from an insurer or a letter of credit from a bank, might be rated AAA or AA; Tranche B, featuring possible loss of interest payments, may be rated in the A/BBB

---

[8] Of the $8b of bonds arranged between 1997 and 2003, $5b were rated BB and $1.3b BBB, the balance in other categories. Based on issuer and investor requirements, this mix is unlikely to change markedly over the coming years.

category; Tranche E, with the potential for complete loss of principal and interest, is akin to a BB-rated security. Note that, apart from enhanced tranches, bonds need not be explicitly rated by the public rating agencies, they may only be 'shadow-rated.'

Though individual tranches carry stated final maturities, actual maturity can be lengthened after an insurable event because claims may be slow to develop; stated and actual maturity may therefore differ. In practice, cedants like long loss development periods, which permit accumulation of a greater amount of claims and help reduce principal/interest repayments. Investors prefer shorter periods, so that they can receive and reinvest their principal/interest. Regardless of the specific length of the claims period, bonds always have shorter loss development periods than insurance (e.g., six months to two years versus several years). While many bonds are multi-tranche and multi-year they are still governed by caps that can be breached before the final maturity. For instance, if a 5-year California earthquake bond has a $250m cap and is subject to a $300m loss event in year two, the issue is effectively extinguished with three years remaining until final maturity.

7.2.1.5   Pricing

Pricing of catastrophe bonds is the focus of much attention given the complex and illiquid nature of the securities. From a theoretical perspective, catastrophe bonds should be priced at a level that approximates catastrophe reinsurance prices, with an allowance for friction costs.[9] Since catastrophe bonds are a substitute for, or supplement to, insurance/reinsurance, the price differential between reinsurance and capital markets issues has an influence on overall activity. There is evidence to suggest that when a hard insurance market develops, catastrophe bond issuance can accelerate (though still remain within a relatively tight boundary, i.e., there is no evidence of a large spike in issuance). Since creating a bond structure tends to be relatively expensive – based on costs associated with forming SPEs/SPRs, preparing documentation, engaging investment banks to underwrite the issue, and so on – it is only justifiable in the cost/benefit framework when other loss-financing alternatives such as insurance are more expensive.

Reinsurance prices, as we have noted in Chapter 6, should be a function of expected/unexpected losses and profit load. Given the linkage between the reinsurance and securitization markets, a catastrophe bond should thus be priced at a level reflecting the risk-free rate, expected and unexpected losses, friction costs, and load. We recall that expected loss can be viewed as a probability-weighted sum of possible outcomes, but must be supplemented by a measure of dispersion that captures unexpected loss. If expected and unexpected losses are properly factored into the pricing, investors should be indifferent to selecting between securities with a low and high probability of loss. However, this only applies when statistical distributions are well defined (e.g., no fat tails); we have indicated that catastrophe loss distributions are not always well behaved, suggesting pricing discrepancies can arise across securities, complicating valuation and trading efforts. There is no single uniform approach to pricing catastrophe bonds, and the relative challenges related to distributions, modeling assumptions, illiquidity, and 'novelty,' are all influencing factors. Some models price the spread

---

[9] Catastrophe bonds are not always tax-efficient, which adds to overall costs. For instance, a ceding company can deduct the cost of an insurance premium from revenues, while an insurer transferring risk via reinsurance can deduct the premium cost from gross written premiums. However, the cost of securitizing risk via an SPE or SPR is not tax-deductible. This means that in otherwise equivalent markets the insurance/reinsurance solution has a built-in cost advantage.

as a constant multiplied by the variance of loss; others incorporate the skewness of the loss profile, while others create a framework where the expected loss is conditional on the occurrence of a given event.[10] Though the high yields that result from various pricing methodologies may be justifiable to a certain degree (e.g., actuarial uncertainty, opacity, illiquidity), they remain well above those of similarly rated corporate high-yield bonds – despite the fact that corporate bonds are reasonably correlated with other financial asset classes (reducing their efficacy in portfolio diversification).

7.2.2 Innovations

As the generic catastrophe bond structure has matured and gained traction with issuers and investors, certain innovations have started to appear, making the market more flexible and allowing participants to match their funding/investing requirements more precisely. Key innovations appearing in recent years include shelf programs, multiple peril issues, multiple trigger issues, notional principal trigger issues, multi-season transactions, direct corporate/sovereign issuance, and other structural enhancements.

7.2.2.1 Shelf programs

During the first five years of the market's existence, catastrophe bonds were arranged and issued on a discrete basis: each new transaction was negotiated and structured by the issuer and intermediary, making the process rather time- and resource-intensive. In 2002, however, Swiss Re developed the first shelf program, allowing multiple issues to be arranged and launched from a single program (much as a corporate or sovereign issuer might do with standard debt issues via a medium-term note or Euro medium-term note program).[11]

The advent of the catastrophe shelf program has injected flexibility into the market, giving frequent issuers, primarily insurers and reinsurers, the ability to launch a bond with a unique set of characteristics (e.g., maturity, peril, trigger type, currency) on relatively short notice and at more reasonable cost. Issuers are likely to create more shelf programs in the future.

7.2.2.2 Multiple peril issues

Through the turn of the millennium the catastrophe bond market was based exclusively on single peril issues. Accordingly, an issuer seeking earthquake cover and hurricane cover would issue two separate bonds, each with its own structure, analytics, and pricing; a more active issuer might launch multiple tranches from a single shelf program (as noted above), but each security would still be considered and evaluated on its own merits. Since that time a number of multiple peril issues have been floated, creating a more efficient way of transferring exposure.

---

[10] Some approaches focus on the probability of attachment as an indication of frequency, and the probability of exhaustion as an indication of severity; if the probability of exhaustion is high, then the potential severity is large, and vice versa. The profit load factor, which must be added to expected losses, is still dependent on the shape of the distribution, which itself requires a gauge of dispersion. There is a direct trade-off between frequency and severity of loss. An investor in catastrophe bonds must consider how much more frequency is acceptable for a given reduction in severity. In fact, this can be examined empirically by observing traded bond prices and fitting a function (taking due account of any seasonality issues where relevant, e.g., hurricane bonds).

[11] In particular, Swiss Re created the $2b Pioneer 'Catsec' program allowing for issuance of specific tranches of securities covering P&C risks attributable to North Atlantic and European windstorm, and California, NMSZ, and Japanese earthquake.

A multiple peril bond contains individual triggers that reference different elements of risk; a breach of *any* of the triggers can lead to a temporary or permanent reduction in principal and/or interest (on a predetermined schedule, e.g., one-third for each of three triggers, or some other combination). For instance, a multiple peril bond may reference earthquake (with a trigger based on a minimum magnitude of x), hurricane (trigger of class y), and flood (trigger of rainfall level z), where x, y, and z can be defined with any degree of parametric precision desired. If any one of x, y, or z occurs, principal/interest are suspended and the issuer is protected.[12]

Multiple peril securities create greater efficiencies for issuers as all exposure requirements can be incorporated in a single security – there is no need to replicate issuance vehicles, structures, or disclosure. Modeling is generally similar to that of a standard catastrophe bond, except in situations where events are correlated (which is relatively uncommon). Multiple peril securities appear to have secured a niche in the market, and future growth seems likely.

7.2.2.3 Multiple trigger issues

The inverse of the structure noted immediately is a bond that requires *all*, rather than one, of the defined events to occur before investor principal and/or coupons are suspended. Instead of a single event creating investor losses (and issuer protection), investors are protected until two (or three) named events are triggered. The aim of this structure is to provide investors with even greater principal protection – at a price, of course, which is a lower yield. The lower yield is appealing to certain issuers, as it makes the cost of risk transfer more competitive with standard insurance/reinsurance – though it does not provide the same level of protection as a standard single trigger security. For instance, a conventional earthquake bond simply requires a particular trigger to be breached in order for principal/coupons to be suspended. Under a multiple trigger issue, principal/coupon may not be at risk until the earthquake trigger is breached, and a second trigger – perhaps related to the overall level of the issuer's losses, the onset of a second earthquake event within a particular timeframe, or some other defined event – is also breached. The multiple events can be structured on a temporal and/or regional basis, and may reference similar or different perils/loss levels.[13]

Multiple trigger bonds are more difficult to model than single trigger bonds, as the correlations and joint probabilities of the two (or more) trigger events have to be properly estimated. The extra layer of analytic complexity adds opacity, which can prove challenging for issuers, investors, and rating agencies. One advantage, however, is the generally higher credit ratings accorded to such issues; since the probability of loss associated with the occurrence of two already small probability events is extremely small, most of the tranches launched to date have been rated investment grade. Growth in this segment of the market is likely to continue as a result of both issuer and investor benefits.

---

[12] For instance, AGF's Med Re provided coverage in the event either a French windstorm or a Monaco earthquake occurred; similarly, the Halyard Re bond provided coverage against European windstorms, Japanese typhoon, or Japanese earthquake.

[13] For example, Swiss Re's Arbor Capital II was based on temporal triggers protecting the insurer in case two or more catastrophes (of any type) occurred within a short time of one another. The motivation for the bond appears to have its roots in the early 18th century, when a major European windstorm and a large Japanese earthquake struck within weeks of one another, causing considerable damage; if the same were to happen in the millennium, the financial impact on the insurance/reinsurance sector would be devastating. Similarly, Electricite de France's Pylon bond supplied second event cover based on the occurrence of two or more French windstorm events. Converium, via the Trinom bond, received second event retrocessional cover based on two separate regional/peril triggers, including European/US windstorm, and US earthquake.

7.2.2.4   Notional principal trigger issues

Another innovation in the marketplace is the notional principal trigger structure. Though not widely used, the concept has gained some attention, and future issuance may increase.[14] Under the terms of the structure a catastrophe bond payout is based on modeled losses rather than actual realized losses (as is common with the conventional trigger structures described above). Losses are estimated by overlaying local intensity on an issuer's portfolio and then applying a damage function and policy conditions to obtain an estimate of insurable losses. This amount is then placed in an escrow account; if an event occurs, the actual physical parameters are input into the model containing the notional portfolio to determine the attachment and loss levels. Since the portfolio remains fixed, moral hazard and adverse selection are minimized; however, the structure requires a detailed post-event analysis to verify principal and interest suspension.

7.2.2.5   Multi-season issues

Though many securitizations have historically been structured as single season/year deals, there has been a growing amount of issuance in the multi-year sector, with 2 to 5-year transactions becoming the norm rather than the exception. A multi-year deal allows issuers to avoid the price fluctuations that can arise when renegotiating cover from year to year (the same annual fluctuations are characteristic of the reinsurance market), and ensures availability of risk capacity on a forward basis. It also results in lower costs as it eliminates the need to reissue securities every year. While these are clear benefits, the modeling effort is more complex as it depends on multiple year events, some of which reset (e.g., hurricanes) and others that intensify (e.g., time-dependent earthquake events).

7.2.2.6   Direct corporate/sovereign issuance

Insurers and reinsurers issued the majority of catastrophe bonds through the early part of the millennium. This is not surprising, as such institutions have the largest amount of catastrophic risk exposure and the greatest need to employ as many loss-financing techniques as possible; they also have the actuarial and financial sophistication to analyze and structure optimal mechanisms.

That said, new issuers have started entering the market. Starting with the first corporate issues by Oriental Land (Tokyo Disneyland) in 1999,[15] companies such as Vivendi (California earthquake) and Electricite de France (French windstorm) have entered the market directly; government/quasi-government institutions such as Zenkyoren (Japanese earthquake and typhoon) and FIFA (all catastrophic perils, including terrorism) have also accessed the market in the millennium. In fact, as companies and sovereign entities become more actively involved in directly managing their risks, more frequent direct issuance is expected.

---

[14] The pioneering issue was Trinom's 2001 $200m, 3-year notes and preferreds, protecting Converium from hurricane, earthquake, and windstorm through three separate notional portfolios.

[15] In May 1999, Oriental Land, owner/operator of Tokyo Disneyland, launched a $200m, two-tranche parametric deal: the first tranche was intended to protect the company against economic losses caused by business interruption from an earthquake in the vicinity of Tokyo Disneyland, while the second was designed to supply post-loss reconstruction financing. The first tranche, a $100m, 5-year floating rate note issued by the Concentric Re SPR, featured a parametric trigger: regardless of the amount of specific damage to the theme park, the payout was linked to parameters related to earthquake magnitude, location, and depth; the closer and larger the earthquake to the vicinity of the park, the greater the effective protection for Oriental Land. The second tranche, a $100m, 5-year floating rate note issued through the Circle Maihana SPE, was designed to provide reconstruction funding in the aftermath of a defined event.

7.2.2.7   Other structural enhancements

Several other catastrophe bond innovations have surfaced in recent years that demonstrate the growing creativity of the marketplace. For instance, various issues have been launched where investors receive an enhanced coupon if the index value of a named peril remains below a specific threshold, or no coupon if it rises above it; this is precisely equal to a bond with strip of embedded digital options that provide an enhanced coupon or zero at each evaluation date.[16] Bonds with variable coupons that fluctuate with changes in an issuer's risk profile have been floated, giving the issuer the ability to dynamically manage a risk portfolio over time.[17] A synthetic catastrophe bond has been developed as a combination of a standard catastrophe bond and an option to issue a bond if the reinsurance market hardens and makes it economically cheaper to obtain cover in the capital markets; by incorporating the option, the issuer preserves the flexibility of deciding on issuance until a future time, when need and market dynamics may be different.[18] The first 'true' securitization has also been arranged, based on a portfolio of specifically identified insurance contracts rather than a general portfolio of non-specific contracts.[19] All of these enhancements suggest that capital markets intermediaries and investors are becoming more comfortable in dealing with catastrophic risk.

7.2.3   Market focus and direction

As the catastrophe bond market becomes more established it is gradually assuming a new focus and direction. Most of the changes since the launch of the original issues in 1997 have been gradual, building on usage by issuers and acceptance by investors. Notable items regarding market focus and direction include:

- Larger deal size, with single transactions averaging more than $200m.
- A greater number of multi-year deals and direct corporate/sovereign issues.
- Expanded mix of perils and regions. The dominant risk references continue to be US/Atlantic hurricane, California earthquake, European windstorm, and Japanese earthquake, but bonds with perils such as Taiwan earthquake, Monaco earthquake, European hailstorm, and general terrorist disruptions have started to emerge. The growing universe of spatial and peril references makes it easier for dedicated catastrophe portfolio managers to diversify their asset holdings and improve mean excess returns.
- Cheaper costs for issuers and lower returns for investors, as the 'novelty' factor declines and more investors come to understand the mechanics of the product; the turn towards a greater amount of index/parametric structures has fuelled this trend as investors are not required to understand the specific portfolio construction of individual issuers. Lower costs

---

[16] For instance, in 2002 Winterthur issued subordinated convertibles with hail-based catastrophe coupons. Investors received a coupon that was one-third greater than standard convertibles as long as the number of auto claims from hail/storm damage remained below 6000, and no coupon if claims exceeded 6000; the deal was thus a package of a subordinated bond, an equity option, and a strip of digital options referencing hail damage.

[17] For instance, a Taiwanese insuer has launched a variable coupon bond linked to its changing residential earthquake insurance portfolio.

[18] For instance, Allianz Risk Transfer created an option on a bond (which it purchased from investors through Gemini Re) that gave it the right to issue a 3-year bond with principal and interest repayments tied to European windstorm and hailstorm if losses reached a pre-specified trigger amount. If loss experience rose above the threshold, Allianz had the right to exercise the option, issuing $150m in standard catastrophe bonds to investors/option sellers (the 'forward' nature of the commitment entailed a dimension of credit risk, e.g., being certain that the option seller (investor) would be financially willing and able to provide funds when (if) exercise occurred).

[19] For instance, F&G Re created a reference portfolio of 42 individual reinsurance contracts, with F&G absorbing first loss cover and investors providing excess layer cover.

make catastrophe bond issuance an increasingly competitive alternative to reinsurance;[20] that said, catastrophe bonds are still often more expensive than reinsurance.[21]

- Greater comfort among stakeholders (issuers, regulators, investors, rating agencies) that the modeling efforts employed in structuring catastrophe bonds is prudent. Gradually increasing price transparency in the catastrophe reinsurance market has removed some of the opacity that has traditionally surrounded reinsurance contracts, which will ultimately impact catastrophe bond prices.
- Development of dedicated catastrophe bond funds with several billion dollars under management; growing recognition among investment managers that catastrophe risk is largely uncorrelated with other asset classes and can help improve portfolio returns.

Though the catastrophe bond market is still relatively young, and quite modest in overall size when compared with the global catastrophe insurance/reinsurance markets, it presents yet another loss-financing solution for firms seeking to manage their exposures. There seems little doubt that the market will continue to develop and expand, until the point where it becomes a meaningful source of risk capacity. That said, the market still faces considerable challenges, which we consider at greater length at the end of the chapter.

7.3   CONTINGENT CAPITAL

Contingent capital is a general class of financing arranged on an *ex ante* basis that provides a company with a capital infusion on an *ex post* basis. Access to funds is based on the triggering of a defined catastrophic event; if no event occurs, then a firm has no need for additional capital and the facility remains unused. Since contingent capital facilities are arranged in advance of any catastrophic event leading to financial loss, the all-in cost is not impacted by any additional risk premium that might be demanded in the aftermath of a catastrophe (i.e., lower creditworthiness and less access to liquidity, leading to a higher cost of capital). A firm that attempts to arrange financing after a disaster has weakened its financial condition is likely to face a higher cost of funds; this is especially true if its credit condition has been lowered to sub-investment grade levels. A firm that has been impacted by the same disaster but arranged its capital access in advance will recapitalize its operations at the cost of capital agreed prior to the loss. Unlike catastrophe bonds, which contain aspects of insurance/reinsurance and capital financing, contingent capital is structured strictly as a funding/banking facility or capital markets transaction, with no element of insurance contracting. This means the facility is not one of indemnification, but of funding – which must eventually be repaid/redeemed.[22] Note that in most instances contingent capital can be viewed as a synthetic package of a derivative and capital markets/loan financing, as we shall discuss in the next chapter.

Contingent capital can be structured in various forms; we consider two broad classes, contingent debt and contingent equity, and their individual subclasses, including committed capital

---

[20] Consider, for instance, the evolution of pricing on USAA's bonds: the insurer's inaugural 1997 issue was launched at +576 bps, its 1998 issue at +412 bps, and its 1999 issue at +366 bps. The tightening of the spread was a combination of reduced novelty factor and changes in certain modeling parameters (e.g., events, paths, speeds, storm surge damage) and brought the all-in cost to a level very comparable to USAA's standard reinsurance costs. The original bond had a 97 bp probability of exceedance, a 39 bp probability of exhaustion, and 63 bp of expected loss – meaning investors purchasing the bond received 9.1× the expected loss level. Subsequent issues have fallen to multiples of 3–5× expected losses.

[21] Note that full reinsurance costs are not always included as part of the comparative analysis process; for instance, the direct/indirect costs of reinsurer credit quality, deductibles, termination clauses, settlement delays, and reinstatement premiums, none of which feature in catastrophe bonds, may be erroneously ignored in the cost/benefit analysis process.

[22] The exception is for common stock issues, which remain outstanding in perpetuity unless specifically repurchased in the form of Treasury stock.

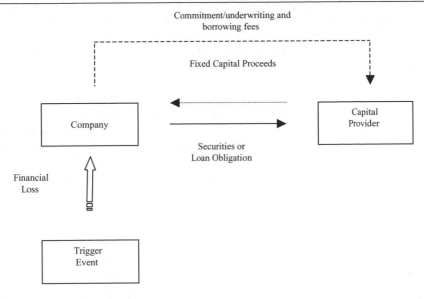

Figure 7.3   Generic contingent capital structure

facilities, contingency loans, contingent surplus notes, catastrophe equity puts, and put protected equity. Before doing so we briefly review a standard structure.

7.3.1   Standard structures

A company creating a generic contingent capital structure first identifies the amount of capital that it may require in the event it suffers a catastrophic loss, and then determines the events that can trigger the loss, and the specific form of loan/security that best suits its needs. If the event occurs, the capital provider supplies funds by taking up newly issued securities or granting a loan at the *ex ante* price. In return, the company pays the capital provider a periodic (or upfront), non-refundable commitment fee (payable whether or not funding ever occurs) as well as an underwriting fee or borrowing charge (payable if financing occurs). Since the capital-raising effort is a committed transaction, the intermediary (generally an insurer, arranging bank or securities firm) is obligated to supply funds as contractually agreed if a trigger event occurs; the company relies on the provider of capital to supply funds when called on to do so and thus assumes the capital provider's credit risk on a contingent basis.[23] Figure 7.3 illustrates the generic contingent capital structure.

The terms of a contingent capital financing can vary widely: loans can be fixed or floating rate, while securities can be issued as common equity, debt, or preferreds.[24] Contingent capital products are created with triggers that are activated by a stated loss level. Like the catastrophe bond triggers noted above, contingent capital triggers can be designed on an indemnity basis

---

[23] For example, a company and a bank (as capital provider) might agree to a $500m capital infusion if the company suffers a loss from a natural disaster. If the trigger is breached and the company loses more than $500m, it expects the compensatory equity infusion from the bank. However, if the bank fails to perform (i.e., perhaps it has encountered financial distress of its own or has actually defaulted on its obligations), the company is left without the vital capital injection it expects, which may be enough to create financial losses or financial distress.

[24] If equity is floated, dilution issues must be considered; if a loan, bond, or preferred is used, details related to leverage, subordination, maturity, covenants, interest rate/coupon (or dividend), and callability must be resolved.

in order to match a company's exposure to a specific loss-making event, or they can be based on transparent market indexes.

Post-loss-financing products such as contingent capital can be used in conjunction with traditional insurance or financial hedges. Since contingent capital is intended for disaster events rather than high frequency/low severity insurance events it supplements, but does not replace, other forms of risk transfer and financing (e.g., a firm might employ an insurance policy to cover its 'close to the mean' risks, and a contingent capital facility to cover upper layers). Ultimately, of course, a company will use contingent capital if the cost/benefit analysis suggests value can be added. Benefits center on the reduction in the cost of financial distress along with potential tax deductibility from ongoing interest payments if debt funding is used. Costs include payment of an upfront, non-refundable fee to secure financing that may never be required (along with additional underwriting/arranging/borrowing fees should financing actually occur). Since contingent capital is a balance sheet and cash flow arrangement (that shares structural similarities with various finite risk programs), it does not provide earnings protection or the tax deductibility characteristics of insurance; in addition, the financing that results must be repaid/redeemed at maturity.

7.3.2 Contingent debt

The general class of contingent debt can be segregated into two subclasses, contingent debt facilities and contingent surplus notes; though other forms of contingent debt exist, these represent the most common mechanisms in the catastrophic loss-financing sector.[25]

7.3.2.1 Contingent debt facilities

Contingent debt facilities are available as committed capital facilities and contingency loans. A committed capital facility (CCF) is funded capital that is arranged prior to a loss, and which is accessible only when two trigger events are breached. Under a typical CCF a company creates a financing program, defining the specific debt it intends to issue upon triggering (i.e., all essential reference characteristics, including seniority/subordination, maturity, repayment schedule, and coupon). The intermediary arranging the facility (e.g., insurer/reinsurer) generally acts as the capital supplier, providing funds in the event of exercise.[26] The first trigger on a CCF is often implicit – that is, the financing option will not be exercised unless it has value, and it will only have value if a loss occurs and the company cannot obtain cheaper funding from other sources. The second trigger is generally related to the exposure that can create a loss requiring funding, but the specific reference event is unlikely to be under the company's control. As with other contingent capital structures, the CCF generally has a fixed maturity date and is intended as a form of financing rather than risk transfer; unlike insurance, which provides a compensatory payment, the CCF creates balance sheet

---

[25] For instance, financial guarantees, which have existed for many decades, are commonly used to transfer risk; however, by virtue of their construction, they also represent a form of contingent financing. In the context of a non-catastrophic or catastrophic risk, a company and a financial guarantor (e.g., an insurer, reinsurer, or bank) agree to a loss trigger that allows the company to access funds from the guarantor. Guarantees of this type are commonly used to protect companies and SPEs against credit losses or residual value claims, but they can also be extended to provide funding of losses created by a specific or general catastrophic event.

[26] In larger or more complex structures the intermediary writing the contingent option might join with a bank (or syndicate of banks) to provide funding; this distributes the funding requirement more broadly across institutions.

leverage that must eventually be repaid. The price of a CCF will be approximately equal to premium and loading, but a portion of the premium may be refundable if the facility is not exercised.

A CCF may contain covenants to protect one or both parties. These might include a material adverse change clause, change of control clause, financial strength/ratios, and so forth. For instance, a company might enter into a CCF to issue $100m of 5-year fixed rate bonds if its production facilities are impacted by a Category 3+ hurricane that creates at least $100m of damage. If the loss occurs ($100m) as a result of the event (Category 3+ hurricane), the company issues $100m of 5-year bonds to the intermediary and receives $100m of funds that it can use to restore its facilities. The intermediary may retain the bonds or sell them to other investors; importantly, the rate on the bonds is fixed in advance of the event (e.g., the spread is fixed with reference to a risk-free benchmark, such as a government bond yield), meaning the issuing company locks in a financing rate regardless of the losses it sustains and its perceived or actual creditworthiness in the aftermath of an event.

The contingency loan, a variation of the CCF, is a bank of line of credit that is arranged in advance of a loss and invoked when a trigger event occurs. Unlike a traditional line of credit, which can be used for any purpose and accessed at will, the contingency loan is only available to cover losses arising from a defined event; if the loss event does not occur, the facility remains unused. In practice contingency loans are used by insurers, reinsurers, and certain public authorities as excess layer loss financing, accessed only once other sources of loss financing have been exhausted (this structure is used in various government insurance/reinsurance programs described in Chapter 9). For instance, an insurer might arrange for a $250m, 5-year contingency loan that becomes available when European windstorm damage creates at least $500m of claims on policies that it has written; for any losses below that amount it may simply rely on standard reinsurance. Since the company has far less flexibility in draw down under a contingency loan than a standard facility (and the probability of draw down is much lower), it pays a smaller fee. As with the CCF above, key terms of the contingency loan are defined in advance, including maximum draw down amount, fixed or floating rate, maturity, repayment schedule, trigger(s), and so forth. Contingency loans are often granted only when the borrower can identify (and in some cases segregate) a repayment source that will remain unaffected in the event a disaster strikes the borrower's other operations. Facilities are often syndicated broadly, so that each participating bank has only a moderate share of what might otherwise be a large commitment.

7.3.2.2   Contingent surplus notes

Contingent surplus notes (CSNs), another form of contingent debt financing, can be issued by insurance and reinsurance companies seeking to protect against catastrophic losses in their portfolios. Under a typical CSN structure an insurer establishes an investment trust, which is capitalized by outside investors through trust-issued notes paying an enhanced yield. The trust invests proceeds in high-grade investments (e.g., AAA-rated bonds) until (or if) the contingent capital is required. If the insurer breaches a pre-defined loss trigger, it issues CSNs to the trust; the trust liquidates the AAA-rated bonds and delivers cash to the insurer, thus providing the necessary post-event funding. In exchange for providing the initial commitment and contingent capital, the investor achieves an all-in yield that is greater than that of similarly rated corporate securities. The insurer, in turn, obtains a post-loss funding commitment in advance at a price

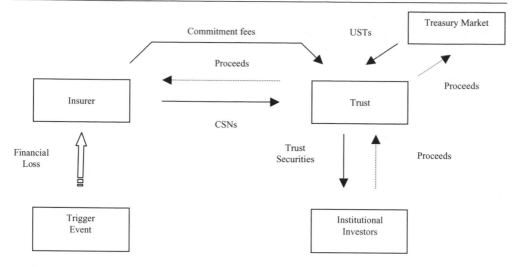

Figure 7.4   Generic CSN structure

that might prove advantageous in a hard reinsurance market.[27] Figure 7.4 summarizes a generic CSN structure.

For instance, an insurer might arrange a $250m 5-year CSN issue that will be triggered if losses in its earthquake portfolio exceed $250m over the next year. The arranging bank identifies several institutional investors that pre-fund a trust for $250m in exchange for an all-in yield equal to the commitment fee plus the return on 5-year US Treasury notes and the credit spread of the insurer. The $250m in pre-funding proceeds are used to purchase US Treasuries; the investors receive notes in the trust reflecting an enhanced coupon. Assuming that in one year several earthquake events occur and create greater than expected loss experience, the insurer issues $250m of 5-year notes to the trust, the trust liquidates its Treasury position and uses the proceeds to acquire the CSNs; the trust now holds the insurance company's CSNs, the insurer receives $250m of cash to help manage its financial position, and end-investors continue to receive the enhanced yield on their trust-issued notes.

In addition to standard CSNs, insurers may also issue surplus notes, which are subordinated securities that function much like CSNs, except that they are issued directly by the company rather than through a trust. Surplus notes typically have maturities of 10 to 30 years and must be approved by insurance regulators. Importantly, these notes increase statutory capital, but not financial accounting capital.

7.3.3   Contingent equity

In some cases a company may prefer, or require, post-loss funding in the form of common or preferred equity rather than debt; this helps ensure that the recapitalization effort does

---

[27] The first CSN, a $400m 10-year note, was issued by National Mutual in 1995. Under terms of the transaction National Mutual was able to access up to $400m in new capital through a trust, which issued surplus notes to investors as needed. In a variation on the standard structure, the insurer was able to raise funds whenever it wanted, and not just in the event of a loss. Apart from National Mutual's credit risk, investors were also at risk to the possibility that the state insurance commissioner would instruct National Mutual to cease paying principal and/or interest if policyholders were likely to be disadvantaged or prejudiced by such payments, i.e., a form of subordination risk.

not increase the debt burden and negatively impact leverage ratios. However, any contingent equity structure that involves the issuance of new common shares creates earnings dilution. In addition, since equity capital is generally more expensive than debt capital, the economics might not be as compelling; the relative costs and benefits must therefore be weighed.

7.3.3.1 Catastrophe equity put

The catastrophe equity put (CEP) is a contingent capital structure that results in the issuance of new shares if a pre-defined trigger(s) is breached. The structure and mechanics of the CEP are similar to the CCF described above, except that equity, rather than debt, is issued if a trigger is breached. In a CEP a company purchases a put option from an intermediary that gives it the right to sell a fixed amount of shares if a catastrophe-based loss trigger is breached during the life of the contract. In exchange, the company pays the intermediary an option premium. In order to avoid dilution, CEPs may be based on the issuance of preferred, rather than common, equity. They may also be structured as convertible preferred shares, with an implicit understanding between the issuer and investors that the preferreds will be repurchased by the company at a future time, prior to any conversion (thereby avoiding dilution). Since the terms of the put option are fixed (e.g., number of shares to be issued and strike price), the post-loss financing is arranged and committed in advance of any loss. If the option becomes exercisable, the company issues new shares to the intermediary, pays any additional underwriting fees, and receives agreed proceeds. The infusion restores capital that may have been lost as a result of a catastrophic event, without increasing the company's leverage.[28]

A CEP is characterized by standard terms and conditions, including exercise event, form of securities, minimum amount of securities to be issued on exercise, time period of coverage, maximum time allotted for issuance of securities, strike price, and specific conditions or warranties (e.g., change in control, minimum net worth (or statutory capital) on exercise, and so on).[29] To reduce the possibility of moral hazard arising from an indemnity structure, CEPs often contain two triggers. The first trigger may be based on the company's stock price, which must fall below the strike price in order to become effective; this is consistent with any option framework, where the derivative will only be exercised if it moves in-the-money. The second trigger can relate to a specific catastrophic loss that must be sustained in order for exercise to occur. Thus, it is not sufficient for a company's stock price to decline – it must be accompanied by a large loss event. In fact, the two triggers are likely to be quite related if losses are large enough; that is, the company's stock price is more likely to fall through the strike price if the marketplace becomes aware that the firm has sustained large losses. CEPs can also be structured with index or parametric triggers instead of indemnity triggers.

---

[28] RLI Corporation, a specialty property liability subsidiary of USA Insurance Company writing excess layer earthquake coverage, joined with Aon and Centre Re in 1996 to create the first CEP. Under terms of the transaction, RLI bought a put option from Centre Re, giving it the right to put up to $50m of cumulative convertible preferred shares to Centre Re if the company's reinsurance lines were to be fully used in the aftermath of an earthquake. The 3-year transaction featured two tranches: one that Centre Re could convert from preferred into common stock in 3 years (50% of the total) and another enabling it to convert into common stock after another 4 years (50%). Implicit in the structure was an understanding that, in the event of exercise, RLI would repurchase the convertible preferreds from Centre Re within the 3 and 7-year timeframes, so that they would never be converted into RLI common shares. This effectively meant the new issuance of capital could be treated as debt for internal and tax purposes, but equity for regulatory purposes. Though the put was more expensive for RLI than standard reinsurance coverage, the firm was not in a position to negotiate a full amount of reinsurance coverage and the new instrument emerged as a viable alternative.

[29] To ensure that the option writer is not forced to invest in a financially distressed company, transactions generally include minimum net worth covenants; if the option buyer's net worth falls below a pre-determined threshold it cannot exercise the option to raise new proceeds.

In addition to securing post-loss equity financing at pre-set levels, CEPs feature at least two other advantages. First, unlike debt facilities that often contain material adverse change clauses that limit or prohibit funding in the event of disruption (either in the market or with the company), CEPs have no such limitations (except for maintenance of minimum net worth), meaning they are virtually certain to be available when needed. Second, the cost of a CEP can compare quite favorably to a standard reinsurance contract because the option purchaser must remain financially viable in order to claim access to funding (the same is not true in a standard reinsurance contract, where the cedant can become insolvent and the reinsurer must still perform on its reinsurance obligation).

Figure 7.5 illustrates the flows of a standard CEP pre- and post-trigger. Note that as in the contingent debt structures above, the intermediary is ultimately responsible for taking up new shares and delivering proceeds if the CEP is exercised; in practice it is likely to distribute the shares to its base of institutional investors.

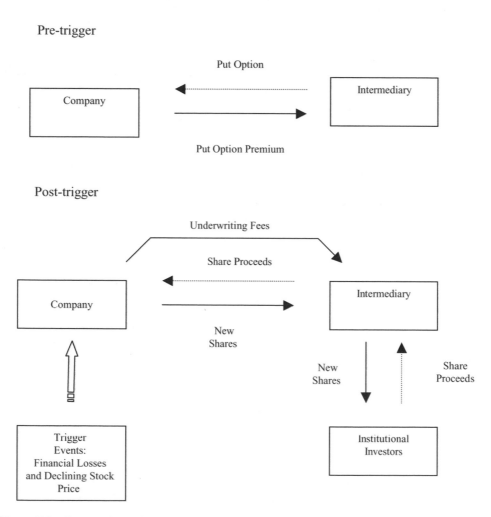

Figure 7.5   Catastrophe equity put

7.3.3.2 Put protected equity

Put protected equity (PPE), a second form of contingent equity, is a mechanism where a company buys a put on its own equity in order to generate an economic gain should the value of its stock decline in the aftermath of a loss. Specifically, a company purchases a put option from an intermediary, defining the number of shares, strike price, and maturity (as in any option). If the company suffers a significant loss, perhaps from a catastrophic event, there is a high probability that its stock price will fall. The company then exercises the contract against the put seller for an economic gain. The economic gain can be used to increase retained earnings or provide a price hedge against the issuance of a new tranche of stock. If the PPE is only used to generate an economic gain based on a decline in the company's stock price (e.g., the company is delivering to the intermediary shares that it purchases in the open market), the addition to equity capital is indirect, rather than direct. That is, it accrues to the retained earnings account rather than the paid-in capital account, meaning the after-tax proceeds will be lower and there will be no share dilution. If the PPE is used to protect the company's issuance of new shares, then the gain on the put serves to offset the increased number of shares that will be floated when the stock is issued at the new lower price. If new common shares are issued, dilution is a factor; if preferreds are used, no dilution concerns appear. Note that unlike the CEP, the PPE does not need to be governed by a specific loss trigger; that is, the company can simply purchase a put on its own stock under the assumption that any sizeable loss will cause downward pressure on the stock price. However, the marketplace can view PPEs negatively. If investors become aware that a firm is buying puts on its own stock, they might be concerned about future bad news; the share price may thus be forced down as investors sell their shares – and not because of any specific loss.[30]

Contingent capital is an important and useful means of arranging post-loss financing before the onset of financial distress; indeed, the optimal time to arrange such facilities is in advance of any potential problem, when the best possible terms can be negotiated. Ultimately, of course, contingent capital products must be analyzed within the cost/benefit framework to determine potential value, and must only be considered as one part of a broader risk management solution.

7.4 CHALLENGES

Capital markets structures, including bonds and contingent capital, may ultimately be the best medium-term solution to meet the growing demand for catastrophic risk capacity. Properly structured, these mechanisms can help fill the void that may ultimately develop in the insurance/reinsurance sector. Capital markets investors and contingent lenders are interested in earning an equitable return based on risks taken; they seek manageable credit and liquidity risks and price transparency, so that they can evaluate opportunities in an unbiased fashion and allocate their capital in an optimal manner. Accordingly, before catastrophe bonds and contingent capital can truly enter the 'mainstream' of the loss-financing sector, they will have to overcome various challenges, including structural flaws (liquidity, transparency, pricing, cost) and regulatory discrepancies.

---

[30] Note that a company can achieve similar results by issuing a reverse convertible bond. While a standard convertible bond gives the investor the right to convert a bond into shares of the issuer, a reverse convertible bond grants the issuer the right to convert the bonds into shares at a specified strike price. The issuer will only exercise the conversion right when the stock price falls below the price where shares offered are worth less than the debt. In fact, optimal exercise occurs when debt is worth more than equity; equity becomes a cheaper source of capital and reduces leverage.

7.4.1   Structural flaws

From the discussion above it should be relatively clear that the market for catastrophe-based capital markets instruments has undergone a gradual transformation over the past few years with instruments becoming increasingly sophisticated and useful. That said, additional structural enhancements are necessary in order to expand the appeal to a broader base of issuers and investors; in particular, securities will have to be:

- Less complex and more transparent. This suggests greater use of index/parametric structures, and perhaps migration of SPEs and SPRs onshore where disclosure and regulation are more direct. It may also require more comprehensive investor education efforts regarding risks and opportunities.
- Accurately priced, indicating a greater need for granular loss data and more transparent modeling. Stakeholders (rating agencies, investors, regulators, issuers) are highly dependent on analytics and may require a greater understanding of the underlying processes used to derive loss estimates.
- Less expensive; to be a consistently compelling supplement to insurance/reinsurance deal fees (2%+, for underwriting, modeling, registration, SPE/SPR formation, legal work, ratings) will need to compress significantly (recalling that reinsurance contracts carry no such fees, though they do contain certain other unique costs of their own, as noted above). To help achieve greater cost savings, transactions will almost certainly have to become more standardized so that they can be replicated with ease. Ultimately, cost is the single most important factor influencing the use of capital markets solutions. If costs can be driven down to levels that consistently approach those found in the insurance/reinsurance market during soft and hard markets, and investors can be persuaded to provide capital at lower yields, capital markets facilities should expand considerably.
- Partially liquid, meaning a larger number of financial institutions will need to become market-makers. While institutional investors purchasing bonds are aware of the liquidity limitations that arise in purchasing high-risk private placement securities, a minimum level of two-way market-making is essential in building a broader base of interest. Greater commonality in modeling can aid in the process.

7.4.2   Regulatory differences

In order to be truly useful, capital markets instruments must be seen as reasonable alternatives to other loss-financing instruments. While aspects of this can be achieved through the structural enhancements noted above, some element must be driven by regulatory harmonization, i.e., placing all available solutions on relatively equal footing regarding rules and regulations. By harmonizing rules, discrepancies that currently exist can be eliminated, helping pave the way for greater participation in the market segment that proves to be most efficient at a given point in time. For instance, US insurers submitting statutory filings can use reinsurance purchases to reflect an improved portfolio position, but cannot do the same with catastrophe bonds they may have issued; this treatment obviously favors reinsurance over bonds, even though the risk-mitigating effects are the same. Other types of regulatory disparities exist and must be eliminated or reduced.

The capital markets will ultimately be required to fill the risk capacity gap that exists whenever large catastrophes strike; the gap will continue to expand as vulnerabilities grow. The situation in the early part of the millennium is not yet balanced: too much investor capital is available in support of high frequency/low severity, diversifiable risks (driving returns down and skewing the overall risk/return profile) and too little capital is still dedicated in support of low frequency/high severity, undiversifiable risks (with very high returns). Until the reallocation of capital occurs, through resolution of some of the challenges we have highlighted, the market for catastrophic loss financing will continue to be primarily a function of traditional insurance/reinsurance and government-sponsored efforts; the largest element of the financial markets will play a limited, though still important, role.

8

Catastrophe Derivatives

Derivatives comprise the second major category of capital market contracts we consider in this book. Like catastrophe bonds and contingent capital, catastrophe derivatives, which are financial contracts that derive their value from the occurrence of a catastrophic event, are in a nascent state of development; basic catastrophe derivatives were introduced as recently as the 1990s and have yet to make significant penetration in the risk management sector. Nevertheless, some derivative structures have considerable potential and may become increasingly important in the transfer and hedging of catastrophe exposures, particularly once key challenges are overcome. In this chapter we discuss the mechanics of catastrophe-related exchange-traded derivatives and over-the-counter (OTC) derivatives; we also consider in detail some of the challenges facing the sector. Before doing so we provide a very brief primer on the major classes of derivative contracts.

8.1 OVERVIEW OF DERIVATIVES

Derivatives have been widely used by individuals, institutions, and sovereigns for many decades. Though basic derivatives date back several centuries, the 'modern era' can be traced back to the 1970s when growing financial volatility[1] and development of financial option pricing methodologies led to the introduction of new instruments and a steady increase in activity. Since that time new asset class references and instruments have been introduced on a regular basis, and growth in certain segments has expanded rapidly (e.g., in interest rate, currency, equity, and credit derivatives).

Listed and OTC derivatives, which provide the holder with an optionable interest, can be used to hedge, speculate, or arbitrage. The fact that derivatives can be used to generate a profit distinguishes them from insurance contracts (which are based on insurable interest and cannot be used to create speculative profits). A catastrophe option, for instance, is not considered insurance since the option buyer does not need to prove that it has sustained a loss to obtain the economic benefit of an in-the-money position; a catastrophe-based reinsurance contract that provides the same economic protection is considered insurance since the buyer needs to prove it has an insurable interest and must sustain a loss in order to file a claim and receive a settlement.

Though derivatives are often used to speculate, many companies use them to hedge their risks; when used as hedges, they are essentially loss-financing mechanisms. Derivatives can be used to neutralize the downside effects of a single risk, diversify a portfolio of exposures (and, in so doing, reduce risk), and provide capacity to engage in additional risk-related business. These goals can be accomplished when a company identifies an exposure it intends to protect or a portfolio it wants to diversify, and arranges a transaction that provides a compensatory payment when (if) the underlying exposure generates a loss. Since derivatives are not structured

---

[1] This was largely the result of the elimination of the post-war fixed exchange rate regime and a rise in inflationary pressures.

as indemnity contracts, a company generally accepts some amount of basis risk. While certain financial risks can be matched quite precisely via derivatives (e.g., specific exposure to exchange rates or interest rates), insurance-related risks often cannot (e.g., specific exposure to catastrophe or weather). The trade-off in accepting more basis risk is a reduction in the specter of moral hazard and a lower cost of risk protection.

Derivatives provide several key benefits that make them an important part of the loss-financing process:

- Some derivative contracts are quite liquid and can serve as cost-effective risk solutions.
- Transactions arranged through the exchange-traded market eliminate credit risk.
- Transactions arranged through the OTC market are highly customizable.
- Insurable interest and proof of loss do not have to be demonstrated; generating a speculative gain is a perfectly acceptable end goal.
- Delays in receiving payment in the event a contract pays off are minimal (i.e., for contracts on insurance-related risks there is no loss development period or claims adjustment process).
- Financial payments to the party holding the in-the-money contract are generally not capped (i.e., there are no policy limits).

Naturally, derivatives also have certain costs/disadvantages, including:

- Coverage of non-standard risks through the exchange-traded market is very limited.
- Liquidity for contracts on non-standard risks is minimal and bid–offer spreads may be very large, adding to the cost of risk management.
- Basis risks can be significant, resulting in imperfect risk hedges.
- Credit risks for certain OTC transactions can be large (i.e., similar to those that might be encountered in the insurance/reinsurance market).
- Certain bilateral contracts (e.g., swaps and forwards) expose a firm to downside payments.

The general class of derivatives can be divided into exchange-traded and OTC contracts. The exchange-traded derivatives marketplace is based on listed futures, options, and futures options, while the OTC market consists of OTC forwards, swaps, and options. There are, of course, various subclasses of exotic derivatives (e.g., complex swaps and options, structured notes), but these are beyond the scope of our discussion.

8.1.1   Exchange-traded derivatives

Exchange-traded derivatives are listed and traded via regulated exchanges (either physical or electronic), with the exchange or its clearinghouse acting as intermediary on every contract. Exchange contracts, which are available on a range of financial and physical reference assets, are defined by common characteristics. Each product has certain standardized features related to contract size, pricing, and maturity, meaning participants cannot customize individual aspects of the contract to suit their needs. However, standardization permits greater contract transparency, allowing liquidity to build and price spreads to compress.

A future is a contract representing an obligation to buy or sell a specific quantity of an underlying reference asset, at a price agreed but not exchanged on trade date, for settlement at a future time. It can be considered a contract for deferred payment and delivery, with a maturity ranging from one month to several quarters (shorter-term futures are available on a limited number of references, but these are rather exceptional). A long futures position – one that is purchased or owned – increases in value as the reference price rises and loses value when the price falls. A short futures position – one that is borrowed or sold – increases in value as the price falls, and decreases in value as the price rises. All futures (and other listed contracts) are cleared through centralized clearinghouses, which mitigate credit risk by requiring buyers and sellers to post initial margin; positions are revalued daily and those in deficit (i.e., a loss position) generate variation margin calls, which must be met if the position is to be preserved. A futures contract may feature financial settlement (i.e., cash exchange) or physical settlement (i.e., underlying commodity/asset exchange); contracts based on non-physical underlying references, such as catastrophe, temperature, inflation, or financial volatility, can only be settled on a financial basis.

An option is a contract that gives the purchaser the right, but not the obligation, to buy (call option) or sell (put option) the underlying reference asset, at a level known as a strike price, at any time until an agreed expiry date (American option), on the expiry date alone (European option), or at periodic intervals up to expiry (Bermudan option); option maturity can range from one month to several quarters (though, again, very short-term contracts are available on a small number of references). In exchange for this right the buyer pays the seller a premium payment; by accepting the premium the option seller has an obligation to buy or sell the underlying asset at the strike price if the option is exercised. As with futures, options may be settled in financial or physical terms. The maximum downside of a long option position is limited to the premium paid to secure the option. The maximum downside of a short option position is equal to the differential between the strike price and the price of the reference at the time of exercise; in some instances this liability can be very significant, meaning selling unhedged options is a high-risk speculative strategy. (Note that OTC options have similar definitional parameters but can include more unique and complex payout terms and conditions; in addition, OTC options often carry much longer maturities, extending in some cases out to several years. Given their general similarities with exchange options we shall not discuss them further in the OTC section below.)

A futures option is an option giving the purchaser the right to enter into an underlying futures transaction in exchange for a premium. A futures put gives the purchaser the right to sell a futures contract at a set strike price, while a futures call gives the purchaser the right to buy a futures contract at a set strike price. Conversely, the seller of a futures put is obligated to purchase a future if exercise occurs, while the seller of a futures call must deliver a future on exercise.

As noted above, exchange-traded contracts – whether futures, options, or futures options – are defined by certain standard terms that add uniformity to the marketplace. These include:

- Trading units
- Delivery date
- Deliverable asset grades
- Delivery points
- Contract months
- Last trading day
- Other terms and conditions as applicable, including price limits
- Strike price/exercise style (for options/futures options)

8.1.2 OTC derivatives

OTC derivatives, including forwards, swaps, and options, are traded through informal, off-market mechanisms (e.g., telephonically or via unregulated electronic platforms), with each participating institution acting as principal to a contract. Unlike exchange-traded contracts, OTC derivatives in standard form do not flow through clearinghouses or involve posting of collateral in order to mitigate the effects of credit risk (unless one of the two parties is of weak credit quality, in which case a separately negotiated collateral agreement is arranged).[2]

OTC contracts are completely bespoke, with all relevant terms and conditions negotiated and agreed between the contracting parties. Contracts can be written on a broad range of references and can be settled in physical or financial terms. This high degree of customization allows development of very precise risk management or investing/speculating solutions, reducing or eliminating basis risks; it also means, of course, that apart from a small number of 'vanilla' derivatives (e.g., standard interest rate forwards and swaps, certain currency and equity options), secondary market liquidity is limited.

A forward is a customized, bilateral, single-period contract referencing a market or asset, with a maturity that can range from several months to several years. Like the futures contract described above, it represents an obligation to buy or sell a specific quantity of an underlying reference asset at a price agreed, but not exchanged, on trade date, for settlement at a future time; settlement may be in cash or physical. Unlike a futures contract, however, a forward contract involves no intervening cash flows (i.e., there is no daily position revaluation and settlement of cash/collateral). A long forward position increases in value as the reference price rises and loses value when the price falls; a short forward position increases in value as the price falls, and decreases as the price rises. Since forwards are bilateral contracts, they can expose either party to credit risk unless exposures are separately collateralized.

A swap is a bilateral transaction calling for periodic (e.g., annual, semiannual, quarterly) exchange of payments between two parties based on a defined reference market or asset, and can be regarded as a package of forward contracts. Swaps, which are generally denominated in notional value terms, have maturities extending from 1 to 10+ years (though long-term transactions are reserved for counterparties with the best credit ratings or those willing to post collateral). Like forwards, swaps are bilateral OTC contracts and can expose either party to credit risk.

Swaps and forwards are defined by various terms, including:

- Notional amount
- Underlying reference index
- Maturity
- Payment frequency (for swaps only)
- Settlement terms
- Forward (fixed) reference price
- Floating reference price

OTC derivatives are often managed on a 'net' basis, which reduces the exposure generated by the individual transactions comprising a portfolio. Netting, which is accomplished through the use of a master netting agreement in a jurisdiction that accepts the legal basis of net exposures, allows parties to lower their counterparty credit exposures from a gross to a net basis.

With this basic primer on exchange and OTC derivatives as background, we now consider the state and mechanics of the catastrophe derivatives marketplace.

---

[2] Note that in recent years exchange clearinghouses have been marketing their clearing services (e.g., collateralization, revaluation, margin calls) to the OTC marketplace in hopes of generating additional business; some OTC participants use third-party clearing arrangements to reduce their credit risks.

8.2   EXCHANGE-TRADED CATASTROPHE DERIVATIVES

Exchange-traded catastrophe derivatives have had a mixed history of activity and have become temporarily dormant in the early years of the millennium. Whether future endeavors will be successful remains to be seen, but a properly designed exchange contract could create a critical mass of interest; growth in related markets, including catastrophe bonds and OTC catastrophe derivatives, might aid in the process.

The earliest attempts at introducing a catastrophe risk contract date back to 1992, when the Chicago Board of Trade (CBOT), one of Chicago's three listed derivative exchanges, developed catastrophe futures based on an index created by the Insurance Services Office (ISO); the ISO index was a compilation of catastrophe loss ratio data gathered from more than 100 participating companies. After the futures contract met with virtually no interest in its first year, the exchange introduced options on futures in an attempt to spur growth, but was unable to generate any meaningful activity; both contracts were abandoned shortly thereafter. The CBOT reviewed the original contract design to identify flaws and potential for enhancements; the most significant reasons for the contract's lack of appeal related to use of the ISO index (which many participants regarded as opaque), the short loss development period for claims (e.g., one quarter versus several years on a standard catastrophe insurance policy), and the high contract fees. Armed with this information, the CBOT redesigned its contract, introducing a cash-settled option in 1995 based on the more transparent, and widely used, PCS index. PCS tracked nine loss indexes for the exchange (including references for national and regional sectors, as well as high-risk states such as Florida, Texas, and California) through a daily survey of 70 participants involved in catastrophe risk. The CBOT created two separate contracts, the large cap option (covering exposures of $20–50b) and the small cap option (exposures below $20b); the contracts featured longer loss development periods (two and four quarters) and lower fees. As part of its marketing effort the exchange attempted to convince potential participants that cost-competitive synthetic XOL reinsurance layers tied to a recognized loss index could be created by assembling particular PCS option spreads (e.g., purchase of a low strike call and sale of a higher strike call). Though the PCS contract fared better than the original ISO offering, it was unable to attract enough activity to make it a truly competitive alternative to other catastrophe risk solutions, and was abandoned in 2000. Several reasons have been cited for the failure of the contract: lack of natural hedgers on both sides of the market (a prerequisite, certainly over the medium term, in ensuring contract success), lack of a deep OTC catastrophe derivative market to provide additional liquidity and pricing references, lack of transparency, and excessive basis risk arising from an insufficiently granular index.

The ill-fated Bermuda Commodities Exchange (BCE) attempted to introduce a catastrophe derivative contract of its own at about the same time. In 1996 the Bermudan Parliament authorized the development of the BCE as a forum for listing and trading catastrophe derivatives. The BCE was intended as a mutual exchange with a separate clearinghouse owned by various highly rated industry players (to ensure a strong credit rating for the clearinghouse itself). The BCE intended to list catastrophe options based on the Guy Carpenter Catastrophe Index (GCCI), an index comprised of loss data from 39 global insurance companies. Unlike the PCS's total dollar loss measure at the state/regional level, the GCCI produced industry loss ratios at a more detailed level (e.g., ZIP code/postal code). The BCE options were also designed to be structurally different from the CBOT's, paying out on a digital or binary basis (e.g., 100% payout above the strike, 0% below the strike) rather than a standard intrinsic value basis (e.g., increasing amounts as the contract moves further-in-the-money). Though considerable planning and effort went into the development phase, the exchange was unable to gain sufficient support from the reinsurance industry, which saw flaws with the structure of the contracts (e.g., digital payout, 100% margin), the index (e.g., GCCI had a strong homeowner loss focus), and the fees. The BCE project was ultimately abandoned.

No other global derivative exchanges offer listed catastrophe derivatives. Though countries such as the UK, France, Germany, and Japan are exposed to various catastrophic perils, local exchanges have not noted enough demand for specific listed contracts on such risks. However, the New York-based Catastrophe Risk Exchange (CATEX), founded in 1995, has emerged as a quasi-exchange conduit for matching cedants and insurers/reinsurers on P&C insurance contracts, including those related to catastrophe risk. Although CATEX is not a formal regulated exchange and does not trade standardized contracts through a clearinghouse, it brings together multiple parties in a central forum so that they can execute risk covers in an organized fashion. In practice, participants (who must be subscribers) use CATEX's technology platform to post exposures they seek to cover or protect. Once posted and matched, the two parties conclude discussions in a private setting; CATEX might therefore be regarded as a hybrid listed/OTC transaction-matching conduit.

8.3   OTC CATASTROPHE DERIVATIVES

As noted above, the OTC derivative market is based on customized structures, with two parties to a contract agreeing all terms and conditions on a transaction-specific basis. The same applies with OTC catastrophe swaps: two parties, such as two insurers and/or reinsurers or a company and an insurer, enter into a negotiated transaction that allows them to achieve certain goals related to ceding or accepting risk exposure. In this section we consider two main types of OTC catastrophe derivatives, the catastrophe reinsurance swap and the pure catastrophe swap, along with certain variations on the theme.

8.3.1   Catastrophe reinsurance swaps

The catastrophe reinsurance swap is a synthetic financial transaction that exchanges a commitment fee for a contingent loss payment based on the occurrence of a catastrophic loss; in this sense the swap is the financial equivalent of a reinsurance contract. Indeed, the swap provides many of the same benefits as reinsurance and securitization but avoids the structural complexities and costs associated with facultative agreements or full catastrophe bond issuance. A catastrophe reinsurance swap is typically negotiated as a financial derivative contract (e.g., via the International Swap and Derivative Association master agreement), though this may require use of a capital markets subsidiary or transformer, as noted below.

In the standard catastrophe swap an insurer pays a reinsurer a floating rate (e.g., LIBOR) plus a spread over a multi-year period in exchange for a loss payment related to a pre-defined indemnity, parametric, or index event. If the event occurs and creates a loss, the reinsurer provides the ceding swap party with compensation and assumes the claim rights through subrogation; if it does not occur the transaction terminates, with the insurer's portfolio remaining unchanged. The insurer essentially creates risk capacity through the swap by transferring a portion of its catastrophe portfolio to the reinsurer. For instance, an insurer might agree to pay a reinsurer LIBOR+300 bps over 3 years in exchange for $50m of US Atlantic hurricane capacity based on a parametric trigger, where a Category 3+ hurricane making landfall between Miami, Florida and Charleston, South Carolina, and causing at least $500m of industry-wide

Pre-catastrophe

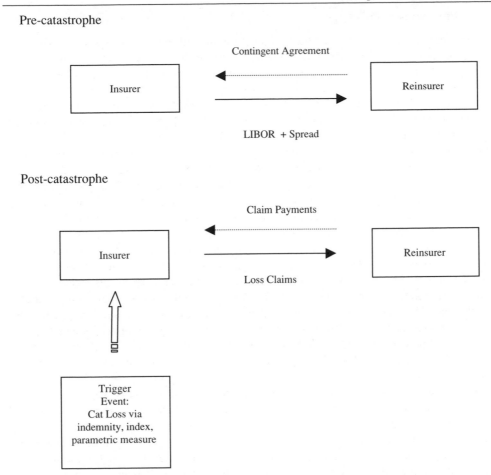

Figure 8.1   Catastrophe reinsurance swap

damage, provides the insurer with $50m of loss coverage. By arranging the swap the insurer reduces the risk in its portfolio by $50m and can either lower its capital allocation or write new risk-related business. Figure 8.1 summarizes the flows of a generic catastrophe reinsurance swap.

In practice global insurers and reinsurers with portfolios that are large enough to require active management, and which seek alternative, and complementary, risk management methodologies, dominate the market for catastrophe reinsurance swaps.[3] Financial intermediaries might also write such swaps to gain exposure to particular perils. However, an insurer with a small catastrophe exposure would almost certainly not arrange a swap, opting instead for a standard reinsurance contract with premium deductibility features and a familiar contractual and legal framework.

---

[3] For instance, insurers such as Swiss Re and Mitsui Marine are active swap parties; in a sample transaction Mitsui Marine and Swiss Re arranged a reinsurance swap where Mitsui paid Swiss Re LIBOR+375 bps and Swiss Re accepted $30m of contingent exposure to Tokyo earthquake, triggered on a parametric basis.

8.3.2   Pure catastrophe swaps

The pure catastrophe swap is a synthetic transaction that allows institutions to exchange un-correlated catastrophe exposures from existing portfolios. Since the risks being swapped are uncorrelated, participants can achieve greater portfolio diversification, reducing their overall levels of risk exposure; they can also gain exposure to perils that they may not be able to access directly. For instance, a Japanese insurer with an excess of Japanese earthquake risk may wish to reduce its concentrations by swapping a portion of its portfolio for an uncorrelated risk, such as European windstorm; a French insurer, actively writing European windstorm risk, may wish to diversify its own portfolio and agree to accept Japanese earthquake exposure in exchange for a portion of its European windstorm portfolio (in practice the two parties might be matched through a reinsurance broker). Depending on the expected loss levels of the two perils, there may also be a net payment between the two. If a Japanese earthquake strikes and creates losses under the original insurance contracts, the loss payment obligations become the responsibility of the French insurer rather than the Japanese insurer as a result of the swap (and vice versa in the event of a European windstorm). In practice the Japanese insurer will make claims payments to its cedants and then expect to receive the same amount as restitution from the French insurer under the terms of the agreement; the swap in this instance can be seen as a pure indemnity transaction (though similar structures can be created on parametric or index basis). In some cases a swap might involve the exchange of multiple, though still uncorrelated, perils, such as California earthquake for a combination of Monaco earthquake, Japanese typhoon and European windstorm; indeed, virtually any mix of catastrophic perils can be included in a swap.[4] Figure 8.2 summarizes a generic Japan/California pure catastrophe swap.

As with the catastrophe reinsurance swap, the most active users of pure swaps are those with risk portfolios that are large enough to require rebalancing (e.g., insurers, reinsurers, financial intermediaries, and certain hedge funds with dedicated reinsurance risk portfolios). The swap can be arranged through standard reinsurance agreements, thus appearing more as a swapping of reinsurance risks rather than a true derivative, or it may be documented in the form of a financial derivative. When executed as part of a standing financial derivative program risks can be exchanged on a relatively quick and cost-effective basis.

8.3.3   Synthetic OTC structures

Though most activity in the OTC catastrophe derivative market is based on the two types of swaps described above, it is important to note that some of the catastrophe bond and contingent capital structures noted in the last chapter are effectively packages of 'vanilla' securities and derivatives that result in the creation of synthetic funding/risk transfer instruments. For example, the contingent capital facility and catastrophe equity put discussed in the last chapter are actually packages of options and debt or equity securities, where the option is exercisable by the issuer if a trigger event occurs. In both cases the triggers are digital options, or derivative contracts with only two payoff states (rather than a continuum of payoffs that characterize

---

[4] For instance, Swiss Re and Tokio Marine entered into a 1-year, $450m swap where Swiss Re exchanged a portion of its California earthquake exposure for a portion of Tokio Marine's Florida hurricane and French windstorm exposure; simultaneously, Tokio Marine swapped a portion of its Japanese earthquake portfolio for Swiss Re's Japanese typhoon and cyclone risks. Tokio Marine later executed similar transactions with State Farm Insurance, with the two insurers swapping portions of their earthquake exposures (e.g., NMSZ for Japan).

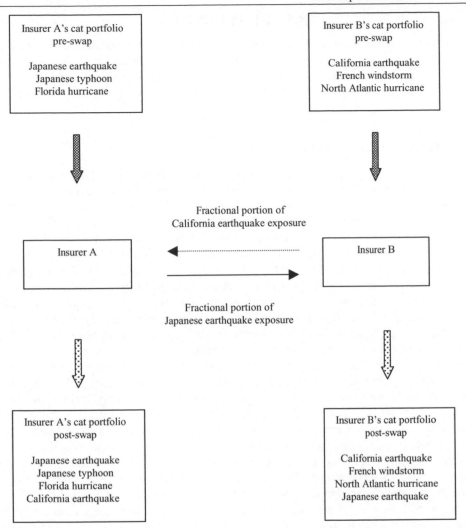

Figure 8.2   Japan/California pure catastrophe swap

standard options): triggered and exercisable or not triggered and not exercisable. Similarly, a synthetic catastrophe bond that permits issuance of a bond in the future if a trigger event occurs is simply an option granting the issuer the right, but not the obligation, to issue a bond, together with an underlying bond that comes into existence upon option exercise. The embedded option gives the issuer control over the decision on whether to issue new capital (which, in practice, will only be exercised when the option is in-the-money, e.g., a disaster occurs and depletes the issuer's capital base). The high degree of customization surrounding these synthetic instruments means that resulting transactions are illiquid and that models drive initial pricing and ongoing valuation rather than quoted prices; nevertheless, very precise enhancements are clearly available for institutions seeking specific risk management or investment results.

8.4   CHALLENGES

Like other risk management products we have discussed in Part II, catastrophe derivatives face certain challenges, including those related to index construction and basis risks, lack of contract transparency, one-way markets, pricing difficulties, and regulatory barriers. These challenges will have to be resolved by direct participants and other stakeholders before further expansion can occur.

8.4.1   Index construction and basis risks

We have noted earlier the gradual migration in the capital markets from indemnity structures to index structures. While indexes yield some obvious benefits, including greater transparency and lower moral hazard risk, they must be approached with diligence. This is particularly true in a developing market sector like catastrophe derivatives, which lacks a critical mass of activity and experience and must therefore be structured properly. We have cited examples of failed contracts in the exchange-traded sector, where the ISO and PCS indexes underlying the CBOT's futures and options proved to be ineffective: the ISO index was not granular or transparent enough, while the PCS index suffered from an excessive focus on residential exposure at the expense of vital, and sometimes more significant, commercial exposures. The large basis risks resulting from the selection of these indexes meant that the derivatives were ineffective as hedging tools (i.e., too uncorrelated with exposures being hedged/transferred). Until the exchange-traded sector can identify catastrophe indexes that more precisely match the needs of end-users and intermediaries, basis risks will continue to plague contract design.

The same problem is generally applicable to OTC derivatives, particularly as the marketplace attempts to develop a more standardized approach to pricing and swapping risks.[5] A base of secondary OTC activity can only form once indexes that minimize basis risk become accepted. (Obviously, at a discrete transaction level this becomes a secondary issue; since transactions are arranged between two parties as private contracts, the specific non-indemnity indexes used as reference points can be specifically negotiated.) While some intermediaries are willing to accept basis risks when managing their portfolios, there are limits to the amount of exposure they can run; proper index construction is therefore vital. A potential solution is for exchanges and intermediaries to use the same index triggers that are most commonly used for the key perils securitized through catastrophe bonds (e.g., California earthquake, Japan earthquake, Florida hurricane); since the catastrophe bond market has enjoyed some success with index structures, patterning derivative contracts after the same metrics may be a reasonable approach.

8.4.2   Lack of contract transparency

Derivative contracts that are based on indemnity triggers eliminate basis risks, but give rise to other complications, including moral hazard. Just as important, bespoke indemnity transactions add a degree of opacity to the marketplace, making it more difficult for standard references to develop and a critical mass of liquidity to build. The same challenges do not exist in the financial derivative markets: though each individual transaction is customized, the underlying references are common (e.g., interest rate contracts often use LIBOR as a floating rate benchmark, US index contracts use the S&P500, and so forth). In catastrophe derivatives non-index

---

[5] Much as the temperature derivative market has done with indexes such as heating degree-days and cooling degree-days.

transactions require an examination of specific portfolio exposures to ensure proper pricing and indemnification; this means that each individual contract remains opaque, which does little to help build a two-way market.

8.4.3   One-way markets

One of the primary reasons for the relative lack of success in developing a robust market for catastrophe derivatives relates to the difficulties in locating the risk-taking side of the transactions. While hedgers of catastrophic risks routinely express interest in using catastrophe derivatives as another tool to manage exposures, those that are naturally willing to supply capacity (e.g., insurers, reinsurers) already have access to efficient tools that allow them to fulfill the function, including insurance/reinsurance and catastrophe bonds. Inducing them to regularly use derivatives, which may have unfavorable/uncertain pricing, excessive basis risks, complexity, and opacity, may be a difficult task. Other possible risk suppliers, such as hedge funds and investment management groups, may lack the requisite expertise/mandate, or may prefer to participate through the purchase of catastrophe bonds. As a result, the risk capacity that is essential in building liquidity has yet to materialize, meaning the market remains one-way.

8.4.4   Pricing difficulties

We have already mentioned the pricing challenges that arise from dealing in catastrophe risk, and the same challenges extend to pricing of catastrophe derivatives. Successful derivative markets (e.g., interest rates, currencies, equities) exhibit very robust modeling processes that allow for smooth pricing, hedging, and market-making. Though the actual modeling processes in such cases can be computationally rigorous, the mechanisms and results are transparent and can be used with confidence.

The same confidence is still lacking in catastrophe derivative modeling. It is clear that advances in pricing catastrophe derivatives have been made over the past few years. For instance, in a standard process a model for an implied loss distribution can be selected, implied parameters can be estimated either from observed prices on related assets (e.g., catastrophe reinsurance contracts, catastrophe bonds) or via simulation, and potential losses on a derivative contract can be computed. However, many challenges remain – including several of those we have already mentioned (e.g., lack of data, difficulty creating loss distributions and estimating tail risk, and so forth). In addition, pricing contracts that are based on jump processes rather than the standard diffusion processes that characterize many financial assets further complicates matters. Until these general pricing challenges are overcome, overall activity is likely to remain limited.

8.4.5   Regulatory barriers

One of the central impediments to growth in the OTC catastrophe derivative market relates to regulatory barriers that limit the type of business certain regulated entities can conduct. For instance, though insurers and reinsurers have benefited in recent years from deregulation measures (which is helping fuel the convergence we described in Chapter 7), many are still required to use separately capitalized subsidiaries to engage in derivative transactions.[6]

---

[6] This rule applies generically to all derivatives, including those based on interest rates, equities, currencies, credits, and catastrophe.

Similarly, banking institutions that are interested in hedging catastrophe derivatives by writing catastrophe insurance contracts must generally do so through separately owned and managed special entities, such as Bermuda transformers.[7] In both cases these regulatory rules create additional structural/organizational burdens and, more importantly, extra costs. When these additional costs are considered as part of a loss-financing strategy, a specific transaction may be less economically compelling than other risk management alternatives. Other forms of regulation can slow the pace of derivatives activity. For instance, accounting, legal, and tax treatment differences that appear between financial institutions and insurers/reinsurers can lead to arbitrage opportunities that drive business, but can also create valuation, interpretation, and accounting treatment differences that favor or prejudice particular types of transactions (e.g., a bank marks-to-market its derivative risks, an insurance company does not mark its insurance risks; a bank can trade derivatives on a secondary basis, an insurer cannot do the same with its policies; a bank uses specific legal forms (ISDA master agreement) to define and document its derivative transactions, an insurer uses its own proprietary insurance forms, and so on).

Catastrophe derivatives are still in an underdeveloped state, and have not begun to approach their potential in serving as useful risk management tools. That said, the outlook for derivatives in the loss-financing sector must be regarded as positive, particularly as the challenges noted above are overcome, and as other instruments of the catastrophe-based capital markets continue to expand.[8] It is worth stressing that the catastrophe derivatives will never become as widely used as other financial derivatives, as the core size of the catastrophe risk transfer market is much smaller than that of interest rates, currencies, equities, and credits. Nevertheless, such contracts have an important niche role to play in a marketplace that increasingly demands hedging capacity and profit opportunities.

---

[7] Class 3 Bermuda insurers are authorized to write and purchase insurance/reinsurance, and can covert insurance/reinsurance contracts into derivatives and vice versa. Since the transformer can buy/sell both classes of instruments and match obligations on each side, the process becomes transparent to the bank and insurer – each party can acquire or shed risk in the most efficient manner while adhering to appropriate rules and accounting conventions. The process is not inexpensive, however, and the extra costs can impact the economics of proposed transactions.

[8] It is important to recall that the credit derivative market, which has become very large and vibrant, took several years to establish. Though the underlying dynamics of the credit market are rather different, and the absolute size of the risk base is much larger, the market suffered from many of the same difficulties plaguing the catastrophe derivative market, e.g., one-sided markets, illiquidity, modeling complications, and so forth.

9

Public Sector Management and Financing

The catastrophe risk management solutions we have discussed in the past few chapters are driven by the private sector; voluntary loss controls and private loss-financing mechanisms allow catastrophic risks to be managed efficiently. And, while the solutions are obviously critical to effective risk management, they are not always sufficient. The public sector must play a role in the risk management process when private sector risk capital is insufficient, financial mechanisms are inadequate, loss controls are disregarded, or when centralized coordination can accomplish certain goals more efficiently. In this chapter we consider the primary responsibilities of the public sector in catastrophic risk management, including *ex ante* loss control measures, insurance/reinsurance programs, *ex post* crisis management, and post-loss financing and subsidies. We also consider a number of key challenges facing these public sector mechanisms.

9.1 FORMS OF PUBLIC SECTOR INVOLVEMENT

Individual nations, states, and municipalities use public sector mechanisms to varying degrees, depending on the nature of local practice, resources, and goals; nevertheless, virtually all locales that are exposed to disaster risk feature one or more of the processes we consider in this section. At a minimum government authorities often implement non-financial controls, such as prevention measures, crisis management programs, and financial regulations. Others may supplement these with loss-financing programs, including state-sponsored insurance/reinsurance and post-loss financing. Cross-border financial assistance is also quite common, with wealthier industrialized nations and supranational organizations assisting poorer nations via grants, subsidies, and soft loans.

9.1.1 *Ex ante* loss control measures

We recall from Chapter 5 that loss control is a key form of risk management. Companies, sovereigns, and individuals exposed to catastrophe risk can take basic steps to help reduce the likelihood and/or impact of financial loss in the event of disaster. While loss control measures are often voluntary, they may also be driven by minimum standards mandated by regulators or government authorities. Indeed, safety measures are so important in reducing the burden of post-loss financing that some believe government and supranational organizations should place even greater efforts on developing and enforcing proper *ex ante* prevention programs.

We have indicated that zoning, construction, and engineering techniques can reduce the probable maximum loss associated with a particular disaster. Though installing or retrofitting safety measures represents an upfront investment, the efforts are often cheaper than the costs associated with post-loss financing. Accordingly, the public sector is wise to encourage, and even mandate, the use of minimum structural and non-structural building codes. This approach is especially critical in developing nations that lack an effective insurance mechanism or risk

Table 9.1 Average insurance penetration for select perils/regions

Country	Peril	Average insurance penetration (%)
Holland	Flood	<10
Germany	Flood	<10
USA	Flood	<10
Japan	Earthquake	5
Italy	Earthquake	20
Mexico	Earthquake	10

capital base by which to transfer/fund losses. In addition to zoning and construction standards, public agencies may be responsible for developing and implementing *ex ante* warning systems that advise the local population center of an impending threat (e.g., hurricane, tsunami), allowing coordination of safety and evacuation plans; this can be seen as an important form of centralized government loss control.[1]

9.1.2 Insurance/reinsurance

As we have noted, insurance/reinsurance remains the single most important private sector mechanism for managing catastrophic risks. But techniques of insurance are not limited to the private sector. In some countries private sector insurance is supplemented by a pure national program or a private/public partnership; this is generally necessary when private sector insurance penetration is low (as noted in Table 9.1), private risk capital is lacking, or the risk community is too small to adequately spread the losses.[2]

Government involvement may also be necessary when a risk appears to be temporarily/permanently uninsurable (e.g., terrorism), the theoretical losses and capacity demand are too large for the private sector to handle on its own (e.g., Florida hurricane), the correlation between individual risk events is high and creates excessive concentrations (e.g., certain flood areas), or the availability of international insurance/reinsurance is unstable or unpredictable (e.g., hard market cycles). Government programs can be designed to provide exposed private parties (i.e., individuals, companies, or insurers) with supplemental insurance or reinsurance, or they may serve as the sole source of coverage if capacity is unavailable from the private sector. When public programs are properly structured they can fill an important void and should be regarded as supplemental rather than competitive. The ultimate goal of government involvement in loss financing is to ensure continued financial and economic stability within the local marketplace.

Government programs may be structured as direct insurance to cedants (i.e., agented by private insurers on behalf of the government and combined in risk pools for proper diversification and management), or reinsurance to insurers that are writing cover for cedants. Alternatively, a government may require private sector insurers to provide coverage to cedants in respect of certain peril coverages; to avoid skewing the risk profiles of insurers, the government may allow them to levy surcharges.

---

[1] Such warning systems cannot be used in all perils, of course; for instance, while there is often sufficient advance warning for tsunamis, hurricanes and extra-tropical cyclones, there typically is not for earthquakes or industrial accidents.

[2] Note that narrow local or state government programs have limited ability to diversify exposures as local/state claims are likely to be highly correlated in the event of a disaster. Federal/national programs are more effective in diversifying risk.

Consider, for instance, the case of French flooding and windstorm, two perils that have historically created significant damage throughout the country. Prior to 1982, private sector insurers were generally unwilling to supply meaningful coverage of either peril, and the public at large expected the government to provide restitution in the event of loss. The French government then passed a law requiring insurers writing non-life policies to include disaster coverage (allowing them to charge an incremental, albeit modest, premium for doing so). The law also permitted insurers to reinsure, on a discretionary basis, 40% to 90% of the catastrophic portion of the policy with the state reinsurance company Caisse Central de Reassurance (CCR).[3] Though the government can still supplement insurance payouts with special grants or subsidies, the system has proven effective, and continues to exist two decades after its formation.

Public programs can therefore be structured as stop loss insurance or reinsurance of last resort, ensuring that some minimum (and maximum) level of coverage is provided to cedants or ceding insurers. The choice of insurance versus reinsurance depends on the depth and sophistication of the local marketplace, the amount of available risk capital, and the ability of a system to attract international reinsurers or retrocessionaires.

Claims financing under such programs is generally a combination of retentions, reserves (accumulated through the levy of special surcharges on standard policy premiums), standard lines of credit,[4] contingent capital, and multiple XOL layers. The use of multiple layers is common as the costs associated with each layer decline as the probability of occurrence associated with each layer decreases (as in any standard risk/return trade-off); this can be seen by comparing the rate on line (a measure of the cost) versus probability of occurrence. A government program can also be established as a pool, grouping together all common risks in a single portfolio; retentions and reinsurance agreements can still be used, but the pool stands ready to absorb upper layer risks. For example, instead of developing a program with a 25% retention, 70% quota share, and 5% XOL layer, the program can be restructured to include a 25% retention, 30% quota share and 55% pool transfer. The pool, which acts as upper layer protection, may yield cheaper loss financing than the standard XOL structure. Figures 9.1 and 9.2 illustrate sample layers of protection that might be found in government insurance and reinsurance programs.

The issue of whether a government insurance program should be mandatory or voluntary is widely debated; both forms are used, though there is some belief that voluntary programs may not be sustainable in the long term as they may be too expensive to operate without a critical mass of risk transfer. Voluntary programs often rely heavily on initial government contributions or pre-funding via capital markets issues, with funds recouped through taxes or special assessments; mandatory programs allow capital to accumulate so that a proper surplus reserve can be funded over time.

When a government acts as an insurer/reinsurer it must protect against moral hazard, and can do so by establishing minimum best practice underwriting standards (just as any private sector insurer/reinsurer might do), as well as retentions, coinsurance, and caps. We can imagine a situation where an insurer in a state of financial distress assumes a great deal of additional risk since it knows that a 'bailout' mechanism exists; the insurer then faces two prospects: strong returns on the additional risk it writes if claims experience is favorable and an eventual return to a healthy state, or weak returns if claims experience is poor meaning almost certain collapse

---

[3] Note that CCR, which is responsible for providing reinsurance, setting premium rates, declaring catastrophes, and developing risk prevention measures, also operates the National Guarantee Fund, which provides crop protection for agricultural disasters.
[4] Lines of credit are commonly used, particularly when insufficient reinsurance capacity exists.

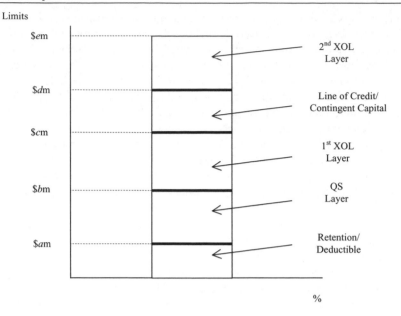

Figure 9.1   Government catastrophe insurance program

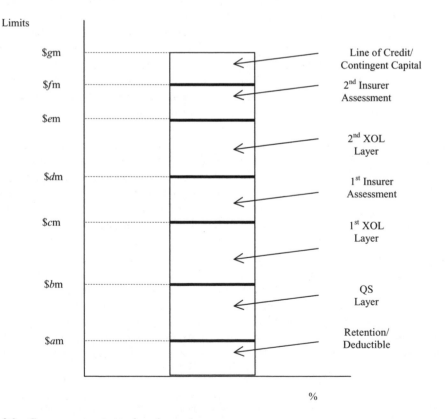

Figure 9.2   Government catastrophe reinsurance program

and bailout by the government. A government program may also reduce incentives for cedants to monitor the activities of private insurers. Furthermore, any program that ultimately provides individuals or businesses with financial assistance in the form of free or subsidized insurance eliminates incentives to enact loss control measures. Care must also be taken in the design stage to ensure proper coverage and pricing; if a government-sponsored insurance or reinsurance program underprices its capacity, it challenges private sector efforts; since these programs are intended to work in partnership with private sector mechanisms, aggressive pricing provides no specific benefit. In addition, programs that are pre-funded through the accumulation of premiums and/or reserves are an attractive source of government funds that can theoretically be applied to other programs or requirements; public sector insurance/reinsurance conduits should be ring-fenced so that assets can only be used to pay claims arising from the onset of a disaster. Indeed, some national programs are managed by independent parties that cannot be influenced by political forces to protect against this type of eventuality.

Since insurance/reinsurance functions on the basis of risk pooling, there may be instances when a government program is simply too small to achieve the necessary diversification; in addition, the costs associated with structuring and operating a program for a small base of participants may be unattractive. In such cases it may be advantageous for several countries with catastrophe exposures to create a joint regional pool;[5] this improves risk diversification possibilities and introduces economies of scale.

To illustrate how government insurance/reinsurance can function in practice we briefly review several sample programs.

9.1.2.1   USA: Flood

The USA has a long history of government-sponsored disaster relief dating back to 1803; more recent efforts are based on the Disaster Relief Act of 1950, which established a permanent relief fund and granted the executive branch broad discretion in declaring disasters. Subsequent amendments were created to address scope, subsidies, mitigation requirements, coordination, and so forth. The first significant program of the modern era was the National Flood Insurance Act of 1968, which resulted in the creation of the National Flood Insurance Program (NFIP) as a mechanism to provide individuals, companies, and communities with supplemental financial protection against flood risk (which may be uninsurable through private sector insurance mechanisms). NFIP provides insurance to property owners choosing to subscribe through payment of a premium; by writing coverage at a national level, NFIP is able to diversify its flood risk portfolio more effectively than a state or regional program. However, in order to protect against future losses, NFIP requires that communities develop ordinances that restrict new construction in high-risk floodplain areas, and that new construction meet minimum standards; if these requirements are not met, a community is not permitted to participate in the pool.

9.1.2.2   Hawaii: Hurricane

Hawaii was one of the first US states to develop a catastrophe insurance program. The catalyst for the state's Hawaii Hurricane Relief Fund (HHRF) was Hurricane Iniki, which battered the

---

[5] This is particularly true when the exposures are all somewhat unique, e.g., hurricane in one country, earthquake and volcanic eruption in a second country, and so forth. This can lead to lower expected losses in a given year and a more efficient use of scarce risk capital resources.

islands in 1993 and caused private insurers to begin canceling their coverage. Under the HHRF program insurers can write insurance cover with or without hurricane protection; those choosing not to offer their own cover must then make available to interested parties the HHRF policy attachment, which incorporates a 10% deductible and a policy cap. The HHRF's claims-paying ability is based on a combination of initial deductibles, retention by insurers participating in the program, reinsurance purchased directly by the fund, a letter of credit, and pro rata assessments on participating insurers, in that sequence. Although HHRF was originally intended to operate on a temporary basis (e.g., until the millennium, when private insurers were expected to return to the marketplace) it continues to exist, working in partnership with the private insurance sector.

9.1.2.3   Florida: Hurricane and windstorm

Following the devastation of Hurricane Andrew in 1992, commercial and residential property owners in the state of Florida faced an immediate insurance crisis: in order to strengthen their financial operations and rebalance their risk profiles, insurers sought significant premium rate increases and announced their plans to cancel a large number of policies. Though the state insurance regulator granted a portion of the rate increases, it limited the number of policies cancelable in a given year/region in order not to leave a significant amount of property owners uninsured (e.g., not more than 5% cancellation in one year, or 10% in a given county). It also required new insurers expanding within the state to write at least 20% of their business in hurricane-prone counties such as Dade, Broward, and Palm Beach. However, when it became clear that many policies would not be renewed over ensuing years, the state created the Residential Property and Casualty Joint Underwriters Association (RPCJUA) as an insurer of last resort (in fact, the program was modeled after a similar, though smaller, windstorm insurance effort created several years earlier, i.e., the Florida Windstorm Underwriters Association [FWUA], which provides insureds with coverage against windstorm damage in coastal areas; FWUA, a private association that pools risks in eligible areas, obtains its own coverage from reinsurance, a pre-funded bond, and a letter of credit). The state also developed the Hurricane Catastrophe Fund (HCF) as a mandatory reinsurance pool to provide coverage to private sector insurers; any insurer writing hurricane coverage in the state is required to purchase its reinsurance from the fund (though they have the option of selecting coverage levels, e.g., 45%, 75%, or 90%). HCF's claims-paying ability is funded through mandatory insurer premiums and emergency borrowing capacity. By the early part of the millennium HCF featured more than 260 participating insurers, suggesting some degree of success in drawing private sector insurers back to the Florida hurricane insurance market.[6]

9.1.2.4   California: Earthquake

California's experience with earthquake coverage parallels Florida's experience with hurricanes. Specifically, after insurers and reinsurers paid out claims for Northridge they began applying for rate increases and canceling policies; since the state requires insurers to offer earthquake cover with homeowners' policies, some insurers ceased writing business entirely. Realizing that severe underinsurance would result, the state limited the cancellation rate on

---

[6] Despite a decade of success in bringing private insurers back to the market the significant hurricane events of 2004 (e.g., four major landfalls in 6 weeks) caused some withdrawal and greater use of the RPCJUA.

existing policies and established the California Earthquake Authority (CEA) as a state-run, privately financed program to offer supplemental earthquake cover through local insurers. Under the program insurers writing homeowners' business in the state can offer their own policies or a CEA policy (covering each primary residence up to a stated maximum amount after a 15% deductible); CEA bears the resulting risk and meets claims through an insurer-contributed reserve, multiple layers of reinsurance, lines of credit, and excess insurer assessments. Despite the existence of private and public sector mechanisms, homeowner coverage against earthquake remains relatively modest, at only 20% statewide (select metropolitan areas are higher, e.g., 25–40%). The primary reasons for the low penetration include small maximum coverage amounts, exclusions of appurtenant structures, and relatively high premiums.

9.1.2.5   Japan: Earthquake

Japan created the Japan Earthquake Reinsurance Company (JER) in 1966 to reinsure private insurance companies providing primary earthquake insurance coverage to homeowners (on a voluntary basis). Under the terms of the program insurers can reinsure up to 100% of their earthquake policies with JER, which is fully backed by the government (JER also retrocedes a portion of its risk in the international reinsurance markets). Despite the existence of the program overall penetration is relatively low (10% nationally and less in specific urban centers), in part because of relatively high premiums and 50% coinsurance levels.

9.1.2.6   Turkey: Earthquake

Turkey has experienced many devastating earthquakes over the years. In order to cope with insufficient private sector loss financing the Turkish government established the Turkish Catastrophe Insurance Pool (TCIP) in 2000, requiring all registered property owners to purchase a minimum amount of earthquake cover from the pool. TCIP is based on the solidarity principle, where exposed parties in less vulnerable areas pay a higher relative premium to cover those residing in more vulnerable areas (e.g., a cross subsidy, which is generally only possible when coverage is mandatory).[7] Each standard policy provides up to $20 000 in coverage in exchange for a premium that varies by location, and is designed primarily to give small homeowners access to protection that would otherwise be unavailable to them. Local insurers distribute TCIP policies, and may provide additional coverage of their own, if they wish. Within 1 year of launch TCIP featured 2m subscribers, and has added more since that time; indeed, the success of the Turkish effort has caused other countries in the region with catastrophic exposures to consider similar measures (e.g., Greece, Algeria, Iran, India).

9.1.2.7   Global: Terrorism

Countries with a history of terrorist activity, such as the UK and Israel, developed government-sponsored terrorist insurance programs during the 1980s and 1990s to reinforce modest private sector efforts. For instance, the UK developed Pool Re in 1993 as a mutual reinsurer

---

[7] Note that in order to reduce the potentially negative effects of correlation, at least 50% of TCIP's assets must be invested outside of the Turkish market (under the assumption that a catastrophic local earthquake would cause local financial assets to plummet in value and leave the pool with insufficient funds to meet claims).

to cover losses from private insurers writing terrorism coverage; the need for this scheme became apparent following the increasingly significant terrorist activities carried out by the Irish Republican Army (which was responsible for many events, including the City of London/Dockland bombings of 1992 and 1993). Insurers now provide cedants with separate cover (e.g., independent of standard P&C policies, and charged at a percentage above P&C rates based on one of four locations) and cede any excess risk they do not wish to preserve to Pool Re, which is directly backed by the UK government; Pool Re effectively acts as a reinsurer of last resort. Israel created a similar state-backed program, the Property Tax and Compensation Fund, which covers losses triggered by politically motivated violence.

Prior to the events of 9/11, P&C fire insurance policies in many countries covered fire/explosion damage regardless of cause, except for war or civil commotion; apart from countries previously impacted by terrorism, coverage was not generally part of the war exclusion cause.[8] This meant that insurers and reinsurers writing cover against businesses affected by 9/11 were forced to pay out substantial claims. In the aftermath, many insurers and reinsurers cancelled their coverage (e.g., 45 US state regulators allowed insurers to drop terrorism coverage from policies), forcing alternate government solutions to be created – particularly in the USA, Canada, Germany, and France, which had never dealt with the matter in a comprehensive manner. Governments attempted to fill the insurance void as quickly as possible for both economic and political reasons.

For instance, in 2002 France established Gestion d'Assurance et Acts de Terrorisme (GARET), where primary insurers providing cover to French individuals/institutions cede to the GARET pool any covers related to terrorist-based property damage or business interruption in excess of €6m. The GARET pool provides coverage in layers: the first €250m is retained by participating insurers acting in unison, the next €750m is ceded to international reinsurers, the next €500m is guaranteed by the French Republic, and any excess is borne by the state-owned reinsurance company, CCR. In 2002 Germany created Extremus AG, a reinsurer owned by private German insurers and reinsurers that insures against terrorism risk directly through participating insurers. The program is voluntary (with minimum coverage of €25m) and premiums are based on the amount of coverage rather than the location of the property. Extremus' shareholders provide the first €1.5b of cover, international reinsurers the next €500m, and the German government the next €8b.

In late 2002 the USA signed into law the Terrorism Risk Insurance Act (TRIA), with an original expiry date of December 2004 (extendible to 2005 and perhaps longer). Under the terms of TRIA, the US government participates in damage coverage of terrorist acts as a reinsurer, meaning insurers must first make available terrorism cover to cedants. The process requires a violent and coercive act to be committed in the USA, on a US carrier, or a US carrier/mission abroad, and the overall insured loss across all lines of risk must exceed $5m. The government absorbs 90% of losses exceeding an insurer's retention, up to $100b per year, and reclaims the difference through policy surcharges.[9]

---

[8] For instance, US terrorism coverage was included as part of standard commercial P&C packages and as an unnamed peril in all-risk policies. Coverage remained intact even after the first World Trade Center bombing of 1993 as the country had been relatively terrorism-free; the Oklahoma City bombing of 1995 did little to change coverage as most physical destruction occurred on government property, meaning private insurers bore few of the losses.

[9] The insurance industry used catastrophe models to price risks under TRIA, dividing groups into high, medium, and low-risk tiers. Initial pricing of $0.10/$100 of property in the high-risk group (e.g., New York, Washington DC) was criticized by those who felt business would be driven away by the cost, and was eventually lowered by approximately two-thirds. Under the terms of TRIA insurers must disclose the specific price they are charging for the terrorism portion of their P&C coverage, injecting some degree of transparency into the process.

Approximately one year after TRIA was formed penetration remained at a relatively low 20% (33% for New York), primarily as a result of the costs (e.g., 20% more than a standard P&C policy), fading memories of 9/11, and growing belief that the probability of occurrence had declined with the creation of greater safety measures.[10]

The long-term outlook for government-sponsored terrorism coverage programs is uncertain. A central question hinges on whether terrorism fits the definition of an insurable risk as described in Chapter 6 – specifically, whether terrorism is quantifiable, sufficiently homogenous that it can be diversified, fortuitous, and transferable through the payment of an economically reasonable premium. If the risk is insurable, private sector mechanisms may ultimately play the dominant risk management role; if it is not, government intervention will be required on an ad hoc or permanent basis. In fact, some degree of state involvement is likely to persist over the medium term; national authorities can absorb extreme losses more easily than private sector institutions and can create mandatory requirements that allow accumulation of a larger amount of risks (which can then be diversified and covered by smaller premium payments). They can also impose permanent property surcharges that can be used to fund a terrorism fund reserve over time.

Government involvement is also consistent with public policy – since terrorism is a national problem, some argue that it should be handled by the public rather than solely or primarily by the shareholders of insurers, reinsurers, and other financial intermediaries.[11] In fact, a partnership between the private and public sector may emerge as the preferred model, with insurers/reinsures retaining some risk before ceding to national pools or state-sponsored reinsurers.

9.1.2.8   Other programs

Various other countries, regions, and states have created programs to focus on one or more catastrophic perils. For instance, New Zealand developed a program as early as 1944 to cover government-defined uninsurable risks, including earthquake, flood, tsunami, volcanic eruption, and hydrothermal activity. Spain established the Consorcio de Compensacion de Seguros (CCS) in 1941 to provide direct coverage of loss created by a range of natural disasters and socio-political events. The CCS is funded through mandatory premiums and a state guarantee. Direct insurance coverage from the CCS is obligatory for 'extraordinary risks' (indirect losses from business interruption are not covered and must be obtained from the private sector); policies generally have deductibles ranging from 10–15% and maximum policy caps that depend on the nature of the risk. The state of Texas established the Texas Windstorm Insurance Association (TWIA) in 1971 to provide wind and hail coverage to communities along the coast; the program resulted from various damaging hurricanes that made landfall during the 1960s. TWIA, structured as a P&C pool, provides approximately 20% of residential wind/hail coverage and 50% of seaward cover in the state and derives its claims-paying ability from assessments on pool insurers, the state-run Catastrophe Trust Fund, and various layers of reinsurance.

---

[10] In fact, such behavior appears to be consistent with the market for natural disaster coverage, with cedants purchasing insurance immediately after an event, and then allowing coverage to lapse as the time since the damaging event passes.

[11] In the extreme, if the private sector is unable to mobilize sufficient risk capacity to provide adequate coverage and the government cannot, or will not, provide proper pre- or post-loss financing mechanisms, individuals and companies may be forced to move from high-risk to lower-risk terrorist target zones (e.g., from downtown New York City to the outlying suburbs). This may be interpreted by terrorist groups as a successful outcome, and embolden them to attempt further disruption. It might be argued, then, that a government is responsible for providing adequate financing capacity so that terrorists are not seen as victorious. This particular characteristic is not, of course, found in natural catastrophes.

Naturally, not all government-sponsored programs are successful. Some are not structured properly and lead to adverse incentives (e.g., continued development in at-risk zones) and societal burdens (e.g., cross-subsidies between high- and low-risk areas), while others are simply too small or inefficient to provide a meaningful amount of protection. For instance, in the USA the Federal Crop Insurance Program is intended to provide the agricultural sector with protection against catastrophic crop damage from extreme heat, drought, rainfall, hail, severe frost, and so forth. The program is based on highly subsidized insurance policies that individual farmers can purchase on a voluntary basis. However, since the government can (and, in practice, does) make supplemental ad hoc payments to farmers suffering from the effects of damage, there is little incentive for farmers to purchase the subsidized insurance. The end result is a program with very high costs to taxpayers and very low subscription rates.

Note that many of the state/national programs described above are not structured to handle a mega-catastrophe that generates losses in the billions of dollars; limited financial risk capacity (even after considering the multiple layers that often characterize a program) means that direct federal/national government involvement may still be required.

9.1.3 *Ex post* crisis management

Crisis management is generally considered to be one of the primary functions of government or a centralized public authority. Properly structured, it permits coordinated action and reaction related to a catastrophic event, allowing resources to be allocated when/where necessary, emergency situations to be addressed as quickly as possible, and economic and social order to be restored as soon as practicable. Crisis management plans cannot be overly detailed; flexibility is generally desirable so that the emergency response can be 'tailored' to the specific characteristics of an event. That said, a plan must cover the essentials, including:

- Mobilization of security
- Enactment of search and rescue missions
- Allocation of health care resources and shelter
- Establishment of logistical support
- Restoration of public services
- Assessment of damages
- Communication of vital intra- and inter-region information

A typical 'chain of command' model, which may be overly rigid, can be replaced by a matrix of communication and coordination, giving regional or specialty sectors the autonomy to respond as required. Robust *ex post* crisis management can thus be seen as a collection of general *ex ante* plans and flexible response.

Many advanced and developing nations have crisis authorities that are responsible for creating pre-crisis plans and post-event relief. For instance, the USA started expanding federal disaster relief in the 1960s as industrialization and wealth levels outpaced the private sector's ability to cope with each new disaster. The government ultimately created the Federal Emergency Management Agency (FEMA) in 1978 to coordinate disaster programs and activities across government agencies. While FEMA now administers the flood program described earlier, its primary role is to ensure that economic and humanitarian relief is brought to bear quickly and efficiently in the aftermath of a disaster, and that local and state authorities commence reconstruction and repair efforts on a timely basis. Many other countries feature similar agencies, and the same efforts often exist at the supranational level.

9.1.4   Financing and subsidies

Post-loss financing and subsidies are a central focus of the public sector. While government financing occurs to some degree in all nations that are impacted by disasters, it is particularly prevalent in emerging nations. As we have already seen, industrialized nations generally feature sophisticated private (and public) insurance/reinsurance mechanisms and capital markets instruments, as well as large pools of risk capital; the need for direct government assistance is therefore comparatively small, except under extremely severe disasters.[12]

The same is not always true in developing nations: local insurance markets are generally in a very nascent state, and may be limited to the provision of very basic health and/or life coverage and non-catastrophic P&C cover; catastrophic risk insurance is often not available, even in countries that are heavily exposed to disasters.[13] Similarly, capital markets are often in a formative stage; they may only feature basic corporate bond and equity financing and are unlikely to be able to support derivative activity or insurance-linked securitization. In addition, the absolute amount of available risk capacity is often small. Local ability to provide catastrophe-based capital or hedging is therefore extremely limited (we consider the relative lack of market access in greater detail below).

Dearth of private sector loss financing in developing nations should not be surprising. In a system of finite resources, government authorities are more likely to deal with high frequency/low severity events and the health and welfare development priorities that are essential to daily living; low frequency/high severity events may be a secondary priority (even though in countries such as Mexico, Bangladesh, Indonesia, and the Philippines the incidence of disasters and the size of losses seem periodically to dominate the government's agenda). Accordingly, many of these developing nations cope with the financial burden of disasters by relying on international aid, grants, and subsidies from industrialized nations and supranational organizations.[14]

Facilities may be structured as outright grants, subsidies, or 'soft loans' with very long maturities and little or no interest charges.[15] Note that in certain instances aid is specifically linked to the implementation of loss controls in order to reduce the impact of future events; these linkages may or may not be successful – much depends on the commitment of the receiving government and the monitoring capabilities of the donor organization. In addition to grants and loans supranational organizations, such as the World Bank and International Finance Corporation (IFC), support post-loss financing mechanisms through contingent credit facilities used to finance catastrophic layers of national reinsurance programs placed by government or

---

[12] This is particularly true when disasters impact large population centers and create social dislocations, or when agricultural production is disrupted and food supplies are threatened, e.g., even industrialized nations with well-established private insurance mechanisms, such as the USA, Belgium, France, Australia, Denmark, and Germany, routinely supply their agricultural sectors with disaster funds, free insurance coverage, and/or ad hoc restitution in the aftermath of a catastrophe. Direct public assistance also tends to occur in the aftermath of earthquakes; while all perils can be costly, the structural damage associated with ground movement is often so significant that many are left without shelter or transportation, meaning government funding and assistance becomes especially critical. For instance, the US government provided approximately $12b in federal disaster funding following Northridge.

[13] Consider, for instance, that catastrophe-prone South Asia accounts for approximately 20% of the world's population, but less than 0.5% of global P&C insurance premiums, and even less of catastrophic P&C premiums.

[14] Naturally, some emerging nations have sufficient resources to help finance a portion of their own post-crisis requirements and may choose to establish dedicated funds in support of the effort. If these are to form part of the *ex post* risk management process, however, they must be available when needed. Consider, for instance, Mexico's FONDEN fund, a post-loss relief conduit that is responsible for financing/subsidizing disaster reconstruction (though, curiously, not for helping transfer risk exposures); while its theoretical role is vital and well intended, it has routinely suffered from a shortfall in resources from 1996 through the millennium. Resource availability in times of crisis is thus questionable.

[15] For instance, the World Bank provided $7.5b in post-loss grants and loan financing from the early 1980s into the millennium. It also developed the Disaster Management Facility in 1998 to provide cross-border coordination of disaster prevention/mitigation to reinforce the concept of loss control.

private sector insurers, or through guarantees of specific capital markets issues. While all of these financial infusions are important, there is evidence to suggest that in some instances recipients allocate resources inefficiently or erroneously.

Over the medium term developing nations that are at risk to disaster must consider mechanisms for pre-funding disaster reserves. By doing so they reduce the deadweight costs of post-event borrowing or the reallocation of capital funds from other planned investments that can create a slowdown in economic growth.

In some instances local, state, or federal governments assume direct responsibility for financing and repairing damaged public infrastructure, including roadways, government buildings, schools, hospitals, communications centers, and transportation facilities (e.g., in the USA, the Department of Transportation is responsible for much of the country's transportation infrastructure). Since infrastructure is part of the public domain and typically managed by government authorities, it is logical that financing of any damage be a government responsibility. In practice, such federal and state programs are often funded through taxes and intertemporal deficit financing, suggesting some amount of the loss burden is borne by future generations of taxpayers.

Current realities of catastrophe, vulnerabilities, and national resources mean that public sector institutions are periodically required to subsidize a certain amount of losses for those that have suffered from a disaster. This is unlikely to be an optimal solution over the long term as it essentially means that individual and corporate taxpayers, rather than risk capital investors, are responsible for covering losses. However, until more sources of risk capacity are available across perils and regions, such mechanisms are likely to remain in place.

9.1.5 Financial regulation

Government authorities often regulate intermediaries involved in the provision of risk management services; this can help ensure all parties are treated equitably. While those operating in free market economies tend to prefer a minimum of regulation, certain standards related to catastrophe risk can be regarded as beneficial – this is particularly true since the sector suffers from lack of comprehensive loss and exposure data and relies on complex modeling efforts to generate loss estimates and minimum capital levels. Supervisory requirements may be based on:

- Common data standards related to property, damage, building codes.
- Model assumptions and back testing.
- Standardized insurance/reinsurance/derivative terms and conditions (consistent with rules and legislation).
- Maximum insurance/reinsurance retention levels.
- Minimum solvency/capital standards for suppliers of risk capacity.

Such financial regulations are intended primarily to reinforce prevention and private sector loss-financing measures, and ensure that exposed parties are adequately protected. Since public sector authorities are often the only ones that can properly enact and police such regulations (apart from a limited number of self-regulating organizations), the responsibility belongs to the government.

9.2   CHALLENGES

The public sector clearly has an important role – and some might argue duty – to play in the catastrophic risk management process. Nevertheless, government involvement gives rise to certain challenges, including voluntary versus mandatory measures, public and private sector responsibilities, and lack of market access.

9.2.1   Voluntary versus mandatory measures

One of the key challenges facing public sector officials is determining whether a risk management guideline should be voluntary or mandatory. Measures that are strictly voluntary reduce government intervention and upfront enforcement costs. However, such measures may have limited effect and may create greater *ex post* costs (e.g., through subsidies or loans to affected parties). Measures that are mandated via formal regulation or law must be enforced: while the *ex post* costs may decline (to the extent enforcement is effective), the cost of administering and monitoring the measures increases. In addition, government intervention in the daily affairs of the private sector grows, a feature many believe to be a disadvantage.

Consider, for instance, the creation of stringent building codes designed to protect commercial and residential structures from catastrophic damage. If the building codes are voluntary, developers and builders may ignore them, as the extra costs involved may make projects economically unfeasible. This means standards will remain unchanged, suggesting that private sector risk intermediaries and the public sector (i.e., taxpayers) will absorb any loss-making event. If the codes become mandatory (under the argument that those occupying a building, as well as those in proximate buildings that might be affected by a neighboring collapse, will be safe), development may be slowed, halted, or moved to other locations that feature more 'flexible' alternatives. In addition, though post-disaster costs will decline, the expenses associated with reviewing building plans and inspecting on-site developments will increase. The optimal approach is not immediately apparent, and may actually be situation-specific. Some compromise solution may be found in providing modest financial credit for those adhering to the standards, though this again represents a cost. It is relatively simple to extend the same analysis to the retrofit of existing structures to meet new voluntary standards. Some studies suggest that property owners are unwilling to retrofit structures, even if they are located in high-risk areas, as it is difficult to justify spending incremental funds to protect against a low probability event. Forcing retrofits may create an unmanageable economic burden for some property owners, regardless of the potential *ex post* benefits. Similar arguments can be made for the purchase of insurance for those residing or operating in a high-risk area. Requiring homeowners or companies that occupy buildings in a fault zone, floodplain, or storm surge area to purchase a minimum level of private insurance protection is a possible solution; forcing public entities to purchase coverage from the private sector can reinforce the role of private insurers. However, these actions may simply force migration to locations without any requirements. Simply recommending the purchase of insurance, or even offering some amount of insurance at a subsidized price, may not create a critical mass of participation.

Another source of mandatory versus voluntary involvement relates to insurance rate-making. In some countries regulators require a state or national insurance regulator to approve premiums for non-catastrophic and catastrophic cover. The intent is to ensure that ceding individuals and companies are not forced to pay egregious sums for the purchase of essential cover. While this can be a relatively straightforward process for high frequency/low severity risks (which, as we have noted, can be estimated with a reasonable amount of precision through actuarial processes), it may be less clear for catastrophic risks. We know from our previous discussion the difficulties that can arise in pricing catastrophic insurance cover; in some cases a conservative pricing level may be difficult to justify or defend, meaning that a mandatory review and approval may not result in an equitable decision. While an insurer may be able to justify a particular rate based on its risk modeling, a regulator may feel proposed price increases are politically unacceptable; this may benefit cedants in the short term, but can undermine the process in the medium term as insurers may ultimately be unwilling to write cover at 'subsidized' rates. This is particularly true when regulators require insurers to preserve minimum solvency ratios; if an insurer cannot price its risk at a fair premium it will be unable to justify the use of capital and adhere to solvency requirements, and will simply curtail high severity/low frequency business. Conversely, a voluntary rate review process does little to protect cedants from potential price gouging by insurers. In such cases cedants requiring cover have no recourse or alternative, and must pay the stated price for protection. The ultimate solution may be a mandatory process that allows insurers to levy the premiums they regard as fair if they can properly justify their requirements through robust modeling; indeed, as modeling techniques continue to evolve, justification of rate-making should improve. Insurance regulators that devote resources to understanding and analyzing the modeling process (in light of both historical experience and simulation activities) may be well positioned to make equitable decisions (e.g., in Florida, the Commission on Hurricane Loss Projection Methodology is actively involved in evaluating the accuracy of models and the fairness of pricing).

9.2.2 Public and private sector responsibilities

Public sector officials must consider the optimal level of government involvement in disaster risk management, and how public sector initiatives should interact with those created by the private sector. This is a complex issue that typically depends on the specific characteristics of a national jurisdiction, its social forces, financial intermediation capabilities, and economic resources. In general, however, we observe that in many countries private insurance/financial intermediation is used to protect private property and private sector enterprise, while public support is used to protect public property (e.g., hospitals, schools, roadways) as well as private property exposed to flood and other uninsurable risks. When proper private sector mechanisms are lacking or inadequate (as in certain developing nations), the public sector generally assumes a larger role, until private mechanisms can be developed (a process that may take years or decades to achieve). While this is an 'ideal' mix of responsibilities, in practice the process is much more challenging. Consider, for instance, a situation where a fully developed private sector risk function exists, but experience with specific natural or man-made disasters leaves insurers/reinsurers and other intermediaries unwilling to provide risk protection (either through outright refusal to supply new cover, lapse/cancellation of existing cover, or excessively large charges on new cover). This is not, of course, a theoretical argument, but one that appears in practice (e.g., terrorism coverage post-9/11, hurricane coverage post-Andrew). The government may choose to intervene by limiting the price that capacity providers can charge, or limiting the amount of cover they can cancel or withdraw. Such government involvement may be seen as unacceptable in a free market context. Alternatively, the government may let risk capacity providers withdraw and attempt to substitute through use of a government-sponsored loss-financing program of its own. This, of course, may place an additional burden on local taxpayers, who have to fund future losses if a sufficient reserve is lacking. Creation of a temporary or permanent industry-wide XOL cover (based on a recognized index) to diversify and finance risk intertemporally may be one solution; such an overarching policy could provide cover even if private sector mechanisms are not active. While theoretically interesting it, too, has several potential drawbacks (e.g., selection of a proper index, containment of moral hazard risks, excessive government intervention).

There may also be instances where the public and private sector must agree on the degree to which a risk is uninsurable. Since insurance can only function when an exposure is deemed to be insurable, government involvement may increase temporarily or permanently in the aftermath of a crisis that creates risk that is uninsurable. This definition can obviously change over time, as the dynamics of a risk change. For instance, in the aftermath of the 9/11 attacks, terrorism was deemed by the insurance/reinsurance industry to be uninsurable and coverage was withdrawn. In the USA, this necessitated government involvement and creation of TRIA for a period of several years. Two years after the attack the private sector began considering the risk insurable, leading to a gradual curtailment of government involvement (for a time, at any rate). Of course, some risks are considered to be uninsurable, meaning government involvement can become semi-permanent; this is true in many countries of flood risk.

9.2.3   Lack of market access and capacity

Perhaps the greatest challenge facing public sector authorities in some countries is lack of reliable access to pre- and post-loss financing mechanisms. We have noted above the relatively small role insurance/reinsurance and capital markets solutions play in providing loss financing to those located in peril-prone emerging nations; far greater reliance has historically been placed on international financial assistance and/or reallocation of internal investment resources. While this has been a manageable, if rather cumbersome, way of coping with the economic effects of disaster, it will become more difficult as population, urban migration, and local asset values continue to rise. As vulnerabilities expand, each new catastrophe becomes a larger financial burden, and finite resources and lack of access to essential risk management tools create the potential for significant shortfalls. Government authorities in these nations must be prepared to aggressively seek access to insurance/reinsurance and/or capital markets financing on a regular basis. Though access can theoretically be arranged at a corporate level, the effort may be more effective at the sovereign level; this suggests the creation of government-sponsored insurance programs such as those mentioned above, which can then be reinsured at a macro level by the government in the professional market. Similar access can be created within the capital markets sphere. Stronger market access may also be possible through local deregulation measures. Emerging nations that are willing to allow international insurers and financial intermediaries to offer loss-financing solutions may create a competitive environment where local and international institutions can supply the risk and financing capacity that is so vital to proper risk management.

An associated point relates to volatility of access. There are instances where small nations (e.g., Caribbean nations) are able to arrange for adequate levels of catastrophic insurance coverage when international risk capacity is in strong supply and premium rates are relatively low. However, capacity can become constrained when an excess of global claims occurs; smaller nations may feel the effects directly (withdrawal of direct insurance cover) or indirectly (curtailment of reinsurance capacity); at a minimum they may be faced with higher premium rates.[16]

Indeed, when the international markets are unstable, the effects on smaller markets are often magnified. Accordingly, access can be regarded as uncertain: it may exist for a period of time when general market conditions are strong, but vanish in the aftermath of disasters and the start of a hard market cycle. The long-term solution may lie in the development of a base of local private capital that can be deployed to assist in the pre- and post-loss financing effort.

Though public sector assistance and guidance is essential for all nations (particularly for risks that are temporarily/permanently uninsurable, or where devastation is so large that short-term financial assistance is essential), it is clearly most important for countries that are in an emerging state and at risk to one or more perils. Countries that are financially vulnerable to the effects of catastrophe must take certain minimum actions to ensure that their populations and economies are adequately covered. Ideally, developing nations should follow a program that includes safety education, basic loss control techniques in dwellings and commercial structures, and essential (and possibly subsidized) insurance coverage (e.g., the government as provider of insurance to property owners, with the resulting exposures ceded in the international reinsurance market).

Lack of capacity surfaces as another potential challenge. As noted, though most public sector programs are structured to provide adequate financial coverage for small to medium catastrophic losses, few are equipped to handle a mega-catastrophe. The growing level of vulnerabilities simply sets the stage for a devastating amount of losses; even the onset of two moderately large events at approximately the same time may be sufficient to create serious financial strains in both industrialized and developing nations. This problem will continue to grow as vulnerabilities expand, and can only be resolved through simultaneous use of multiple mechanisms: public funding, private sector insurance/reinsurance, and deep capital markets access. Unfortunately, not all of these elements are in a desired state of readiness. Such efforts must also be accompanied by a greater focus on vulnerabilities; government authorities must be much stricter about enforcing development regulations and/or insisting on mandated coverage.

---

[16] Consider, for instance, that during the mid-1990s several Caribbean nations faced premium rates that were two to three times higher than usual as a result of capacity constraints.

10

Outlook and Conclusions

Anecdotal and empirical evidence suggests that individuals, companies, and sovereigns are becoming more sensitive to the social and economic effects of catastrophe. The growing size of losses, which is a direct result of increased vulnerabilities, along with more intensive media coverage, have sensitized larger segments of the population to the potential consequences of earthquake, hurricane, windstorm, terrorism, industrial accidents, and other disasters. Ultimately, this awareness should help strengthen the risk management effort. As we conclude our work we summarize aspects of the discussion by focusing on future challenges and how these may influence risk management activity; we consider several themes, including loss control, quantification, loss financing, government participation, and general management.

10.1 LOSS CONTROL

10.1.1 Loss control implementation

Loss control measures must be seen as the essential first step in the management of catastrophe risk. Any individual, company, or nation that enacts basic safety and loss prevention measures helps preserve value in the event of a disaster. To be sure, loss control measures demand an investment of time and economic resources, but the final result is often justified in the aftermath of a damaging event; as a reminder of the importance of loss control we note again that an estimated 25% of the losses associated with Hurricane Andrew could have been avoided by simple building code compliance. While progress has been made in this area, use and acceptance are far from uniform. Stronger efforts to broaden the use of mitigants must be undertaken by government authorities, lenders, insurers, and developers; this is particularly vital in emerging nations, which lack a strong loss control discipline or loss-financing mechanisms/risk capital, and feature very significant vulnerabilities.

It is also important to consider the reactive nature of loss control policies. In many instances loss controls are imposed in the aftermath of a disaster, meaning some degree of human and economic damage must first be sustained. Loss control methods must become more anticipatory or proactive in order to minimize human and economic costs, as we note in greater detail below; thoroughly examining the lessons of history prior to the onset of the next major natural or man-made catastrophe is likely to be the best solution towards implementation of 'forward thinking' loss control solutions.

10.1.2 Enforcing urban planning

We have noted that techniques of avoidance and resistance can dramatically reduce vulnerabilities and loss levels, particularly in developed urban areas. Urban planning, based on non-structural and structural rules/guidelines, is central to the process. While formal urban planning exists in many industrialized nations it does not exist or is widely ignored in many emerging nations; indeed, illegal squatter settlements, inferior construction materials, and lack of building standards place lives and infrastructure at risk. Ultimately, uncontrolled growth in spreading metropolitan areas increases vulnerabilities and places an enormous financial strain on national resources when events strike. Accordingly, enforcement of minimum urban planning standards is a necessity. If a government is providing loss financing on a direct or indirect basis (e.g., through subsidized insurance or reinsurance programs or outright grants), it has the authority to demand behavioral reform and should be prepared to exercise such authority. If this does not occur as a matter of priority, the economic and social costs in some regions may become untenable.

10.2   QUANTIFICATION

10.2.1   Modeling requirements

The quantification effort has progressed dramatically over the past two decades. Analytic firms and intermediaries have diligently refined and updated their methodologies with each new event, improved the quality of data collection and granularity, and extended frameworks to cover other natural and man-made catastrophes such as tornadoes and terrorism. Risk assessment has improved with scientific and engineering advances, and computing power has allowed the implementation of more comprehensive and realistic simulation routines. However, the effort is not yet complete. Analytic firms and intermediaries, working in concert with government authorities, must strive to obtain even more accurate and granular vulnerability data (particularly in emerging nations). They must also continue to partner with scientists, engineers, and industry experts to obtain better scientific, behavioral, and geopolitical inputs in order to create even more accurate modeling platforms. Limitations will always exist, of course. Models are not predictive and a 'black box' capable of anticipating the relative location, magnitude, and time of the next extra-tropical cyclone, flood, or terrorist attack is simply not a realistic goal; this must be well understood by all participants. But if models can be refined to yield more accurate loss exceedance curves and associated risk management output, then they will allow for better risk management actions.

10.2.2   Transparency

Considerable benefits can be derived from injecting transparency into the catastrophe modeling process. While most modeling efforts developed by analytics firms and intermediaries are based on proprietary information/intellectual property, the community of stakeholders would be better served by making the quantification process as transparent as possible. This approach has worked to good effect with many aspects of financial risk modeling, where detailed methodologies are widely publicized in order to create a base of understanding and interest, but where sufficient proprietary information is retained in order to preserve the necessary competitive advantages. In general, the world of catastrophe risk still suffers from an excess of opacity; this relates equally to insurance, reinsurance, and capital markets solutions, where modeling details are typically only made available to very proximate stakeholders (e.g., rating agencies, third-party clients, and regulators). Greater transparency, short of disclosing very proprietary information, could help promote understanding among a base of potential users, which would ultimately foster more participation.

10.2.3   Complexity of terrorism

We have noted at several points the unique characteristics of terrorism. Unlike natural disasters, which are governed by the laws of science and nature, terrorism deals with the unpredictable qualities of human nature. And, unlike natural disasters and industrial accidents that face spatial and/or temporal boundaries, terrorist groups can choose to strike an almost limitless number of targets at any time. While it might be argued that 'high-value' targets that do the most damage are the real threats and are actually quite limited in number, a change in mindset or *modus operandi* to strike unexpected, or low-value, targets alters the dynamic considerably. Together, these elements make potential threats more difficult to identify, model, and manage – suggesting that the possibility of damage and losses is extremely unpredictable.

The realities of the 21st century indicate that the terrorist threat is likely to impact any part of the world at any time; the resulting damage may be direct (e.g., loss of life, destruction of property) or indirect (e.g., social instability leading to interruption of activities, business). Modeling cannot underestimate this dynamism. While efforts have rightly been placed on magnitude rather than frequency or location, caution must be taken in refining models to the next step. Developing analytics that attempt to generate information about frequency or location may be overly simplistic, and may actually create a false sense of comfort.

10.3   LOSS FINANCING

10.3.1   Vulnerabilities and risk capacity

Vulnerabilities are clearly on the rise. The growth in global population, urban densities, and asset values means that potential social and economic losses are greater than ever before. Importantly, the trend is likely to continue. Growth in vulnerabilities means, of course, that sufficient risk capacity must be made available to protect against financial loss. It is worth remembering that finite capital resources must be used for all exposures: not just the catastrophic risks we have covered in this book, but the much more prevalent non-catastrophic risks that affect daily activities. This suggests that deeper access to the institutional capital markets is imperative. The insurance and reinsurance markets cannot absorb all requirements on their own; public sector programs must be added to provide additional support, but the ultimate medium-term solution rests with the enormous pools of capital that investors already allocate to non-catastrophic risks.

The application of capital markets solutions to catastrophic risk is in a formative stage. We have noted that the first catastrophe bonds appeared as recently as 1997 and issuance has averaged approximately $1–1.5b per year since then (though structures are becoming more innovative); contingent capital and catastrophe derivatives have emerged only gradually as alternative risk transfer mechanisms. Issues related to cost, transparency, design, and regulation must be resolved to bring these instruments to the forefront. Given the overall size of the global capital markets and rapidly expanding vulnerabilities, there can be little doubt that these instruments will play an increasingly important role. Indeed, as mechanisms such as catastrophe bonds become more widely accepted in the portfolios of investment managers (and as greater familiarity is gained with modeling processes), it is likely that select instruments will join the mainstream of the capital markets. It is possible to conceive of a point in the medium term where insurers act as the primary originators of catastrophic risk and then transfer the bulk of their exposures to the capital markets, distintermediating reinsurers from their traditional role. Alternatively, insurers may continue to pass precise catastrophe exposures to reinsurers, who may then transfer risk to capital markets investors via index-linked securities (so retaining a certain amount of basis risk).

Though various risk management techniques are available (both theoretically and practically), the specter of potentially enormous losses from one or two mega-catastrophes means that new sources of risk capacity must be developed on a continuous basis. This is a critical point, but one that tends to be ignored when a mega-catastrophe has failed to appear for a period of time. Only when a significant financial disaster strikes might the system discover that it lacks sufficient capacity – leading to upward pressure on prices and a worsening of the cost/benefit proposition for end-users. Foresight in the development of alternative capacity is essential.

10.3.2   Discriminatory funding and insurance

Banks and insurers are central to post-loss financing of commercial and residential properties and other valuable assets. Without support from the financial sector development would undoubtedly be slowed, perhaps dramatically. That said, banks and insurers have historically done a poor job in limiting funding and insurance coverage of properties and assets located in hazard-prone areas – meaning that their actions contribute directly to the accumulation of vulnerabilities. Banks that are willing to fund property developments on a hurricane-exposed coast, or insurers that agree to provide catastrophic covers against damage in the floodplain, are encouraging developers and property owners to build and purchase such properties – increasing vulnerabilities and potential losses for bank and/or insurer investors (and, in more extreme cases, taxpayers). Since these intermediaries have a crucial role to perform in expanding development, they must be more diligent in redirecting resources away from the most hazard-prone areas; at a minimum they must require borrowers/cedants to apply more stringent loss control measures before supplying financing and insurance cover.

10.4   GOVERNMENT PARTICIPATION

10.4.1   Optimal government role

The optimal nature and extent of a government's involvement in catastrophic loss financing is still widely debated, and there appears to be no single 'correct' answer to the issue – much depends on the specific economic, regulatory, and social status of individual nations. Emerging nations lacking the sophisticated insurance and capital markets mechanisms we have discussed in Part II require significant government involvement. This can take a variety of forms, including government-sponsored catastrophe insurance/reinsurance, subsidized premiums or premium rebates, and direct subsidies (as well as education and risk mitigation incentives from a loss control perspective). Government participation must also exist in nations with advanced mechanisms attempting to cope with temporarily/permanently uninsurable risks or mega-catastrophes.

In the main, however, the ultimate goal for all nations might indeed be a focused role for the public sector; this ultimately reduces taxpayer burdens and limits government involvement in private activities. In a deregulated, free market economy with proper capital allocation mechanisms and sufficient capital, the private sector should be able to accommodate loss-financing needs, and innovate when risk capital appears to be in short supply. Over time the government's role in loss financing should be reduced to special circumstances where risks cannot be managed solely by private sector mechanisms, i.e., a mega-catastrophe, or where significant public policy interests exist, e.g., terrorism, nuclear contamination.

10.4.2   Limited government resources

As the world's population continues to expand, economic resources/assets grow in value and associated vulnerabilities increase; it is therefore important to consider the reasonable and rational limits of government participation in post-loss crisis management and financing. In the aftermath of a serious catastrophe, a government may find itself unable to provide all of the social and economic support that is required to overcome dislocations and place economic growth back on track. It is easy to note the considerable strains that can occur with the onset of any single large catastrophe (e.g., the Kobe earthquake, 9/11 terrorist attacks, the Indonesian tsunami). It is therefore not too difficult to project what might occur in the face of two or more relatively large events occurring at approximately the same time: financial losses would place an enormous stress on the local and national economies, social disruption would almost certainly intensify as a result of lack of basic resources and shelter, existing financial/investment plans would be disrupted, and so forth. Governments need to consider the potential consequences of resource scarcity and plan accordingly; this is best done by incorporating extreme scenarios in loss control rules and crisis management plans. Possible solutions include easing the burden on vulnerable areas by limiting expansion, ensuring that robust loss mitigants are in place, making certain that sufficient (discriminating) risk financing is available, and ensuring that taxing/borrowing mechanisms allow for additional emergency fund raising. National emergency/crisis management centers must create actionable social programs and authorities must be prepared to reallocate financial resources from discretionary sources on relatively short notice when true emergencies appear. Since even these activities may not be sufficient to overcome a devastating strike, national governments must consider formal ways of pooling knowledge and resources to assist one another in times of severe need. Such cooperative cross-border arrangements, formalized in advance of any crisis, can cover a broad range of areas, from loss financing/capital allocation to post-event disaster relief. Plans to access temporary capital from supranational organizations should also be developed.

10.4.3   Adverse incentives

We have noted in the last chapter the very important role that the public sector plays in financing catastrophic risk losses. In some countries the government remains the single most important source of post-loss financing and therefore performs a vital function. However, this role can also create adverse incentives and place private sector risk suppliers at a disadvantage. A government that provides its citizens and/or corporate sector with post-loss financing for free (or at heavily subsidized rates) creates at least two effects: it encourages individuals and companies to develop or undertake activities in at-risk areas, and it discourages them from implementing loss mitigation/financing measures. To overcome this challenge, governments must consider alternative approaches, such as enforcing urban planning measures more strictly, granting a greater percentage of aid to those pursuing development in lower-risk areas, requiring implementation of minimum safety controls, or mandating the purchase of a minimum level of insurance; by doing so, some adverse incentives will be removed. In addition, such actions can create greater business opportunities for private sector risk capital providers.

10.4.4   Market deregulation

Deregulation of institutions, markets, and mechanisms that can be used to transfer, reduce, or hedge catastrophic risks must be seen as an imperative for global regulators. Since active risk management through efficient solutions is still the best way of coping with catastrophe, regulators must encourage the private sector to mobilize capital and create solutions that can absorb exposures. For instance, we have noted that insurance penetration in some hazard-prone countries is relatively low (e.g., Japan, Korea, Taiwan, Mexico). Some of this is due to local legislation that limits the amount of cover that can be provided for particular perils, while some is due to restrictions placed on foreign insurers, reinsurers, and other intermediaries seeking to do business in the country (e.g., in some national systems three or four domestic insurers control more than 80% of the insurance/reinsurance market).[1] In order to help expand insurance density, deregulation measures, such as those that loosen domestic caps and increase foreign insurer access, should be implemented.[2] These actions can provide much needed risk capacity, and create price competition that results in lower premiums and fees for those seeking coverage. They can also lead to the development of new products, such as 'standalone' catastrophe insurance that can be purchased separately from other P&C or liability coverage (rather than as part of a more expensive package). All of these factors ultimately help individuals and companies exposed to catastrophe cope with their risks efficiently.

The same is applicable across industries. We have noted that regulations often prevent insurers and banks from engaging in one another's businesses (or, where they are not specifically barred, still require use of cumbersome and expensive structural enhancements, e.g., dedicated, capital-intensive, subsidiaries); this means risk capacity may be confined to a single sector, or the costs of accessing capacity may be prohibitive. Deregulation of these barriers should be considered as a matter of priority so that growing vulnerabilities can be transferred across sectors efficiently.

10.5   GENERAL MANAGEMENT

10.5.1   Sub-optimal management

Some catastrophe exposure is almost certainly not being managed optimally, despite the availability of various private sector mechanisms. Many firms choose to retain portions of their high severity/low frequency risks, either unknowingly or as part of a total capital program that combines all risks in a self-insurance scheme. This high level of catastrophe risk retention is contradictory, as the very risks that have the potential of creating a situation of financial distress remain on the corporate balance sheet. In addition, government-supported programs encourage risk-taking at public expense; de facto subsidies through cheaper premiums or post-loss 'bailouts' lead to excessive risk-taking. These management approaches appear to be the result of perceived costs of protection, relative infrequency of events, and knowledge that the government stands ready to assist in times of need. Optimal risk management through one or more of the techniques we have described in the book can only be accomplished through proper

---

[1] Indeed, in some national systems the control of market share is still a valued factor, regardless of the profitability of the business; this means that insurers/reinsurers that remain focused on market share in an environment where margins continue to compress may be underpricing their risks, including those of a catastrophic nature. The end result may be an increased incidence of financial distress. National systems that are driven by profitability and enterprise value creation rather than market share may be better placed to avoid problems.

[2] These can be supplemented by domestic measures that limit the ability of domestic insurers to underprice their business in order to retain market share, e.g., smoothing earnings, manipulating reserves, and so forth.

education and transparency, and through enforcement of government rules that discourage the creation of vulnerabilities in at-risk zones.

10.5.2 Sustainability of solutions

Government authorities are sometimes tempted to enact *ex post* solutions to address perceived problems/shortcomings in the aftermath of a disaster. While this may be a natural, and well-intended, reaction, it is vital to consider whether such responses are truly sustainable over the long term. For instance, in the wake of a terrorist act, authorities may increase military resources, intensify the public display of law and order, and suspend civil liberties for a period of time. These must only be seen as temporary actions, however, as they cannot (and perhaps should not) be maintained over the long term.

Knowing this, it is interesting to speculate on whether they are truly useful. If such actions simply serve to calm psychological fears of the public, then they may indeed have some use; however, if they are intended to dissuade or prevent future attacks – that is, lower the frequency of occurrence – then they may be of very limited use, as terrorists will simply wait until the temporary fears wane and the operating environment returns to its pre-attack state.[3] The same might apply to the creation of new safety standards in the aftermath of an industrial disaster, enactment of a new fuel-burning policy in the wake of a large forest fire, and so forth. It is important to investigate whether loss control measures taken in response to the latest occurrence are relevant in preventing, mitigating, or managing future events – if not, the time and costs may not be justifiable.

10.5.3 Preparing for the mega-catastrophe

The specter of the mega-catastrophe looms large, and most experts agree that it is simply a question of time before an event of tremendous force impacts society and a national, or even global, economy. It is obviously impossible to know precisely when and where such an event might occur, but the probability of having to cope with an event of $100b+ grows with the passage of time. Fundamentally, managing through such a process will demand the *ex ante* and *ex post* efforts and resources of both the private and public sectors. Preliminary discussion and preparation on how countries or regions might manage through such a crisis is essential; development of a general crisis management framework to cope with the $100b+ event (rather than a more likely $1–10b event) should be a priority driven at the national level by countries that are truly at risk (e.g., USA, Japan, France, Mexico, China, India).

10.5.4 Amalgamated solutions

It is becoming increasingly clear that coping with catastrophic risk in a rapidly growing world can only be accomplished through an amalgam of solutions – combinations of loss control, loss financing, and risk reduction conducted in a cooperative manner by the private and public sectors. Peak catastrophic vulnerabilities far outweigh the ability for any single risk management solution, marketplace, or capacity provider to manage the resulting losses, meaning close partnerships must develop between sectors and across national boundaries. Sharing of loss data, modeling, technology advances, and education/safety measures can help in the process;

---

[3] For example, does the creation of TRIA and the Department of Homeland Security create sustainable loss control change?

deregulating markets so that capital can flow more freely to support risk capacity needs is also essential.

10.5.5   Learning from past events

Every natural or man-made disaster that occurs must be taken as a learning opportunity. The very risk mitigation, modeling, and financing efforts that comprise the area of catastrophic risk management should be analyzed, verified, and critiqued in the aftermath of an event. New fallibilities and areas for improvement may be revealed, or the efficacy of existing methods may be supported. Where necessary, adjustments can be made to protect against future events. In practice, analytics firms and intermediaries make adjustments to their models and portfolios when they are presented with new information, data, and results from the latest catastrophic event. Others involved in the process (e.g., financial intermediaries, government authorities, crisis management organizations, rating agencies, individual firms) should perform a similar exercise so that the effects of each devastating event are thoroughly examined.

It is quite clear that catastrophic risks, which have the potential of creating widespread destruction and financial loss, have to be managed actively in order to reduce the specter of loss. This becomes increasingly true as national populations expand and overall vulnerabilities increase. Despite the fact that catastrophic risks have a relatively low probability of occurrence, they cannot be ignored or managed passively. The prudent individual, company, and nation must be prepared to cope with exposures through a combination of loss control, loss financing and, where possible, risk reduction. Equally, private and public sector forces must be prepared to work in a cooperative fashion to ensure physical and financial safety for those at risk. In the end, most natural and man-made disasters cannot be eliminated, but their effects can be limited, reduced, or transferred through the development and use of a proper risk management program.

Bibliography

Abbott, P. 2002. *Natural Disasters*, 3rd ed. Boston: McGraw Hill.

Alexander, D. 2000. *Confronting Catastrophe*. Oxford: Oxford University Press.

Banks, E. (ed.). 2001. *Weather Risk Management*. London: Palgrave Macmillan.

Banks, E. 2003. *Alternative Risk Transfer*. Chichester: John Wiley & Sons.

Banks, E. and Dunn, R. 2003. *Practical Risk Management*. Chichester: John Wiley & Sons.

Best, A.M. 1999. Exposing catastrophe risk. White Paper, New York.

Borden, S. and Sarkar, A. 1996. Securitizing property catastrophe risk. *Current Issues In Economics and Finance*, Vol. 2. New York: Federal Reserve Bank of New York.

Brillinger, D. 1993. Earthquake risk and insurance. *Environmetrics*, Vol. 4(1).

Britton, N. and Oliver, J. (eds). 1997. *Financial Risk Management for Natural Catastrophes*. Sydney: Aon Group.

Camerer, C. and Kunreuther, H. 1989. Decision processes for low probability events: policy implications. *Journal of Policy Analysis and Management*, Vol. 8.

Canabarro, E. and Finkemeier, M. 1998. Analyzing insurance linked securities. Goldman Sachs Fixed Income Research, October.

Cummins, D. and Doherty, N. 1997. Can insurers pay for the big one? University of Pennsylvania Working Paper.

Cummins, D. and German, H. 1995. Pricing catastrophic insurance futures and call spreads: an arbitrage approach. *Journal of Fixed Income*, Vol. 4.

Doherty, N. 1997. Financial innovation in the management of catastrophe risk. *Journal of Applied Corporate Finance*, Vol. 10.

Freeman, R. 2000. Estimating chronic risk from natural disasters in developing countries: a case study on Honduras. Paper presented at Annual Bank Conference on Development Economics, Paris.

Froot, K. 1997. The limited financing of catastrophic risk: an overview. National Bureau of Economic Research Working Paper.

Froot, K. (ed.). 1999. *Financing Catastrophe Risk*. Chicago: University of Chicago Press.

Froot, K. 2001. The market for catastrophe risk: a clinical examination. National Bureau of Economic Research Working Paper.

Froot, K. and Posner, S. 2001. The pricing of event risks with parametric uncertainty. *Geneva Papers on Risk and Insurance*, Vol. 27(2).

General Accounting Office. 2003. Catastrophe insurance risks: status of efforts to securitize natural catastrophe and terrorism risk. Washington, DC: GAO.

Guin, J. and Saxena, V. 2002. Extreme losses from natural disasters – earthquakes, tropical cyclones and extratropical cyclones. Boston: Applied Insurance Research.

Gurenko, E. and Lester, R. 2001. Managing catastrophe risk exposures in South Asia: the role of the World Bank. Washington, DC: World Bank.

Harrington, S. and Niehaus, G. 1999. *Risk Management and Insurance*. Boston: McGraw-Hill.

Insurance Services Office. 1996. *Managing Catastrophe Risk*. New York: ISO.

Insurance Services Office. 1999. *Financing Catastrophe Risk: Capital Markets Solutions*. New York: ISO.

Intergovernmental Panel on Climate Change. 2001. *Climate Change 2001: Impacts, Adaptation, and Vulnerability*. Cambridge: Cambridge University Press.

Jaffee, D. and Russell, T. 1996. Catastrophic insurance, capital markets, and uninsurable risks. Wharton Financial Institutions Center, Working Paper 96–12.

Kovacs, P. and Kunreuther, H. 2001. Managing catastrophic risk: lessons from Canada. Presentation at ICLR/IBC Earthquake Conference March 2001, Simon Fraser University, Vancouver.

Kozlowski, R. and Mathewson, S. 1997. A primer on catastrophe modeling. *Journal of Insurance Regulation*, Vol. 15:3(Spring).

Kreimer, A. and Arnold, M. (ed.). 2001. *Managing Disaster Risk in Emerging Economies. Disaster Risk Management Series*, Vol. 2. Washington, DC: World Bank.

Kreimer, A., Arnold, M. and Barnham, C. 1999. Managing disaster risk in Mexico: market incentives for mitigation and investment. Washington, DC: World Bank.

Kunreuther, H. and Michel-Kerjan, E. 2004. Dealing with extreme events: new challenges for terrorism risk coverage in the US. University of Pennsylvania Working Paper 04–09.

Lakdawalla, D. and Zanjani, G. 2003. Insurance, self-protection, and the economics of terrorism. RAND Institute for Civil Justice Working Paper WR-123-ICJ.

Lane, M. 2000. *Pricing Risk Transfer Transactions*. Kenilworth, IL: Lane Financial.

Lane, M. and Beckwith, R. 2003. *2003 Review of Trends in Insurance Securitization*. Wilmette, IL: Lane Financial.

Lee, J. and Yu, M. 2002. Pricing default-risky Cat bonds with moral hazard and basis risk. *Journal of Risk and Insurance*, Vol. 69(1).

Lewis, C. and Murdock, K. 1996. The role of government contracts in discretionary reinsurance markets for natural disasters. *Journal of Risk and Insurance*, Vol. 63.

Major, J. 2002. *Advanced Techniques for Modeling Terrorism Risk*. New York: Guy Carpenter.

Marsh and McClennan. 1998. *The Evolving Market for Catastrophic Event Risk*. New York: M&M/Guy Carpenter.

May, P. 1985. *Recovering From Catastrophes: Federal Disaster Relief and Politics*. Westport, CT: Greenwood.

McGhee, C. 2004. Market update: the catastrophe bond market at year-end 2003. *MMC Securities Research Report*.

Mesrazos, J. 1997. The cognition of catastrophe: preliminary examination of an industry in transition. Working Paper, Wharton Risk Management and Decision Processes Center, Philadelphia.

Moss, D. 1998. Public risk management and the private sector: an exploratory essay. Harvard University Working Paper 93–073.

Parisi, F. and Herilhy, H. 1999. Modeling catastrophe reinsurance risk: implications for the Cat bond market. *Standard and Poor's Structured Finance Special Report*.

Pollner, J. 2001. Managing catastrophic disaster risks using alternative risk financing and pooled insurance structures. World Bank Technical Paper No. 495.

Porter, B. and Lee, S. 2002. The role of catastophic modeling in ART. *Journal of Reinsurance*, Vol. 9(3).

Porter, B. and Virkud, U. 2002. *Catastrophe Models: Where They Came From and Where They're Going*. Boston: Applied Insurance Research.

Risk Management Solutions. 2003. *1703 Windstorm Retrospective*. Santa Barbara, CA: RMS.

Risk Managment Solutions. 2004. *Northridge Earthquake 10 year Retrospective*. Santa Barbara, CA: RMS.

Royal Society. 1998. *Preventing Natural Disasters: The Role of Risk Control and Insurance*. London: Royal Society.

Rubin, C., Cumming, W., Renada-Tanali, I. and Birkland, T. 2003. Major terrorism events. Working Paper 107, University of Colorado, Natural Hazard Center.

SCOR. 1996. *Are Natural Catastrophes Insurable?* Paris: SCOR Re.

Shah, H. and Nakada, P. 1999. Managing and financing catastrophe risk. Special Report, RMS and Oliver Wyman.

Stone, J. 1973. A theory of capacity and the insurance of catastrophic risks. *Journal of Risk and Insurance*, Vol. 40.

Swiss Re. 1997. *Proportional and Non-Proportional Reinsurance*. Zurich: Swiss Re Publishing.

Swiss Re. 2000. *Facultative Non-Proportional Reinsurance and Obligatory Treaties – Caution: Faulty Design*. Zurich: Swiss Re Publishing.

Swiss Re. 2000. *Storm over Europe: An Underestimated Risk*. Zurich: Swiss Re Publishing.

Swiss Re. 2000. *Twister: The Professional Reinsurer's Perspective*. Zurich: Swiss Re Publishing.

Swiss Re. 2002. *Terrorism: Dealing with the New Spectre*. Zurich: Swiss Re Publishing.

Swiss Re. 2003. *Natural Catastrophes and Reinsurance*. Zurich: Swiss Re Publishing.

Swiss Re. 2003. *Reinsurance – A Systemic Risk*? Zurich: Swiss Re Publishing.

Tobin, G. and Moritz, B. 1997. *Natural Hazard: Explanation and Integration*. New York: Guildford Press.

US Natural Resource Council. 1992. *The Economic Consequences of a Catastrophic Earthquake*. Washington, DC: National Academy Press.

Winter, R. 1994. The dynamics of competitive insurance markets. *Journal of Financial Intermediation*, Vol. 3.

Woo, G. 1999. *The Mathematics of Natural Catastrophes*. London: Imperial College Press.

Woo, G. 2002. Natural catastrophe probable maximum loss. *British Actuarial Journal*, Vol. 8(V).

Woo, G. 2003. *The Evolution of Terrorism Risk Modeling*. London: Risk Management Solutions.

Woo, G. 2004. A catastrophe bond niche: multiple event risk. Presentation, NBER Insurance Workshop, Cambridge, MA.

Index